PLASTICS FOR JEWELRY

PLASTICS FOR JEWELRY

by Harry Hollander

WATSON-GUPTILL PUBLICATIONS/NEW YORK

PITMAN PUBLISHING/LONDON

To Rufus, again.

Copyright© 1974 by Watson-Guptill Publications

First published 1974 in the United States and Canada by Watson-Guptill Publications,
a division of Billboard Publications, Inc.,
One Astor Plaza, New York, N.Y. 10036

Published simultaneously in Great Britain by Sir Isaac Pitman & Sons Ltd.,
39 Parker Street, London WC2B 5PB
U.K. ISBN 0-273-00805-6

Library of Congress Cataloging in Publication Data
Hollander, Harry.
　Plastics for jewelry.
　Bibliography: p.
　1. Jewelry making—Amateurs' manuals.
　2. Plastics craft.
I. Title.
TT212.H64 1974　　745.59'42　　73-19643
ISBN 0-8230-4027-5

First Printing, 1974

ACKNOWLEDGMENTS

I would like to thank my 95 years young father-in-law Dr. F. G. Ballentine, Professor Emeritus of Latin at Bucknell University, for putting the draft of this book into proper English. I would also like to thank companies such as CIBA-GEIGY, Reichhold Chemicals, Diamond Shamrock, Dow-Corning, Rohm and Haas, E. I. Du Pont, without whose samples, technical literature, and counseling I would never have been able to keep up to date in the evaluation of applicable developments in resins and plastics.

The following people also provided invaluable assistance: Helen Drutt of Philadelphia, who was so helpful in giving me names of artist-designer-craftsmen whom I approached for photographs of their work. She has helped make this a better book.

My photographer Michael Yarrow, of Bradenton, Florida, who did the black and white glossy prints for the twenty projects as well as the color shots of my jewelry. Besides having a full-time job as a staff photographer on a local newspaper, he managed to come through at deadline time with excellent photos. Thanks, Mike.

Don Holden of Watson-Guptill, who got me going on this book in the first place, I am grateful: I learned lots and hope that I have properly passed it on to the readers.

Joan Hugaboom of Fairport, New York, who typed my draft with her usual diligence. I hope we can continue working together.

Watson-Guptill Senior Editor Diane Casella Hines, who beautifully supervised the care and feeding of this book. Writing this book would have been infinitely more difficult if Diane hadn't helped me organize myself. As a matter of fact, she said that she would give me a passing mark in the course!

And to my editor, Sarah Bodine, who made the whole manuscript even more readable and logical, many thanks!

Lastly, I don't want to forget Bill Brown of Penland School of Crafts who gives me his ever-encouraging backing whatever I'm trying to do.

CONTENTS

INTRODUCTION

This book demonstrates simple methods of making jewelry: using synthetic products alone or in combination with older materials such as metal, stone, and organic natural materials like wood and bone. The plastics described in this book are used (1) as molds and other releasing surfaces upon which jewelry may be cast or formed, or (2) as the materials which are formed within these molds and on these releasing surfaces.

Plastic releasing surfaces are usually made from thermoplastics (synthetic resins which can be melted or softened and resolidified), such as cellulose acetate, Mylar, Teflon, Plexiglas (acrylic), and polyethylene.

The plastics that are generally used for casting and forming are called thermosetting resins. They are liquids at room temperature and can be converted to solids through the addition of hardening agents. They may be softened under heat, but generally cannot be liquified again. Included in this thermosetting group are polyester, epoxy, and catalyzed acrylic resins. From these three families, the craftsman can fashion jewelry pieces of pure resin or resins combined with traditional materials. These thermosets are beginning to switch professional jewelers to new tracks that go far beyond conventional silver, gold, and stone.

Another member of the thermosetting family will also be discussed in this book. This group is called the silicones. They are used here primarily as mold-making materials for casting jewelry.

As the projects for this book developed I found that I had included pewter in many of the pieces. This metal melts at around 425° F., a temperature even lower than the working temperature of an increasing number of plastics, and therefore has many advantages for the jewelry maker. Modern pewter, also called Britannia metal, an alloy of tin, antimony, and copper, contains no lead and does not tarnish. It's softer than sterling silver but it has a similar visual warmth. Pewter is readily cast in silicone rubber molds. When covered with epoxy resin "enamels," this metal looks very much like enameled sterling silver.

In this book I'll stress how to use synthetic materials alone and in combination with natural ones. The following guidelines should help you determine how these plastic materials may be best employed:

Visual and tactile beauty must be your first consideration in using the materials described in this book.

Uses not possible with conventional products are an important feature of epoxy resins in particular. Thirty years ago, for example, a clear, rigid, unbreakable, hard, adhesive coating for metal was not available.

Lower cost of materials is certainly a factor, for example, in the decision to use epoxy resin enamels in place of the vitreous enamels.

Lower cost of production is also a very important factor, especially for the professional jeweler. For example, metal-epoxy jewelry, with the exception of pewter, is more rapidly cast than pure metal jewelry. And it takes much less time to get exactly the same effects with epoxy enamels than with the vitreous enamels.

Better physical and/or chemical properties are often obtainable through the use of synthetics. Plastics can be used to make water-clear jewelry which is relatively unbreakable, and certainly shatter-proof.

Compatibility of the resin with older, natural materials will allow for effects that were previously impossible, for example a pin can be made from cast pewter combined with cast epoxy or polyester resins.

Although this book deals with combinations of natural and synthetic materials in the creation of modern jewelry, conventional jewelry techniques will be used wherever necessary and convenient. Innovations will be presented if they simplify older methods or if they will yield something new and different.

It's very important for the serious artist and craftsman to be given the proper working tools; thus, basic resin formulas will be given. In some cases, details will also be given on how to modify them. These basic resin formulas are essential because there are so many ill-defined hobby-shop plastics on the market today—pretty packages at high prices. There are literally dozens of different polyester, epoxy, and urethane resins available. The artist or craftsman usually doesn't know where to go to get the right product, and there's the danger of using a material which, if not properly formulated, won't have the optimum properties. (I've heard many complaints about hardware store epoxy resin glues that don't harden properly even when mixed in the recommended proportions.) The basic formulas presented here are meant to reduce this risk.

In the bibliography are listed a few of the excellent books on designing and making jewelry, which you should consult for in-depth information on making metal jewelry. In this book, the editors and I decided to emphasize but one thing: how to use plastics in the making of jewelry.

Brooch by Bernd Seegebrecht, Freiburg, Germany.
Taken from "Science Fiction" drawings,
925/silver, Plexiglas, and red paint.
Photo by Johannes Schmidt.

YOUR STUDIO AND BASIC EQUIPMENT

The starting point in carrying out the projects in this book is to set up a place to work. The most important consideration is that your work area have good ventilation. Plenty of electrical outlets and good lighting are also necessary. Use 100-watt bulbs in the section of your studio where you'll be weighing materials, sawing, sanding, and buffing. Since you'll continually drop filings during these operations, work on an easily cleanable floor or cover your floor, especially if it's tile, to protect it.

The next consideration is your working surface. A table supporting a 4' x 8' plywood sheet, 1'' thick and covered with 4-mil polyethylene, makes an ideal working surface.

In addition to a worktable, you'll want a stool. Although buffing and polishing are best done standing up, you'll find a stool very convenient for such work as sawing, filing, sanding, and close detail work.

If you don't have a sink in your working area, be sure to have buckets of clean water available. You'll be continually washing your hands with an abrasive soap such as Lava, and drying them with paper towels.

Start buying tools slowly and cautiously. The most important tool to have in the beginning is a scale. Familiarize yourself with the resin systems and processes before you decide on the other tools that will be essential for your work.

WEIGHING TOOLS

An Ohaus triple beam balance (scale) weighs in 1/10 gram units with the accuracy of plus or minus 0.1 grams. It has a built-in magnet so that the beam comes to rest quickly in balancing. I suggest that you pastewax your scale as soon as you get it to keep resin from sticking to it. You can calibrate a dropper for measuring by counting the drops on the balance set to 1 gram. (Photo Courtesy Ohaus Scale Corporation.)

Coffee stirrers, waxed-paper, and/or plastic-coated cups, empty tin cans, and bottles are an integral part of any studio where work is done with liquid thermosetting resins. Weigh all ingredients into the same container so you don't lose any materials which are left sticking to the walls of different cups. (Generally, waxed-paper cups are fine for mixing resins, although a small portion of the wax can dissolve or break loose. For super clarity in the resin surface, I suggest using plastic-coated paper cups.)

HEATING TOOLS

A 250-watt industrial uncolored heat lamp and holder or a more expensive infrared heat lamp is necessary for heat curing. You can use the lamp alone or you can make a box to contain the heat.

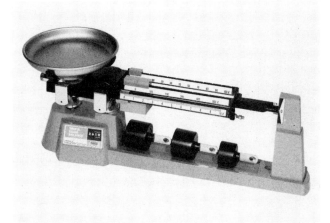

Ohaus triple beam balance.

Cups and stirrers.

Heat lamp.

Heat box.

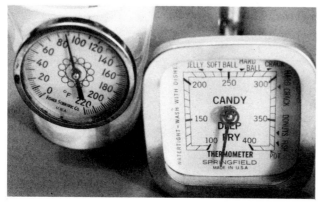

Thermometers.

Electric hot plate.

A heat box is convenient for controlling heat and keeping out dust while curing resinous jewelry pieces. You can buy a laboratory oven from Fisher Scientific (although it is quite expensive), or you can easily make a heat box from six 10″ square sheets of ¼″ to ½″ plywood. Cut a circular hole in one sheet to allow the heat lamp to be raised or lowered from outside the box. Cut a slit in another sheet to use as a spyhole. Spring hinge one side for a door which can close tightly, and then nail or glue the cube together. You can fiberglass the outside of the box to strengthen it if you wish. Tack or glue aluminum foil to the inner walls to distribute heat more uniformly. You can set the box on bricks to obtain the desired height.

A candy/deep-fry thermometer is an adequate temperature-measuring device for the curing of thermosetting resins or you could buy a more expensive laboratory thermometer.

An electric hot-plate or a burner on your kitchen stove can be used to melt materials such as pewter and wax.

A Varaflame torch kit is excellent for soldering metals. It produces a small, hot flame, is easy to light, and is very reliable. (Photos courtesy of the Ronson Corporation.)

JEWELER'S TOOLS

Toothless pliers come in many shapes and sizes. You will need about four different pairs to accomplish most of these projects.

A metal ring mandril and a rawhide mallet are invaluable for shaping and sizing rings. The beauty of hammering with the protection of the rawhide is that it doesn't scratch the metal.

Needle files, available in a variety of shapes, are very convenient for filing in corners and small spaces. Treat these files gently since they are brittle and break quite easily. You'll also need some heavier, half round files.

The Brightboy assortment of rubber abrasives can be used by hand or as attachments for a flexible-shaft motor tool (see ''Cutting Tools'').

CUTTING TOOLS

A flexible-shaft motor tool, which has a variable speed from 0 to 14,000 r.p.m., can be used with a large assortment of attachments. This is an expensive piece of equipment, but it will last a long time.

A hand drill is good for slow drilling, burring, and cutting.

Large metal shears make cutting pewter a pleasure. Placing one of the handles on the floor while you cut will help to make the cutting easier because the floor does half the work.

A jeweler's saw uses 5″ blades which are high-grade but brittle steel. There are about 15 different sizes from #0, the finest, to #8, the coarsest, which will cut through almost any metal. Put the blades in the saw frame so that the barbs face outward. The blade should be tight enough so that it makes a nice middle C ''ping'' when it's plucked.

When sawing plastics and metal, place the piece on a rectangular piece of plywood with a V-cut, called a bench

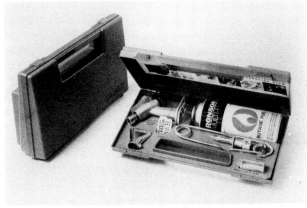

Varaflame torch kit.

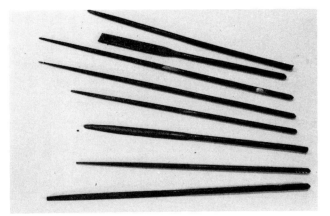

Needle files.

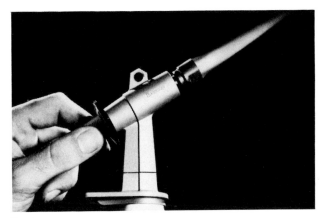

Torch.

Abrasive discs.

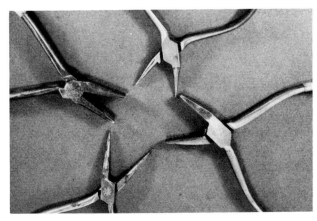

Toothless pliers.

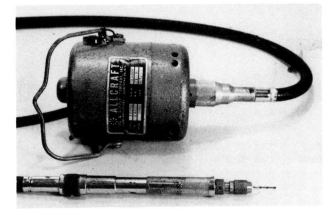

Flexible-shaft motor.

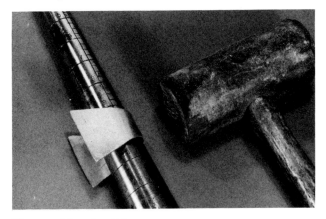

Ring mandril and mallet.

Hand drill.

Shears.

Vise.

Jeweler's saw and bench pin.

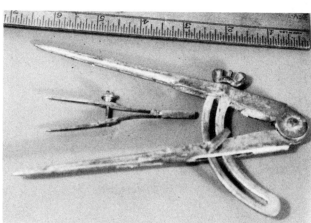

Dividers.

Coping saw.

DISPOSABLE POLYETHYLENE GLOVE

Protective gloves.

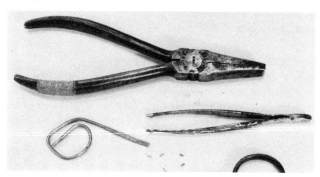

Tweezers.

Dust mask.

pin. Nail, screw, or clamp it to a table top. To cut, hold the saw vertically to avoid breaking blades; turn the piece rather than the saw.

A coping saw or jigsaw with its heavy blade is ideal for sawing pewter, wood, or Plexiglas sheet.

MISCELLANEOUS TOOLS

Tweezers are useful for working with small objects such as solder snippets or paillons. You should always handle solder with tweezers, since it may not adhere well if covered with the natural oil from your fingers.

A small vise is handy for holding jewelry pieces while drilling or sawing.

Dividers are useful for making comparative measurements and for drawing arcs and circles.

SAFETY EQUIPMENT

Polyethylene gloves are cheap and disposable. Wear them when you're working with fiberglass cloth or filaments.

A dust mask should be worn when you work with asbestos or cut fiberglass cloth to avoid getting glass needles in your lungs. Wear long-sleeved, protective clothing if you cut a large amount of fiberglass.

An activated charcoal mask should be worn if you have trouble breathing when you work with polyester resins or acrylic syrups. This mask filters out styrene and acrylic monomer vapors.

Safety goggles are important to wear when weighing chemicals. Go to a safety equipment supply house for goggles that really cover your eyes!

FINISHING TOOLS

Wet-or-dry sandpaper of grits from 180 or 220 to 400 or 600 is usually used wet for sanding resinous castings. If the piece has curves, you can wrap the wet sandpaper around a fairly hard piece of 1½" thick foam rubber to aid in following the contours.

A Westinghouse ⅓ h.p. motor facilitates cut-down and luster buffing. Run it at a speed of 1750 r.p.m. (revolutions per minute) or 2800 s.f.m. (surface feet per minute) for best results on the resins and metals described in this book. Be sure that the buffing wheel doesn't run faster than this or the jewelry piece may become overheated. You'll also need one or two tapered arbors or spindles to hold the buffing wheels.

Buffing wheels are made from a wide variety of materials. For most pieces made from resins and soft metals, use the muslin buffs manufactured by the C. R. Hill Company, (see *Suppliers and Manufacturers*) with thread counts of 86 or 93 (for plastics, the lower thread counts are preferable). I use Hill's 38-730 muslin 6" stitched buffs for all buffing except the final luster. For this, I use Hill's 38-731, a loose muslin buff with a leather center. Don't mix buffing compounds on the same wheel—keep enough buffs handy so that you'll have one for each compound you use.

A Lea buff rake can be used to properly break in new buffs.

Activated charcoal mask.

Safety goggles.

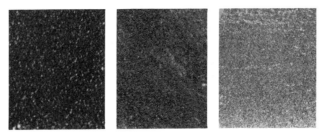
Wet-or-dry sandpapers.

Motorized buffing wheels.

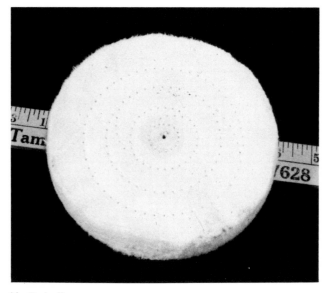

Muslin buff.

Buff rake.

Buffing compound.

Raking removes loose threads and softens the face of the buff. With the rough face of a pumice stone, you can smooth out the buff face to get a fine nap. You can also use the buff rake to clean metal and resin particles from the wheel after use. While the wheel is turning, gently push the rake into it.

Greaseless buffing compounds, manufactured by the Lea Manufacturing Company (see *Suppliers and Manufacturers*), are a pleasure to use since you don't have to spend time cleaning off your piece to see what you've accomplished. Lea Compound C and Learok 765 are cutdown buffing compounds. Compound C can be used right after 180-grit sandpaper to remove scratches still remaining in the plastic or metal surface. Learok 884E is considered by Lea to be a low-luster buffing compound and should be used after Learok 765, on its own 6″ muslin wheel.

Learok 339E is a greaseless aluminum oxide buffing compound that produces a very high luster when used on its own 6″ loose muslin buff. Learok 312 is also used as a final gloss buffing compound. I see little difference between 312 and 339E.

STUDIO PROCEDURES

Arrange and use materials in a reasonable and logical manner. Think ahead.

If working in a group, each person must have his own work area, whether this is an entire table or a portion marked off with tape, where personal tools and supplies can be arranged. Give each person a small tray (an old TV tray or a piece of Masonite, thin plywood, or sturdy cardboard, depending on the load) on which to gather all materials to be weighed. This will discourage grabbing up the wrong can from a crowded table and will provide a definite place to keep cups, sticks, and additives.

Have the weighing area easily accessible. Place your scale on a small piece of polyethylene sheet, which you can change frequently. You can make a weighing area from quartered newspaper or small rectangles of polyethylene film, stacked next to the scale. These disposable sheets may be used on weighing trays or alone. After weighing, dispose of the top sheet. For ease in cleaning, coat all parts of the scale and can-opening tools with MirrorGlaze wax.

Place sticky resin and hardener containers on polyethylene coffee-can covers so that you'll be able to keep your plastic table cover clean.

Label all supplies clearly. When transferring materials to smaller containers, label them immediately.

Transfer materials other than solvents to polyethylene containers (old detergent or shampoo bottles) for ease in pouring.

Keep polyester resin 32-032 in an amber or opaque container or it will cure in sunlight.

Wipe up spills on the scale or table with acetone (which can be obtained in drugstores) or lacquer thinner. Keep small safety cans of these materials at the scale and sink.

General clean-up includes emptying metal trash containers each day. Clean brushes with lacquer thinner, soap, and water. Chip cured resin spills off the work area. Cure out the contents of used cups before reusing them, or throw the used cups away. Remove clothing for cleaning.

NOTES AND CAUTIONS

Avoid physical contact with the resins, curing agents, and catalysts. Wear goggles or glasses when weighing and mixing, and protect hands with gloves or hand creams. Wash hands frequently with Lava soap and water and dry with paper towels. Use hand creams such as Silicare by Revlon, which contains silicone, to replace skin oils.

Don't smoke while handling resinous materials because they're highly flammable.

Don't eat in your work area. You could easily contaminate the food with resins from your hands or mistake a cup of resin for a cup of coffee.

Maintain adequate ventilation. In warm climates, this is usually no problem; you just keep the windows open. In cold climates, you should change the air in your studio a minimum of six times per hour by opening windows or by using fans to move air in and out. Wear a vapor mask or work near an exhaust fan if you can't move the air in the room.

Be very careful when using epoxy hardeners. RC-125 is alkaline and gives off the most vapors. 956, called a safety hardener, gives off minimal vapors, but it should not be heated or touched. RC-303 stinks, but there's no problem with vapors. HH 1065B requires good air circulation because it gives off vapors while heat curing. N-001 and B-003 seem to be no problem and are the safest curing agents used in this book.

Large amounts of MEK Peroxide(MEK-Px) pose a fire hazard through spontaneous combustion.

Wear goggles or glasses and tie back loose clothing and hair when using the buffing wheel.

First aid products you should have on hand include an eyecup, adhesive tape, gauze pads, Band-aids, tincture of methiolate, tincture of green soap, and cream (allo cream) or ice, when available, for burns.

If you get chemicals in your eyes or mouth, flush them immediately with cold running water for 15 minutes and then see a doctor.

Bob Natalini's studio. Photo by Jeffrey Hannigan.

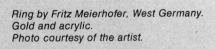

Ring by Fritz Meierhofer, West Germany.
Gold and acrylic.
Photo courtesy of the artist.

FINISHING YOUR JEWELRY

Finishing is an exciting part of the jewelry-making process. After casting any piece of jewelry, much work is often necessary to bring it to the desired finished state. There are a number of ways to finish your piece; depending on the way you want the surface to finally appear, you can use finishing methods whose results range from a matte to a high-gloss finish.

FILING, RUBBING, AND SANDING

The first step in finishing, no matter what surface you want, is either to rough-file the piece using a heavy half file or the appropriate shape needle file (shown in *Your Studio and Basic Equipment*), or to shape the piece on a stone grinding wheel. Be sure not to let the resin get too hot or it may melt and mar the piece. You can prevent such a catastrophe by dipping the piece intermittently in cold water or by continually running water over the stone as you work.

You can give a metal or powdered-metal piece a Swedish-type finish merely by rubbing in one direction with steel wool to produce a dull matte or brushed surface. Such a surface is often more desirable than a highly polished finish which, especially on sterling silver or gold, can be easily marred.

For any other finish, after you've rough-filed and ground the piece, you should sand it with wet-or-dry sandpaper of increasing grits from 180 or 220 to 400 or 600. Depending on the size and delicacy of your piece, you can sand either by holding the piece and rubbing the sandpaper over it or by securing the sandpaper and rubbing the piece over it. For the latter, you can use a piece of glass or any flat surface to support the sandpaper, securing it with rubber cement when dry sanding. When wet sanding, the sandpaper will adhere well by itself. Use two or three layers of sandpaper to give a slightly cushioned surface for delicate pieces. When rubbing the sandpaper over the piece, you can sand by hand or wrap a sheet of wet-or-dry sandpaper around a stick or hard piece of rubber, which provides a flexible, rounded surface, to aid in following the contours of the piece.

BUFFING PROCEDURES

Buffing to produce a semi-gloss or high-gloss surface can be done either by hand or with an electric buffing wheel. Hand buffing takes a lot of time, but you can polish as brightly and highly by hand as you can on the wheel by using a series of special sanding cloths manufactured by the Polysand division of Micro-Surface Finishing Products, Inc. (see *Suppliers and Manufacturers*), which have grits down to 8000.

You can also hand polish using a piece of cotton or wool flannel wrapped around and stapled to a wood paint-mixing stick. Mix up a slurry of jeweler's powdered tin, aluminum, or cerium oxide and water, apply this to the hand buffer, a rub it against the piece. Another interesting product for hand buffing is Alphalap "PS" manufactured by J. I. Morris (see *Suppliers and Manufacturers*), which is even more efficient than cotton flannel. Write for a sample.

When buffing with an electric buffing wheel, run the motor at a speed of 1750 r.p.m. (revolutions per minute) or 2800 s.f.m. (surface feet per minute). Be sure that the buffing wheel does not run faster than this or the piece may become overheated. Using this speed with 6" muslin buffing wheel works beautifully for buffing both the resin systems and the metals described in this book. (Some experts suggest the use of cotton flannel or wool cloth buffs for high polishing.) Hold the piece tightly and press it lightly against the wheel to get the best results. Keep moving the piece gently back and forth across the buff.

FINAL FINISHING

The final finishing is usually divided into cut-down and luster buffing. *Cut-down buffing* is the operation that produces a semi-gloss finish from a dull-sanded surface. *Luster buffing* involves polishing the surface to a highly reflective, mirror-like finish.

Cut-down buffing is done with abrasive compounds such as Compound C and Learok 765. When using Compound C, apply it to the buffing wheel and let the wheel run for about a minute before buffing your piece. Compound C contains some glue; when exposed to air on the running wheel, the water in the compound evaporates so that the compound becomes fast to the wheel and doesn't get glue on your piece. Then gently push the piece against the "dressed" wheel. Be especially careful during the initial cut-down steps, because abrasive compounds can cut into your piece with a vengeance. Be sure to keep moving the piece back and forth across the wheel.

For the final luster buffing, apply the polishing compounds, Learok 884E and 339E, to separate buffing wheels and gently push the piece against each wheel in turn. If you want to add a bit of protection after you have satisfactorily polished your piece, you can rub some MirrorGlaze wax onto it and polish it right away with a soft cloth.

CAUTIONS FOR GRINDING, BUFFING, AND POLISHING JEWELRY

Wear unbreakable protective goggles (Lexan plastic are currently the strongest).

Roll sleeves up to the elbows.

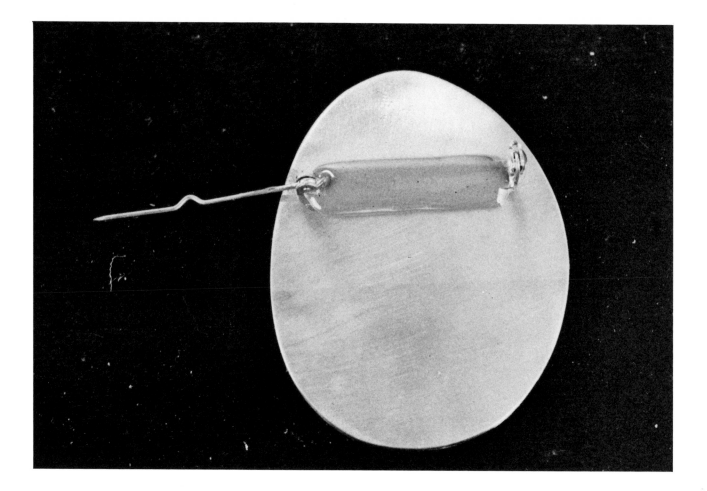

(Above) Pinback adhered with epoxy adhesive.

(Right) Hole drilled, to hang a pendant.

Tie back loose or long hair.

Wear no dangling jewelry.

Have good light and ventilation.

Never take you eye away from the spinning wheel and the jewelry piece.

Hold the piece as tightly as you can to prevent its being thrown out of your hands. Always hold it with both hands for good guidance and safety.

Always angle the piece down in the direction in which the wheel is turning. Angling up may tear the piece out of your hands.

Don't press the piece too hard against the grinding or buffing wheel. The jewelry may become overheated and burn you, or the resin may soften and mar the piece. A suction device to collect the grindings is most helpful.

ANNEALING (HEAT TREATING)

Finished acrylic pieces may be fixed by annealing, or heat treating. This insures that they won't distort or craze as time goes by. Crazing is the appearance in the surface of the acrylic casting of very fine, hair-line cracks. These can be caused by contact with a solvent or when excessive heat is applied to the resin surface. Annealing also clears up any moisture clouding that may occur on the surface of the resin during curing.

Generally, the resin casting in jewelry pieces is too thin to produce crazing problems. To clear up clouding, place your *cured piece* in a heat box (see *Your Studio and Basic Equipment*) or in your oven set at 140°F. for several hours. *Note*: never place an uncured piece in an oven, and never set the oven higher than 150°F., as insufficiently cured resin or too-high temperatures may cause the methyl methacrylate monomer to vaporize and could result in an *explosive vapor concentration in the oven*. As an extra precaution, when using your oven to anneal pieces, leave the door slightly ajar. As long as there is some ventilation, there will be little danger of an explosion with resinous materials. If you should have problems with crazing or want to insure against crazing in the future, place your cured piece in a heat box or oven set at 150°F. for 24 hours.

ADHERING PINBACKS

Jewelers solder pinbacks to gold and silver jewelry brooches. However, since it's not always possible to use solder on jewelry made from resin systems, here are some alternative methods of adhering pinbacks:

On jewelry made with acrylic resins such as Plexiglas, it's best to use acrylic adhesives such as PS 30, made by Ca-

dillac Plastics, or Tensol 7, made by ICI. You can buy these acrylic cements ready-made in a two-part kit which includes benzoyl peroxide as a hardening agent. You can also make your own acrylic adhesive from HH 772 as shown in the formula in Project 1, "Formulas." For adhering pinbacks to all other jewelry pieces, whether made from metals, metal powders mixed with either epoxy or polyester resins, or straight polyester or epoxy resin systems, you should use an epoxy resin adhesive. The epoxy adhesive is easy to make and safe to use.

To adhere a pinback with epoxy adhesive, outline the area to be glued with Scotch tape in order to stop the adhesive from spreading. Then lightly rough the area with 0 fineness steel wool. Clean the area with detergent and water and dry it with a Q-Tip. Then clean it with mineral spirits. After this, *do not touch* the area; the natural oil in your fingers will prevent good adhesion. Similarly rub with steel wool and clean the pinback.

Add a very thin layer of the well mixed adhesive (see Project 9, "Formulas") to the marked-off area. You can add 300-mesh powdered tin or other metal to this formula to make a stronger joint.

Carefully lay the pinback on the freshly applied adhesive. Place the piece about 12″ away from an infrared lamp and leave it there until hard. While the piece is still warm, lightly cut away any excess adhesive with a small, sharp knife.

HANGING THE PENDANT

If you want to hang a pin as a pendant, use needle-nose pliers to bend a half-circle or half-loop in the center of the pinback bar. You can then slip the cord or chain into this loop when you want to hang the pin.

To hang a pendant without a pinback, you must slowly and carefully drill a hole in the pendant. In order to make the hole correctly, use a sharp-pointed tool (a nail or the end of a center punch) to mark the spot where you want to drill.

Plan the angle at which you want to drill. Generally, a hole drilled at a 45° angle will look better and will make a stronger channel. If possible, use a drill bit attached to a flexible-shaft motor tool (see *Your Studio and Basic Equipment*). It's usually best to drill through a side edge or corner of the piece so that the hole won't mar the front surface. If you want to make a 1/16″ channel, use a 1/32″ drill bit to start the hole and then switch to a 1/16″ bit. This "two-bit" method usually produces cleaner results.

In local hobby shops you can usually find inexpensive chains, strips of leather, or thin plastic "cord" with which to hang the pendant, or use materials available from companies such as C. R. Hill (see *Suppliers and Manufacturers*).

Necklace by the author
Pewter, sterling silver,
heat-formed Plexiglas,
and HH 772 acrylic resin.
Photo by Mike Yarrow.

PART ONE ACRYLIC RESINS

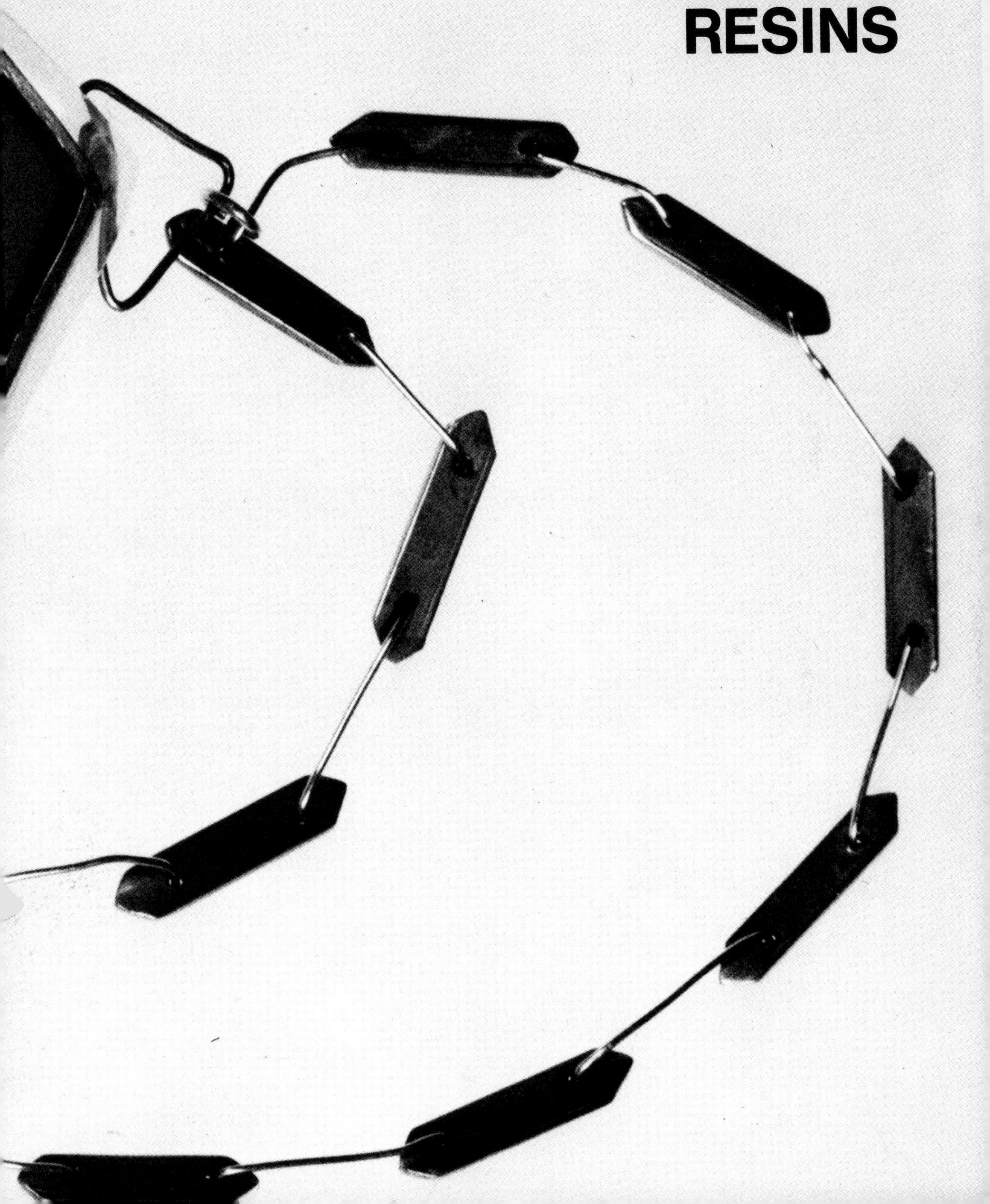

ACRYLIC RESINS

Methyl methacrylate polymers, which are used to make acrylic resin sheets, castings, and adhesives, are best known under the trade names Lucite, Plexiglas, Acryloid, Perspex, and so on. For the past 25 years artists and craftsmen have been using this glass-like, synthetic, organic (carbon-containing) material to make sculpture and jewelry. Since it has generally been too difficult technically and financially for the average sculptor or jeweler to do his own acrylic castings, the practice has been to use sheet acrylics. These plastic sheets are cut and/or shaped under heat and vacuum or pressure conditions and are often bonded together with special acrylic adhesives that don't show at the joint.

TRANSPARENT GLUES

Bonding acrylic sheets together can be done with chlorinated solvents such as methylene dichloride or ethylene dichloride. These solvents, which should only be used for gluing pieces that will be kept indoors, must be used with good ventilation since they are volatile and give off toxic fumes. Here is the formula for a modified solvent-gluing system which, according to the Rohm and Haas Company, gives excellent joint strength and weather resistance:

Methylene dichloride	60%
Methyl methacrylate monomer stabilized	40%
½ strength Benzoyl peroxide catalyst	2.4 grams per pint

Good results are usually obtained in the bonding operation by first sawing the edge of the acrylic sheet on a table saw equipped with a special blade for cutting plastics. The cut surface of the acrylic sheet should then be sanded smooth on a wet, flat sheet of 220-grit wet-or-dry sandpaper, and the second sheet should be cleaned well. Brace the two sheets firmly together—the surfaces to be glued must be in perfect contact. Fill a syringe with the solvent-gluing system and squirt it along the contact points. If the preparation of the joint is correct, the solvent adhesive will "wick-in" the length of the contact. Any excess solvent can easily be removed by immediately wiping it off. The glued sheets should be clamped for at least 5 hours (see Project 2). For additional information on gluing acrylic sheeting, consult the *Plexiglas Design and Fabrication Bulletin*, 1971 revised edition, which is available from the Rohm and Haas Company (see *Suppliers and Manufacturers*).

With a little practice, acrylic sheets intended for indoor or outdoor use can be glued without forming any air bubbles in the joint. This can best be done using the following formula, which contains an acrylic polymer dissolved in methyl methacrylate monomer:

HH 772 monomer/polymer acrylic syrup	100 grams
HH 772 catalyst	3 grams (3%)
HH 772 bleach	3 grams (3%)

Weigh, add, and mix the catalyst and the bleach well for several minutes in the HH 772 syrup. The catalyst initiates the hardening process, which is called polymerization. After mixing the ingredients well, it's wise to let the solution stand several minutes to allow the air bubbles to surface. If the HH 772 catalyst becomes yellow or brown, it has lost its strength and should be replaced. Store the catalyst in a cold place to prevent this from occurring, but be sure to bring it to room temperature before opening the bottle.

When bonding one piece of acrylic to another with this formula, which is based on a M/P (monomer/polymer) acrylic syrup, follow the same procedure of sawing and sanding as that used for solvent gluing. The next step here, however, is to mask all areas adjacent to the two surfaces to be bonded with clear cellulose (Scotch) tape (see Project 4, Step 3).

Pour the activated adhesive mixture into a squeezable container with a very small opening. A disposable squeeze bottle or a polyethylene baby-bottle bag (Playtex nurser), with a small hole cut in one corner, works well. Lay a small amount of resin along one of the edges to be glued, and place the edge with the adhesive on it next to the other prepared sheet. Brace the sheets and clamp them in this position overnight. Apply no pressure to the joint other than the weight of the acrylic sheet itself (see Project 2, Steps 4 and 5). The next day, carefully remove any surplus resin that has bled onto the cellulose tape by cutting along the glued edge with a sharp knife and then peeling off both the tape and adhering resin.

For some years I have used these M/P acrylic syrups as medium-strength adhesives with good success. For certain projects they may be colored with the same transparent color pastes which are used for both epoxy and polyester resins. In my experience, however, bonded joints have not been as strong as the cast material.

CASTING

It had been in the back of my mind for years that the average person, with no complicated equipment at his disposal, might want to make castings using a clear, liquid, acrylic resin system. After studying much of the technical literature published by such companies as Rohm and Haas and Du Pont, consulting with experts, and doing many experiments, I worked out a method for easily casting pieces weighing up to a pound, using catalyzed acrylic M/P syrup and bleach.

Thick castings (¾" or more) tend to get quite hot and often have to be cured in a mold immersed in cold water. If the resin cures at temperatures above 130°F., bubbles may form as the result of vaporization of the monomer. Before you cast a piece of jewelry, learn the process by running a series of samples using an immersion-type bayonet thermometer. You can also use a glass-stem thermometer wrapped in aluminum foil, which facilitates removal from the cured resin. If your samples still form bubbles when cured below 130°F., decrease the catalyst by 0.5% (for example from 3% to 2.5%).

After you have mixed the HH 772, the catalyst, the bleach, and any colors you want, stir well for at least 2 minutes and pour the mixture into the mold. The resin surface must be covered to keep out the oxygen in the air, which acts to inhibit polymerization (hardening). A solution of water with a few drops of Joy detergent makes a good covering when carefully sprayed onto the acrylic resin surface. Once the resin is hard—this may take several hours—pour off the seal and clean and dry the resin surface. You may need to grind blemishes off the cured resin surface. If the resin cured without generating any heat, it may have a brownish cast. This will usually disappear when the resin is annealed or heat treated (see *Finishing Your Jewelry*).

TABLE OF CATALYST HH 772 FOR ACRYLIC RESIN CASTINGS

Add the appropriate amount of HH 772 catalyst shown in this table to 100 grams of HH 772 M/P acrylic syrup and 3 grams (3%) of HH 772 bleach.

Thickness of resin casting	HH 772 catalyst
⅛"	3 grams (3%)
³⁄16"	2.5 grams (2.5%)
¼"	2.25 grams (2.25%)
½"	2 grams (2%)
¾"	1.75 grams (1.75%)
1"	1.50 grams (1.50%)
2"	1.25 grams (1.25%)

MOLDS

In addition to being covered with detergent solution, the HH 772 system must be cast in an airtight mold in order to keep out the oxygen that would inhibit the curing or hardening of the acrylic resin. Also, because too much heat will cause bubbles to form in the curing resin and mar the casting, it's a good idea to use thin molds so that heat can be removed easily in a water bath if necessary.

With its rigid, non-adhering surface, glass is ideal for molds. You can use a collapsible gasket of rubber or heavy hollow ⅛" PVC tubing between the glass sheets so that they can come together as the resin shrinks—acrylic resins shrink about 15% when cured (see Project 3, Steps 11 through 15). For an easily assembled mold that is also self-releasing, 5-mil to 20-mil cellulose acetate is ideal. The pieces of this mold can be fastened together with ethylene dichloride, which is an instant adhesive, applied with a syringe (see Project 2, Step 4).

Other self-releasing molds such as Mylar, polyethylene, and Teflon may also be used, although they are not as easy to assemble as the cellulose-acetate mold. Polyethylene containers tend to breathe and let in oxygen, which slows down the curing of the acrylic resin. As the resin shrinks during the polymerization, it pulls away from the polyethylene walls and collapses uniformly.

Another excellent method, which jewelers will find interesting, is the use of molds which adhere to the acrylic resin and become part of the piece. Since HH 772 adheres to acrylic sheet, polystyrene (Styrofoam) sheet, and wood, all of these can be shaped to hold the acrylic resin. See the acrylic projects for samples of such molds.

COMPARISON TABLE OF HH 772 M/P ACRYLIC RESIN* WITH 32-032 WATER-CLEAR POLYESTER RESIN**

Since you are now getting ready to take a plunge into a most interesting field, I have prepared a comparative table of HH 772 and water-clear Polylite 32-032 polyester casting resin which you should read over carefully. Don't try to remember the facts, just know where you can find them when you need them.

Properties	HH 772 Acrylic (Uncured)	32-032 Polyester (Uncured)
Composition of resin	Acrylic polymer mixed with methyl methacrylate monomer (reactive diluent †)	Polyester polymer mixed with styrene and other reactive diluents
Composition of catalyst	Benzoyl peroxide in a soluble vehicle	Methyl ethyl ketone peroxide in a soluble vehicle
Comparative volatility	Methyl methacrylate more volatile than styrene	Styrene less volatile than methyl methacrylate
Breathing danger	The safe allowable concentration of methyl methacrylate monomer vapor is 100 parts per million of air, †† (this incidentally, is the same figure as that given for turpentine) No human cases of ill health caused by methyl methacrylate monomer, aside from possible skin injury for a few individuals, have been reported through May 1971, claims Rohm and Haas	The safe allowable concentration of styrene vapor permitted by a medical group is also 100 p.p.m. (parts per million)
Flammability	Very flammable Vapors in confined areas explosive in presence of flame or sparks, or heating elements in ovens; do not use near flames, open motors, sparks, or in home ovens	Flammable Vapors are not considered as explosive hazard for general polyester resin use
Spillage on skin or eyes	Do not let HH 772 get on your hands or body (according to the manufacturers, there are a few individuals who are very allergic to methyl methacrylate monomer); wash off the affected area with mild soap and lots of water; for eye contact, rinse 15 minutes in cold running water and get medical attention	Although styrene is considered to be a much less toxic material, it would be wise to take the same precautions with this monomer as for the methyl methacrylate monomer
Personal protection	When weighing and mixing HH 772 you should wear protective goggles and polyethylene gloves	When weighing and mixing 32-032 polyester resin, wear protective goggles and polyethylene gloves
Studio conditions	Work in the open air if possible or change air in studio 10 times per hour or work under hood with an explosion-proof motorized fan for exhaust	Open air or change air in studio 6 times per hour with exhaust fan
Effect of air on resin cure	HH 772 does not cure well if at all in presence of air—resin system must be covered; deterginated water works well	Air slows cure on surface of 32-032 but resin cures well at room temperature in 24 to 48 hours
Effect of too little catalyst	Resin will not cure out properly	Resin will eventually cure out properly

*HH 772 M/P acrylic resin, manufactured by Polysciences (see *Suppliers and Manufacturers*)

**32-032 Water-clear polyester resin, manufactured by Reichhold Chemicals, Inc. (see *Suppliers and Manufacturers*)

†A material which reacts in the system chemically and which also lowers the viscosity of the other ingredients

††The exposure for an average person over an eight hour period, according to the American Conference of Governmental Hygienists (1967)

Properties	HH 772 Acrylic (Uncured)	32-032 Polyester (Uncured)
Effect of too much catalyst	Resin will heat above 150° F. while curing and bubbles will form in resin	Resin temperature will rise to the point where the heat will cause it to turn yellow and crack
Effective air excluders	Water, SAE 30 mineral oil, Cellophane, polyethylene, Mylar, aluminum foil, and polyvinyl alcohol film	Cellophane, polyethylene, Mylar, and so on
Coloring	Use the same color pastes as you use for epoxy and polyester resins	Use the same color pastes as you use for acrylics
Storage of resin and catalyst	Keep these materials in a cold, dark place, away from sparks, flames, and open electrical equipment; don't leave in direct sunlight	Store these materials in a cool dark place; don't leave in direct sunlight
Transparency and brilliance	More transparent and brilliant than polyester resins	Not as transparent and brilliant as acrylic resins, but more so than epoxy-resin clear "enamels"
Adhesive qualities	Bonds well to acrylic sheet, polycarbonate, polyester resin, wood, and ABS resin	Bonds fairly well to acrylic sheet, polycarbonate, wood; bonds very well to polyester resin and polystyrene
Light piping	Pipes light through a tube like water in a pipe	Does not pipe light to the extent that acrylics do
Volume shrinkage	Measured shrinkage is in the neighborhood of 15%	Average shrinkage about 7.5%
Effect of additional heat curing on hardened resin	Heat curing of finished pieces makes resin more stable and harder; temperature should be regulated no higher than 160° F. so as not to risk any formation of vapor bubbles from uncured methyl methacrylate—leave in oven, which, if possible, should have circulating air	Heat curing of finished pieces makes resin harder and more brittle; temperature should be regulated no higher than 150° F. so as to not have resin yellow from heat—leave in oven 2 to 3 hours
Why use the resin	Curious artists and craftsmen should investigate all usable materials which are applicable to their area; this acrylic liquid polymer has singular characteristics—try it; you may not like it; for jewelry, you may find it incomparable	As an inexpensive substitute for acrylics, polyester has very special characteristics which make it most interesting for jewelry
Cost of resin	Approximate cost of HH 772 will be several times that of 32-032 water-clear polyester casting resin; the increased cost is offset by the brilliance and clarity of the finished piece	32-032 water-clear polyester casting resin is about 2½ times cheaper than epoxy resins

Brooch by Jem Freyaldenhoven,
Georgia State University.
Silver, 14k gold, vacuum-formed acrylic sheet,
nylon rod, and hammer-forged,
bottom-heated, hand-formed Lexan rod.
Photo courtesy of the artist.

HEAT FORMING A PENDANT

In the five projects in Part One, I'll try to show you how to cope with the properties and peculiarities of different synthetic polymers. Before you begin these projects, be sure to thoroughly read *Acrylic Resins* as well as *Finishing Your Jewelry.*

Working with polymerizing (hardenable) acrylic resins has interesting surprises for those who have worked with epoxy and polyester resins. I have spent much time making mistakes as I learned how to use the new HH 772 M/P acrylic adhesive casting syrup. These M/P acrylic syrups cure very well under water but not well, if at all, in air. Unless you prevent these resins from overheating, bubbles can form.

This project will demonstrate how to make a pendant using a 1/16″ acrylic sheet and a liquid acrylic resin called M/P (monomer/polymer) acrylic syrup. After you've mastered acrylic resin system casting, you can investigate the use of mixed media such as exotic woods, metals, and precious or semi-precious stones. In this project you will learn:

How to hollow out an acrylic sheet with heat and hand forming.

How to incorporate pewter into the catalyzed M/P acrylic syrup to bring sparkle to your pendant; it's difficult to produce well-made jewelry solely from resins without being pedestrian.

How to cut, shape, and close up the pewter strips without using solder.

How to color-blend and pour the acrylic resin system into the "cloisons" (fenced-in areas).

TOOLS AND MATERIALS

1. Heat-forming frame. You can make this frame easily and cheaply from two identical 8″ square pieces of ¾″ plywood and four hinges. (See Step 1 for instructions.)

2. Jeweler's tools: saw and blades, drill and bits, shears, pliers, and files.

3. Finishing tools: wet-or-dry sandpaper, 6″ diameter muslin buffing wheels, buffing compounds (Learok 884E for semi-gloss and Learok 339E for polishing).

4. 18-gauge pewter (Britannia metal). You can either buy pewter or make it. (See Project 8 for instructions on how to make pewter.)

5. 20-gauge sterling silver wire.

6. Any brand of 1/16″ clear acrylic sheet, such as Plexiglas or Lucite, 6″ square. You can use scrap pieces of acrylic, cutting them to size by scoring them with

---

FORMULAS

ADHESIVE, CASTING, AND DECORATING RESIN SYSTEM

HH 772 acrylic syrup	20 grams
HH 772 catalyst	0.6 grams (3%)
HH 772 bleach	0.6 grams (3%)
Color pastes	as needed

Add the catalyst and the bleach to the resin system and mix thoroughly. Let stand a few minutes to allow the air bubbles to surface. Add needle-point amounts of color pastes. Use the system immediately.

CURING SOLUTION

Water	1 quart
Joy detergent	5 drops

To cure the resin after you have poured it into the acrylic form, spray the surface exposed to the air with ¼″ of this detergent solution.

---

the sharpened corner of a screwdriver and breaking them on the edge of a table.

7. Polysciences HH 772 monomer/polymer acrylic syrup.

8. Polysciences HH 772 catalyst.

9. Polysciences HH 772 bleach.

10. Joy detergent.

11. Color pastes.

NOTES AND CAUTIONS

See Suppliers and Manufacturers for resins and jewelry materials.

HH 772 M/P acrylic syrup is highly flammable and in certain concentrations the vapors can be explosive in the presence of open sparks or flames. Therefore, work in a well-ventilated room where the air is changed every three minutes, or under a suction hood with a fan run either by compressed air or by an explosion-proof motor.

Wear goggles and polyethylene gloves when you work with these resins and catalysts. If the uncured acrylic resin gets on your skin, wash well with soap and lots of running water. If the resin splashes in your eye, have someone check to see if any resin is visible, and if so, carefully remove it with a clean handkerchief corner. Then wash the eye out with cold running water for 15 minutes and be sure to see a doctor.

Do not smoke, drink, or eat around your working area.

Step 1. Make a heat-forming frame by cutting 5″ x 5″ "windows" in two ¾″ thick, 8″ square plywood boards. Hinge the frames together at one end, using four hinges. At the other end, drill two ¼″ holes at the center of the bias of the corners. Place a 6″ square piece of acrylic sheet inside the frame.

Step 2. Clamp the frame shut with two wing-nuts. Slowly rotate the frame horizontally over a hot plate. Keep the acrylic sheet about 3″ from the heated wires as you move it circularly over the hot plate. The acrylic sheet will first begin to crinkle and then tighten up and look like it did when it was hard. Tap the resin with the rounded bottom of a spoon; when the plastic gives slightly, like a rubber band, the sheet is ready for heat forming.

Step 3. As soon as the acrylic sheet is soft, place it on top of an empty coffee can and push a heat-resistant form such as the tin can used here into the hot plastic to make a hollow in the shape of the pendant. You can usually push the form about 1″ to 2″ into the coffee can. Be sure to hold the shaping form steadily in place while the resin cools. If you're in a hurry, it's possible to cool the acrylic resin faster by pouring cold water into the form.

Step 4. If you're not satisfied with your first efforts, you can reheat the acrylic sheet and repeat Steps 1 through 3. However, you can't usually repeat this procedure successfully too many times.

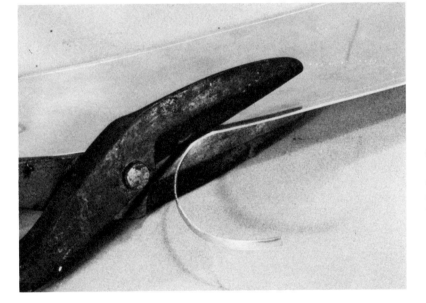

Step 5. Make an internal design for the piece with a set of three pewter squares of different sizes, which will be used as cloisons. To make the first square, score a ¼'' wide strip of pewter by drawing the sharpened point of a nail along a straight edge to provide a guide line for cutting. Cut out the pewter strip with shears; the heavier the cutting shears you use, the truer the cut will be.

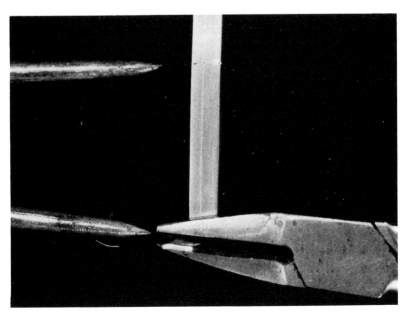

Step 6. Sand the strip of pewter with wet 400-grit wet-or-dry sandpaper, and mark out the dimensions of the squares on the strip. Bend the strip into a square by folding along the marks.

Step 7. In preparation for sawing, score a guide line at an angle on the side where the two ends of the strip will meet. With a jeweler's saw, cut through both ends of the metal at the same time to get a perfect fit. (Cut the pewter on an angle so that if you want to solder with the weak lead solder, the added surface area will give the joint more strength.)

Step 8. Shape the pewter square by hand and with pliers so that the ends fit together without soldering. Make the other two pewter shapes by the same process. Assemble the set to see how it looks before embedding it in the HH 772 acrylic resin system. (If you are bothered by the "open" joints, you can solder them. Pewter soldering is demonstrated in Project 9, Steps 5 through 8.)

Step 9. Wash the three pewter squares with soap and water, dry, and use tweezers to assemble them on the acrylic form.

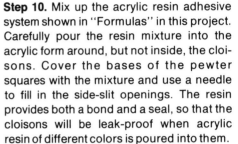

Step 10. Mix up the acrylic resin adhesive system shown in "Formulas" in this project. Carefully pour the resin mixture into the acrylic form around, but not inside, the cloisons. Cover the bases of the pewter squares with the mixture and use a needle to fill in the side-slit openings. The resin provides both a bond and a seal, so that the cloisons will be leak-proof when acrylic resin of different colors is poured into them.

Step 11. Since the HH 772 acrylic system won't cure in the presence of air when catalyzed, cover the resin mixture with the dilute detergent solution shown in "Formulas" in this project. Spray the deterginated water carefully all over the resin until the surface is submerged about ¼". Curing the acrylic resin system takes 2 to 3 hours at 70° F. This time can be cut in half by placing an infrared heat lamp about 10" from the piece, although the extra heat may cause internal bubbles to form. If you object to the bubbles, don't heat cure. The resin is cured when it can't be pierced with a needle. Pour off the water, dry the surface with a paper towel, and place the piece about 10" from an infrared lamp. While still damp, the resin may have a slight haze, but this will completely disappear when the resin is dry.

Step 12. Mix up another batch of the acrylic resin system. Divide the batch into three plastic-coated cups and add small amounts of color pastes until you get the shades you want. Pour enough colored resin into each cloison to make it about ⅞ full. Cover the colored resin with the detergent solution and cure as in Step 1.

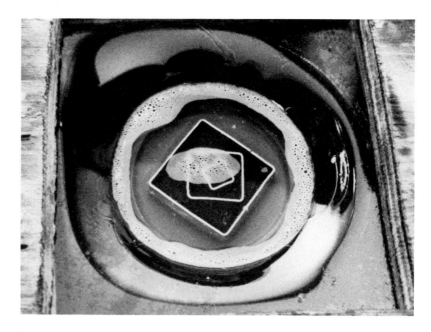

Step 13. Because the resin shrinks about 15% after curing, use another batch of clear HH 772 acrylic resin to completely cover the pewter inlays. Spray the acrylic with the same detergent solution and this time let the piece harden for 3 to 4 hours. Cure under an infrared lamp for a few more hours to get a harder resin surface.

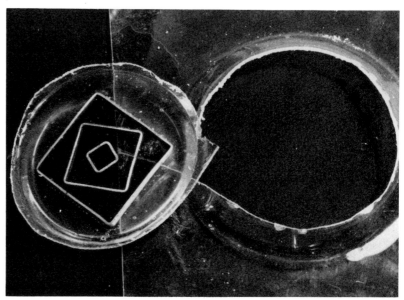

Step 14. Once the acrylic resin is well cured and dry, remove the 6″ acrylic square from the frame. Saw out the pendant shape. It's easier to cut the acrylic if you put a little candle wax on the saw blade while cutting.

Step 15. Roughly shape and smooth the piece with a file.

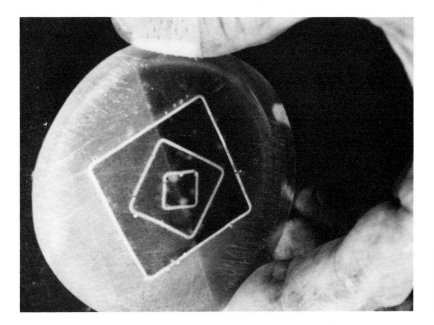

Step 16. Next sand the piece with increasingly fine grades of wet, wet-or-dry sandpaper, from 180 or 220 to 400 grit. (See *Finishing Your Jewelry* for instructions.)

Step 17. I decided to change the shape of the piece shown here for esthetic reasons. When you are satisfied with your piece, buff it with a 6″ diameter muslin wheel running at 1750 r.p.m. and buffing compounds. (See *Finishing Your Jewelry*.)

Step 18. Drill a hole in the piece with a ⅛″ bit and make a double loop through it with 20-gauge sterling wire. Leave both ends of the wire inside the hole to give the hanger a neat appearance.

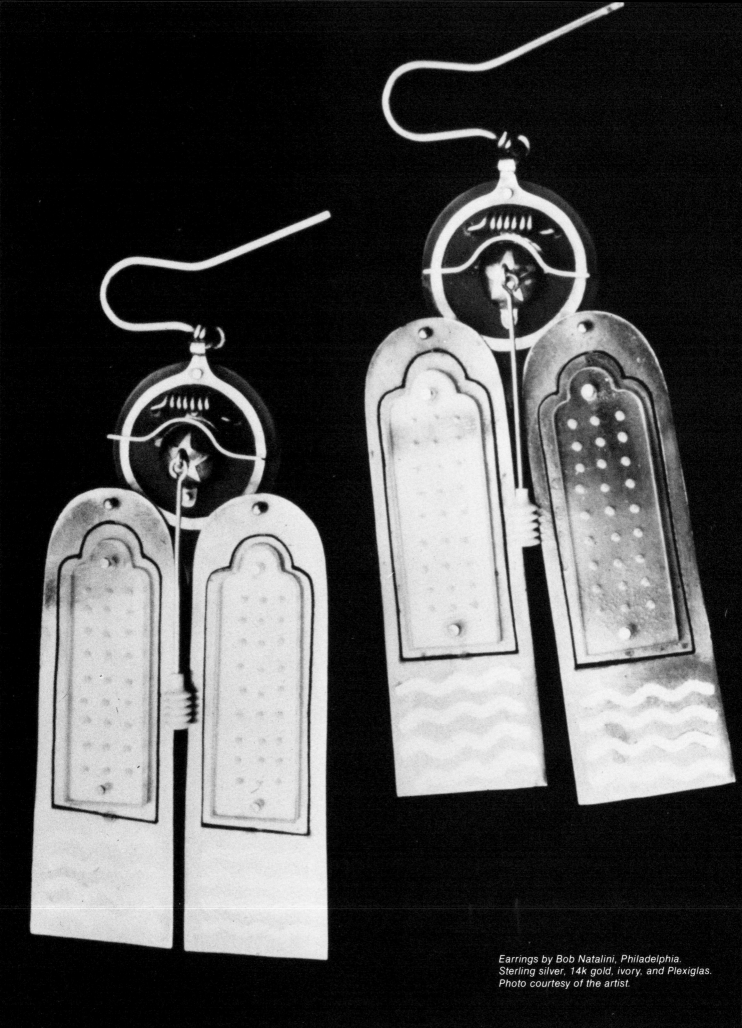

Earrings by Bob Natalini, Philadelphia.
Sterling silver, 14k gold, ivory, and Plexiglas.
Photo courtesy of the artist.

MAKING MIXED-MEDIA EARRINGS

Acrylic resins have glasslike clarity and nearly the brilliance of cut precious stones. Through use over the past 35 years this synthetic polymer has proved to have excellent weatherability and non-yellowing properties. According to the manufacturers, acrylics lose only about 1% of their light-transmitting properties for each five years of outdoor exposure. Jewelry made from acrylics, then, has a long life expectancy. Now that there are methods for working with liquid acrylics, which are easily hardened at room temperature, the jeweler can enlarge his scope if he's willing to learn some new technology.

Throughout this project, as in all the others in this book, I want to emphasize certain information that will enable you to use plastics in any jewelry item. In this project you will learn:

How to bond sheet acrylic and construct a form with or without air bubbles (see also *Acrylic Resins*), using ethylene dichloride for the adhesive and an activated M/P (monomer/polymer) acrylic casting resin for the inbedments.

How to employ mixed media as a simple design technique, taking advantage of the transparent nature of acrylics.

How to enhance the brilliance of acrylics through proper cutting and polishing.

TOOLS AND MATERIALS

1. Jeweler's tools: saw and blades (or band saw), pliers, electric or hand drill and 1/32", 1/16", 1/8" bits.
2. Any sharp tool such as a nail or pointed scissors.
3. Masking and cellulose (Scotch) tape.
4. Infrared heat lamp.
5. HH 572 soft modeling wax.
6. Soft iron binding wire, used by silversmiths.
7. 16-gauge sterling silver wire.
8. Earring findings.
9. Finishing tools: 180-grit to 400-grit wet-or-dry sandpaper, buffing wheels, and buffing compounds.
10. 1/16" water-clear or tinted-clear acrylic sheet, regular or scrap, whichever is cheaper.
11. Needle and size 40 nylon or cotton thread.
12. Ethylene dichloride.
13. Annealing oven or heat box which you can make yourself (optional, see *Your Studio and Basic Equipment*).
14. Polysciences HH 772 M/P (monomer/polymer) acrylic syrup.
15. Polysciences HH 772 catalyst.

16. Polysciences HH 772 bleach.
17. Joy detergent.
18. CIBA-GEIGY Araldite epoxy resin 502.
19. RC-303 curing agent.
20. Color pastes.

FORMULAS

CASTING RESIN

HH 772 acrylic syrup	100 grams
HH 772 catalyst:	
up to ¼" thick	3 grams (3%)
up to ½" thick	2–2.5 grams (2%–2.5%)
HH 772 bleach	3 grams (3%)
Color pastes	as needed

Use this resin system at 70° F. (room temperature). Mix only what you need at any one time. The catalyzed material yellows when exposed to air for ½ hour or more. Add the catalyst, the bleach, and the desired colors and mix well (but not over-enthusiastically) for about 2 minutes. Let the system stand several minutes to allow the air bubbles to rise.

CURING SOLUTION

Water	1 quart
Joy detergent	5 drops

To cure the resin after you've poured it into the acrylic form, spray the surface exposed to the air with ¼" of this deterginated water.

QUICK-CURE RESIN FOR EARRING FINDING DECORATION

Araldite epoxy resin	2 grams
Curing agent RC-303	1 gram (50%)
Color pastes	as needed

Mix the resin and curing agent together for about 30 seconds. Add needle-point amounts of color paste. Stir well.

NOTES AND CAUTIONS

All non-resinous materials are available from local stores, and resins for this project can be obtained through the suppliers listed in *Suppliers and Manufacturers*.

These acrylic resins are relatively expensive, which is one of the reasons why I've found a way to use acrylic cast sheet to cut down the cost to equal that of polyester resin.

Always work carefully with these resins; remember to have good ventilation, wear goggles and gloves, and don't smoke, drink, or eat in the working area.

Step 1. Make three equal-sized, 5½" x 3", rectangles out of 1/16" paper-covered acrylic sheet by scoring them three or four times with a sharp-pointed tool. Break the sheet at the score line by placing it on the edge of a table and bending down and away. Practice this procedure until you can break the sheet smoothly.

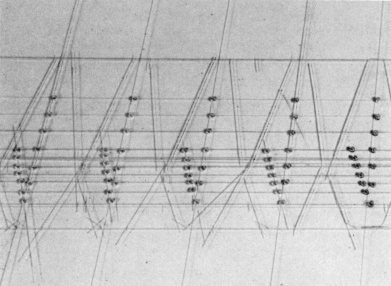

Step 2. Outline a simple design on the outer paper that protects the acrylic sheet. Use a sharp tool to mark the acrylic where you want the holes (to be threaded as part of the design) and drill them with a 1/16" bit. Remove the paper covering and scratch your design on one of the three acrylic sheets. This sheet will occupy the center position of the three-sheet construction for the earrings.

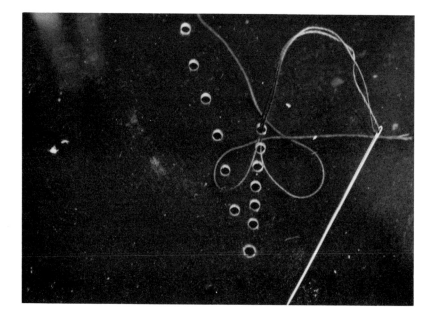

Step 3. However you sew your configuration, be sure to end up at the same place where you started so that you can tie a careful, invisible knot at the "starting point." The only hard part of all this is threading the needle. Sew each design in the sheet. Making two or more earring sets doesn't take much more time than a single pair. If I were going to make a production run, I would make at least 12 patterns.

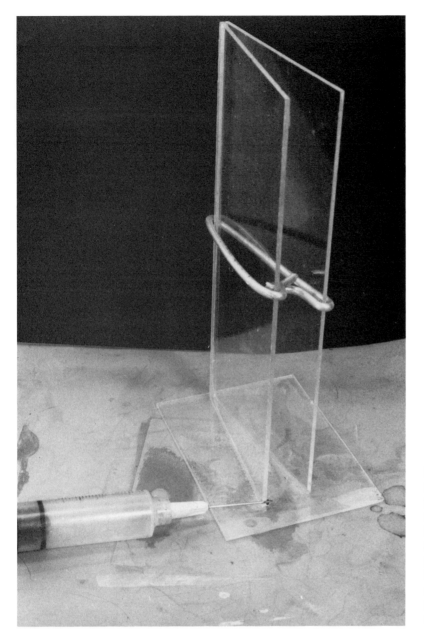

Step 4. The simplest method for constructing the container for the sewn design is to cut two 6″ x 4″ rectangles from 1/16″ Plexiglas. Scotch tape them together so that they form a "V" and then stand the pieces up vertically on top of one of the 5½″ x 3″ acrylic rectangles. The ends of the V should be ⅝″ to ¾″ apart. Squirt the inner and outer edges of the Scotch-taped V with a syringe filled with ethylene dichloride, one of the standard adhesives for acrylic sheet.

Step 5. Use ethylene dichloride to glue the third 5½″ x 3″ acrylic rectangle to the other end of the V. Use soft wire to help hold the V in shape. Turn the V to a horizontal position.

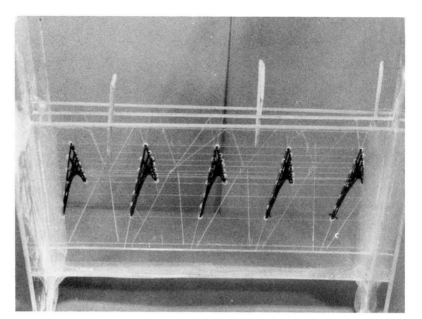

Step 6. Place the sewn rectangle in the center of the V and glue it along the bottom edges. If necessary, insert little wedges for proper spacing. Put HH 572 soft modeling wax over the glue to seal all the inside edges which will be in direct contact with the acrylic pour-in. Use water to test for leaks; if there are any, dry the form, and stop up the holes with more HH 572 wax. Let the ethylene dichloride gluing stand for 4 hours about 18″ away from an infrared heat lamp.

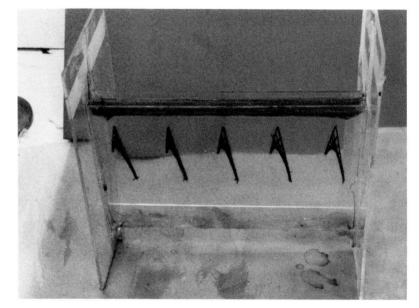

Step 7. Prepare the HH 772 acrylic resin system shown in "Formulas" for this project. You can estimate how much resin to make by weighing the amount of water needed to fill the trough. Remember that the resin system will shrink about 15% when it has finally cured out. Be sure to dry the trough before pouring in the resin. Now fill the V mold with the resin and immediately spray the surface with ¼″ of deterginated water given in "Formulas." Let the resin cure at room temperature. When the resin is about to cure, the acrylic trough will begin to get warm.

Step 8. Bubbles will appear in the thickest part of the casting where the most heat has been generated. I find that the presence of vapor bubbles in the resin creates the feeling of depth. To cure the resin after it has hardened, place the trough in a heat box or oven set at 150° F. for several hours. (Leave the oven door ajar to prevent vapor build-up.) If the resin system is not cured hard enough, you'll have trouble sawing through the acrylic mass. Use a jeweler's saw—or you may find that a coping saw works even better—to cut out the earring pieces. Apply a little oil to the saw blade while cutting to keep it from sticking.

Step 9. Sand the pieces with wet 180-grit, 220-grit, and 400-grit wet-or-dry sandpaper. Buff them with Learok 765, 885E, and 339E compounds applied to separate 6″ muslin buffing wheels running at 1750 r.p.m. or a buffer with the surface speed of approximately 2800 feet per minute. All these buffing compounds are greaseless, so the pieces won't get dirty while being polished. (See *Finishing Your Jewelry* for buffing procedures.)

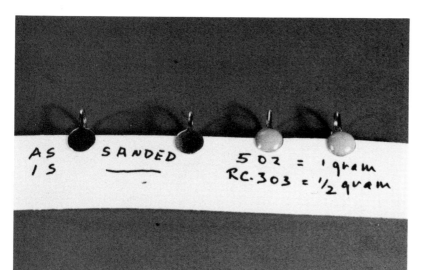

Step 10. To decorate the earring findings, first sand them with 220-grit sandpaper, wash and dry them, and then apply a "jewel" made of the quick-cure epoxy resin listed in "Formulas" for this project. After the resin has cured to a rigid rubberiness, harden it further by putting it about 8″ away from an infrared heat lamp for an hour.

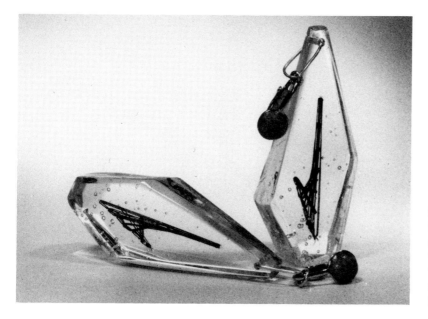

Step 11. The earring finding can be attached in a number of ways; I try to use the simplest. Drill the hole in the acrylic "dangle" with a 1/16″ bit. Shape a piece of 16-gauge sterling silver wire with a pair of needle-nose jeweler's pliers to form the hanging loop.

Necklace by Bernd Seegebrecht,
Freiburg, Germany.
Taken from "Science Fiction" drawings,
925/silver and Plexiglas.
Photo by Johannes Schmidt.

RELIEF PAINTING A NECKLACE

Since the hardest thing about this project is working out a good design, I offer the following hints, which should make this task a little easier. Make each unit in the piece as simple as possible. Good shapes are based on circles, squares, or triangles. Make all units the same size or make pairs in gradually decreasing sizes with one large center piece. Don't make any more units than necessary unless you enjoy lots of work. Five, seven, or nine units should be ample, since generally it's not necessary to hang pieces on the necklace above the collarbone. Plan your color scheme on adjacent hues such as blue and green or blue and yellow. Pure colors are usually gaudy. Traces of yellow or red in blue make it more interesting. Any incised decoration should be executed with the utmost economy. If you're unsure, leave it out. The procedures you will learn in this project are applicable to making any type of jewelry:

How to craft jewelry containing acrylic resin from relatively inexpensive scrap acrylic sheet and catalyzed HH 772 M/P acrylic syrup.

How to add another material such as metal, stone, or wood to make the piece more interesting.

How to saw and solder pewter with solders of different melting points.

How to invisibly attach the pewter loops used to hang the necklace pieces.

How to relief "paint" with "thickened" water to achieve an incised design in the acrylic surface.

TOOLS AND MATERIALS

1. Jeweler's tools: saw, blades, drill and 3/64" bits, files, and pliers.

2. Finishing tools: wet-or-dry sandpaper, wheel or hand buffer, buffing compounds, and buffing spring clamps.

3. Large pair of plumber's shears to cut the pewter (borrow them if you can).

4. Sheet of double-strength glass.

5. A few feet of PVC plastic-covered clothesline.

6. Spray bottle.

7. Annealing oven, or heat box which you can make inexpensively (see *Your Studio and Basic Equipment*).

8. A Ronson Varaflame torch for soldering the pewter.

9. Soft iron binding wire, used by silversmiths.

10. 18-gauge pewter sheet.

11. 16-gauge and 18-gauge sterling silver wire.

12. Tin/lead solder wire, 60/40 high melting and 63/37 lower melting.

FORMULAS

CABOSIL WATER-PAINTING MEDIUM

Water	50 grams
Glycerin	5 grams (10%)
Joy detergent	1 drop
Cabosil	5 grams (10%)

Mix all ingredients together and stir well until you have a homogenous thixotropic (non-runny) mixture, which can then be bottled and kept.

CASTING RESIN

HH 772 acrylic syrup	50 grams
HH 772 catalyst	1.5 grams (3%)
HH 772 bleach	1.5 grams (3%)
Color pastes	as needed

Weigh the ingredients into a container and stir well. Divide the resin mixture into plastic-coated cups and drop in needle-point amounts of color paste. Stir thoroughly.

---

13. Pewter flux, bought, or made from 10 drops of muriatic (hydrochloric) acid dissolved in 1 liquid oz. of glycerin.

14. HH 572 soft, high-temperature modeling wax for gasketing around the pewter pieces.

15. 1/16" acrylic sheet, such as Lucite or Plexiglas.

16. A sable brush.

17. Glycerin, Joy detergent, and Cabosil.

18. Polysciences HH 772 M/P acrylic syrup.

19. Polysciences HH 772 catalyst.

20. Polysciences HH 772 bleach.

21. Color pastes.

NOTES AND CAUTIONS

Remember, you're doing this project to learn how to handle acrylic M/P syrups. The first piece will help point out your mistakes, the second will bring out other errors. Your third should be the best!

Among the variations you should consider is the inclusion of different media such as stones, string, and metal objects (other than copper, which prevents the acrylic resin from polymerizing). But keep it simple.

All materials are available from the resin and jewelry suppliers listed in *Suppliers and Manufacturers*. A few items that are obviously hardware supplies can be obtained locally at more reasonable prices.

Handle the acrylic liquid resins carefully and safely as directed in Project 1, "Notes and Cautions."

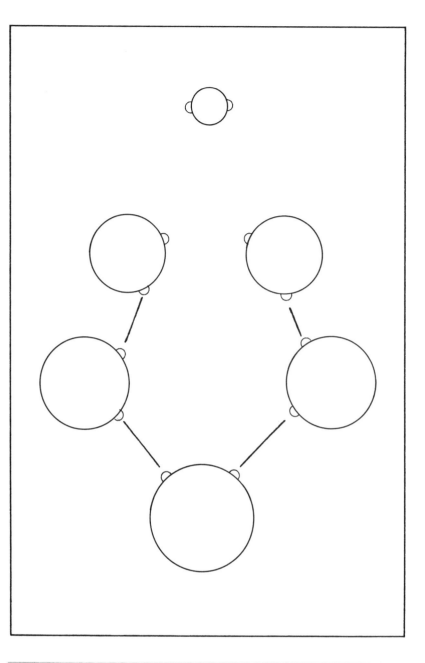

Step 1. Draw your design on a sheet of paper (see the introduction to this project for thought on the design problem).

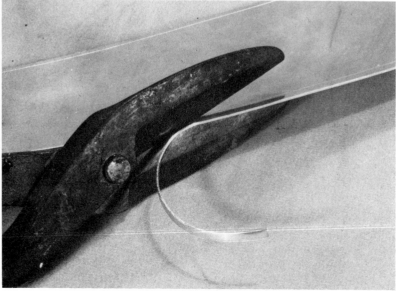

Step 2. Score and cut a strip of ⅛″, 18-gauge pewter. Cut enough strips to fashion the elements of the design. Similarly, cut 1/32″ strips of pewter for the hanging loops. Sand all these strips lengthwise with wet, 400-grit, wet-or-dry sandpaper. This procedure not only cleans the metal but also makes it rough so that it will provide a better adhesive surface for the acrylic resin.

Step 3. With a pair of jeweler's pliers, shape the ⅛" pewter strips according to your design. Overlap the ends of the strip so that wherever the pewter is cut through at the overlap the ends will mesh nicely.

Step 4. Use a jeweler's saw to cut the pewter at an angle at the overlap, and bend the ends together with jeweler's pliers.

Step 5. Secure the pewter circle upright with an L-shaped piece of soft iron binding wire embedded in a heat-resistant asbestos plate. Apply the pewter flux, made from 1 oz. of glycerin and 10 drops of muriatic (hydrochloric) acid (which you can purchase already prepared) to the touching ends. Flatten a small piece of 60/40 tin/lead solder and place it over the joint with a pair of tweezers (see Project 9, Steps 5 through 8). Wave a small butane jeweler's torch (see *Your Studio and Basic Equipment*) slowly back and forth across the joint of the pewter circle. The blue part of the 2" flame should be kept about 3" to 4" from the pewter. When the flux boils off and the solder *begins* to melt, remove the flame. Usually the solder will continue to melt from the residual heat and will "run" into the joint.

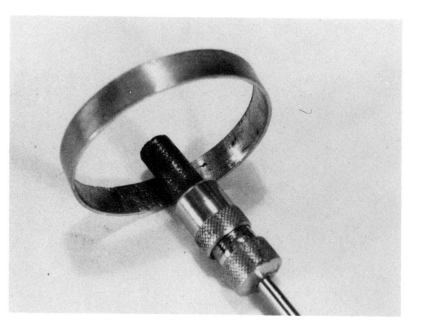

Step 6. After soldering, sand the area of the joint in one direction, following the circle, with wet, 180-grit wet-or-dry sandpaper. If this is done properly, you won't be able to see the joint. Following the 180-grit sanding, use 400-grit wet-or-dry sandpaper to get a good surface for resin adhesion. You can also use Brightboy rubber abrasive to put a matte finish on the metal surface (see *Your Studio and Basic Equipment*).

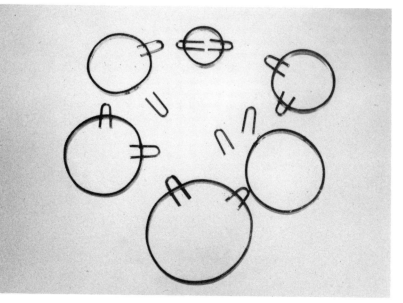

Step 7. Solder all the pewter circles. Then make U shapes from the 1/32″ pewter strips. Drill the circles with a 3/64″ bit to accommodate the U shapes and insert them into the pewter circles.

Step 8. Make solder snippings ⅛″ in length from a flattened strip of lower melting 63/37 tin/lead solder and bend each one to form a V. Perch the upside down V shapes on the legs of the U shapes for soldering. Wave the butane torch gently across the solder, the legs of the U, and the pewter circle.

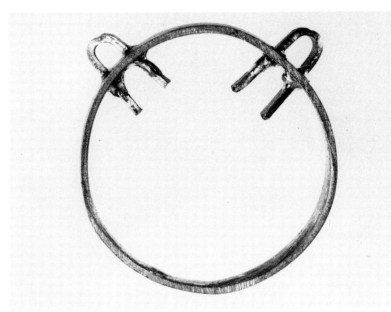

Step 9. Allow the solder to fill up and cover the inner and outer surfaces of the holes holding the U shapes. Cut off the feet of the U shapes with a jeweler's saw.

Step 10. With a needle file (see *Your Studio and Basic Equipment*), carefully file down the excess solder and the leg stumps of the U shapes. Clean the inside of the pewter circle by wet sanding with 400-grit wet-or-dry sandpaper; sand in the direction of the circle rather than across it.

Step 11. Place the pewter circles on a glass plate and surround them with HH 572 modeling wax. The wax prevents the acrylic resin from contacting the exterior surface of the pewter circles. Protect the U shapes as well. Make the interior design with a sable brush, using a non-runny mixture of Cabosil, water, glycerin, and Joy detergent shown in "Formulas" for this project. This relief "painting" creates negative space in the final acrylic casting. Since the HH 772 acrylic casting material does not bond to the glass plate, you can easily remove the non-adhering Cabosil mixture from the surface of the cured HH 772 resin later by washing it off with running water.

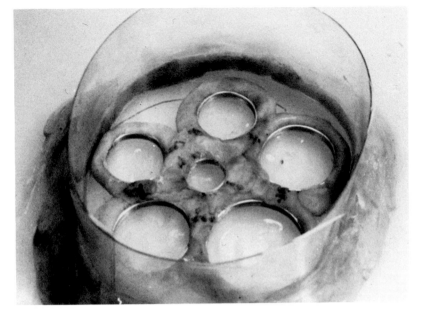

Step 12. Make a collar from a strip of 20-mil cellulose acetate by gluing the overlapping ends with acetone squirted from a syringe, and embed the collar in the soft HH 572 modeling wax. This "container" will hold the water and keep out air while the acrylic resin cures.

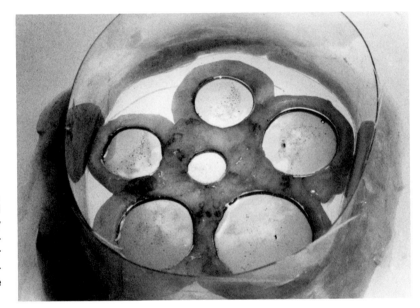

Step 13. Mix up the colored HH 772 system, shown in "Formulas" for this project, and pour it into each circle up to the rim. Spray deterginated water (a few drops of Joy detergent to a quart of water) ¼" deep over the freshly poured acrylic resin HH 772. Allow the resin to cure at room temperature for 3 hours.

Step 14. The resin is sufficiently cured when it can't be penetrated with the point of a needle. Pour off the water, remove the acetate collar, and dry the resin with paper tissues. Place the entire mass about 12" away from an infrared heat lamp for ½ hour, or until the resin is clear and dry.

Step 15. With plastic-covered clothesline, make a fence ¾ of the way around the wax-molded circles. Cover the original glass sheet with an equal-sized sheet of ⅛″ Plexiglas, using the clothesline as a gasket between the two sheets. Secure pressure clamps directly over the PVC (polyvinyl chloride) gasket so as not to distort the flexible Plexiglas. Mix the acrylic casting system from "formulas" for this project. Hold the container upright and pour the HH 772 acrylic resin system into the space between the sheets through the top (the open side). Cure the resin with the air-excluding detergent-solution seal, at room temperature for about 3 hours. Remove the pressure clamps and lift the non-sticking glass plate and the PVC clothesline from the acrylic casting. Wash the Cabosil mixture off the cured resin surface with running water.

Step 16. Saw the pieces of the necklace away from the sheet of Plexiglas. The HH 572 soft modeling wax that covers the outside of the pewter circles and the U shapes makes the job of removing the resin much easier.

Step 17. To get a lens effect, round the edge of the pieces of filing, sanding wet with wet-or-dry sandpaper (from 180-grit to 400-grit), buffing with Learok 884E, and finally, a high-polishing with Learok 339E. According to the Lea Manufacturing Company, you can polish to a super-high gloss by finishing with Learok 312 applied to a clean finish-buffing wheel. For additional information on finishing, see *Finishing Your Jewelry*.

Step 18. Bend a piece of 18-gauge sterling silver wire with jeweler's pliers to form the links of the necklace. Make one link to connect each of the units you've just made.

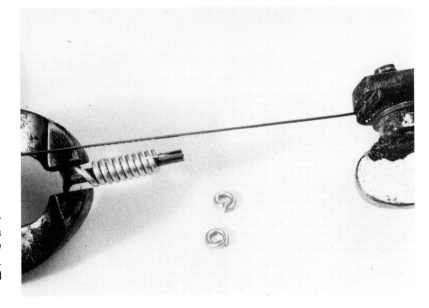

Step 19. Make the "jump" rings by wrapping 16-gauge sterling silver wire around a nail. Clamp the nail in a vise and saw through the coiled wire at a sharp angle. While cutting, you can easily pull the sawed jump rings away from the nail.

Step 20. To finish the necklace, attach the links to the U shapes of each necklace piece with the jump rings. Attach a piece of sterling silver chain to each of the two necklace end units. Buy a safety clasp from a jewelry supply store and attach it to the silver chain with one of the jump rings. Attach another jump ring to the other end of the chain, through which to fit the clasp.

Wall brooch by Jem Freyaldenhoven,
Georgia State University.
Cast, constructed, and electroformed silver,
electroformed gold, and vacuum-formed,
hand-formed, and pierced white Polystyrene.
Photo courtesy of the artist.

ROTATIONALLY CASTING A NECKLACE

An intriguing property of catalyzed M/P acrylic syrups is their ability to cure well under water. This project is based on this fact and will show you:

How to use Plexiglas or Lucite as a casting mold that becomes an integral part of the curing M/P acrylic syrup.

How to cast rotationally with a new method using HH 772 M/P acrylic syrup in the presence of water.

How to fashion a chain for the necklace using heavy Plexiglas and sterling silver links.

TOOLS AND MATERIALS

1. Jeweler's tools: saw and #1 blades; electric or hand drill with 1/16″, 1/8″, and 1/4″ bits; pliers.

2. Finishing tools: 180-grit to 400-grit wet-or-dry sandpaper, buffing compounds (Learok 765, 884E, and 339E) and wheels.

3. A safety catch for the necklace chain.

4. HH 572 soft modeling wax.

5. PVC electrical tape, masking and cellulose (Scotch) tape.

6. Any sharp tool, such as a nail, to score the Plexiglas.

7. 1/16″ water-clear acrylic sheet. Scrap is cheapest.

8. Plexiglas 70 for the links. You can also use the polycarbonate, Lexan, sold by General Electric (see Project 5, "Tools and Materials").

9. Methylene dichloride or ethylene dichloride solvent adhesive.

10. Syringe for applying the adhesive.

11. Homemade annealing oven (optional, see *Your Studio and Basic Equipment*).

12. Polysciences HH 772 M/P acrylic syrup.

13. Polysciences HH 772 catalyst.

14. Polysciences HH 772 bleach.

15. Color pastes.

FORMULA

CASTING RESIN

HH 772 acrylic syrup	50 grams
HH 772 catalyst	1.5 grams (3%)
HH 772 bleach	1.5 grams (3%)
Color pastes	as needed

Mix thoroughly in one container. Divide into plastic coated paper cups and add needle-point amounts of color pastes as desired. Mix well.

NOTES AND CAUTIONS

Materials for the acrylic resin system are available from Polysciences (see *Suppliers and Manufacturers*). All non-resinous materials are available from local stores.

You can make an acetate mold instead of the acrylic mold for this project (see Project 18, Step 1). In this case, remember that the mold is self-releasing and is not part of the final casting.

Any dry and non-oily material, except uncoated copper, may be embedded in the acrylic system.

In this project, there's little air contamination from the volatile methyl methacrylate monomer since the rotating mold is not open to the air. However, as in the preceding project, you are warned to keep HH 772 systems from touching your skin.

Wear protective goggles and polyethylene gloves when weighing and mixing acrylic M/P syrups. (Please read Acrylic Resins and Your Studio and Basic Equipment thoroughly.)

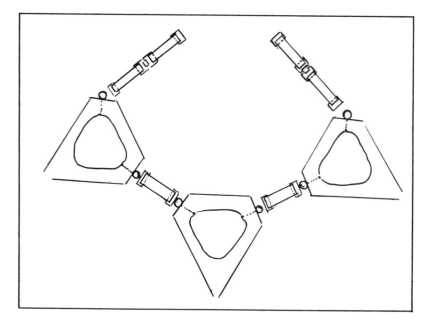

Step 1. Make a simple sketch for the necklace.

Step 2. Break three 1/16″ pieces of Plexiglas, according to the method described in Project 2, Step 1, to make 2¼″ x 6″ rectangles. Put them together to form a prism. Make two 4″ Plexiglas squares for the top and bottom. Drill a ¼″ filling hole in the top square. Hold the "container" together with masking or cellulose (Scotch) tape while preparing to glue. Fill a syringe with ethylene dichloride and squirt it generously on the surface edges of the prism and the contacting edges of the top and bottom Plexiglas squares. Allow the form to set at least 12 hours before filling it or the joint might give way when you pour in the HH 772 acrylic casting resin.

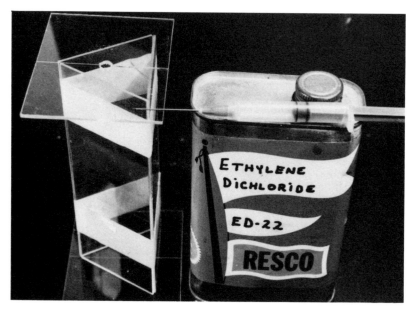

Helen J. Russell

Step 3. As an added precaution, after removing the masking tape, Scotch tape the edges to further seal against leakage. Once you start rotating the mold, it's frightfully messy if it springs a leak!

Step 4. As an extra safeguard, seal the glued edges with HH 572 soft modeling wax by smearing it right over the Scotch tape.

Step 5. Mix the colorless HH 772 acrylic resin according to "Formulas" for this project. Pour the resin into the ¼" filling hole in the top square. *Be sure* to completely cover the inside of the form with a ⅛" to ¼" layer of resin. Add water to fill up the prism. Dry the filling end and seal the hole with PVC electrical tape or masking tape. Then start to rotate the container until the resin stops flowing. This can take up to 1 hour. Rotate the prism by hand, slowly turning the piece in all directions, or lash it lengthwise with rubber bands to a barbecue spit. The rotating may cause bubbles which will form part of the design.

Step 6. Remove the tape seal, reopen the hole, with a ¼" drill if necessary, and empty out the water. Place the container in a heat box or oven set at 150° F. to allow the inside of the prism to dry out thoroughly. (When using an oven, leave the door ajar to avoid vapor build-up.) You can speed up the drying by swabbing the interior of the mold chamber with cotton wrapped around an 8" stick (or a Q-tip). If the inside of the form is not completely covered after curing, repeat Steps 5 and 6 with the colorless HH 772 system and water until all the prism sides are well covered with about ⅛" to ¼" or more of the colorless, cured, acrylic resin.

Step 7. Then repeat Steps 5 and 6 with several layers of HH 772 resin colored with small amounts of transparent color pastes. The colors should be very pale or they'll lose their transparency. I usually add about five layers of resin, the last one being a deep-colored batch.

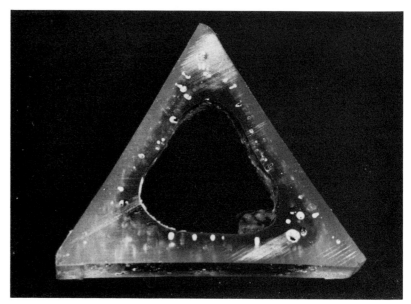

Step 8. Slice the prism pieces ¼'' to ⅜'' thick (or a thickness appropriate to your design) with an oiled coping saw, or use a band saw if available (see *Your Studio and Basic Equipment*). Sand the triangles well with wet, 180-grit to 400-grit, wet-or-dry sandpaper to be sure that all of the deep scratches have been eliminated. If you don't eradicate deep mars in this step, you'll never get them out later.

Step 9. At this point there's no need for additional sanding. Switch to greaseless buffing compounds, starting with Learok 765 applied to its own 6'' muslin wheel, running at 1750 r.p.m. Then buff with Learok 884E and, finally, with 339E to achieve a high polish (see *Finishing Your Jewelry*).

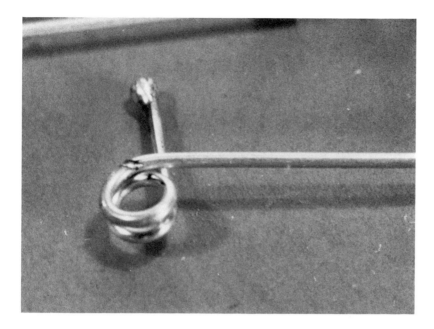

Step 10. Make a little ball at the end of a length of 18-gauge sterling silver wire by melting the wire in the torch flame. Then polish the ball and wire on a buffer.

Step 11. Drill a 1/16" hole in each triangle and pass the wire through it. Twist the wire with jeweler's pliers to make a hanging loop. Saw off the excess wire with a jeweler's saw.

Step 12. To make the links of the necklace use Plexiglas 70, which is stronger than regular Plexiglas. Mark out the links with dividers and cut them out with a jeweler's saw.

Step 13. Sand, buff, and high-polish the Plexiglas 70 links.

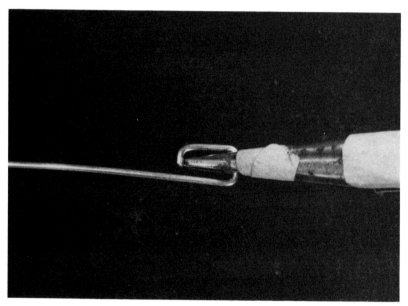

Step 14. Fashion the sterling silver links with a pair of needle-nose pliers that have been marked with masking tape to measure the bending of the wire uniformly. Bend the link around itself to make a rectangle, measuring the other side with a second piece of tape on the pliers. Saw the excess wire off as you complete each link.

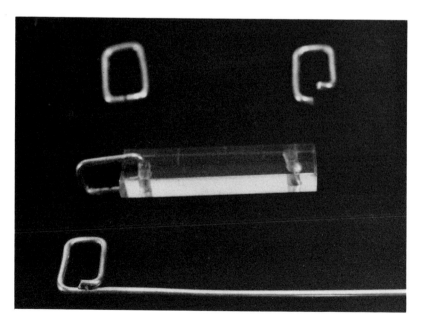

Step 15. Drill a 1/16" hole in the Plexiglas 70 links and bend the sterling silver link into the hole.

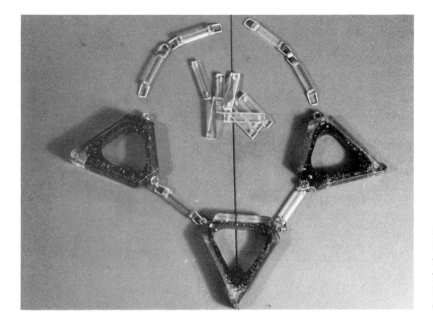

Step 16. Make "jump" rings from the sterling silver wire (see Project 3, Step 19). Attach the acrylic bars and silver links to the triangles with the jump rings. Attach the bars and links in the same way to make a chain of the appropriate length.

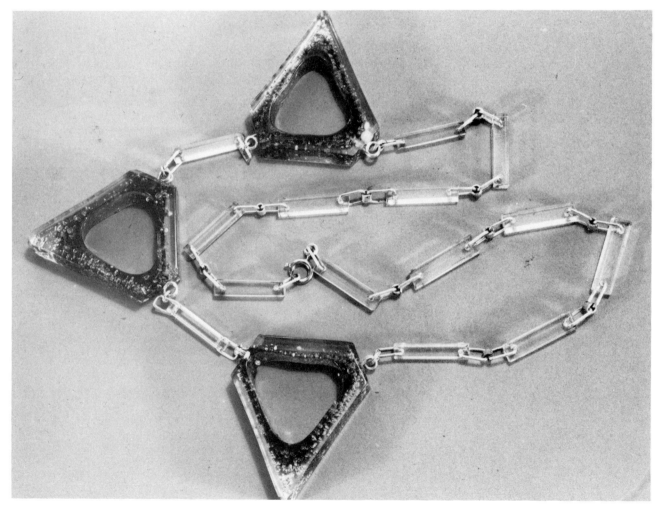

Step 17. To finish this necklace, you'll need to buy and attach a safety catch.

Pendant by Nancy English, New York City.
Sterling silver and vacuum-formed
and silk-screened plastic,
air brushed with acrylic lacquer.
Photo by Catherine Brown.

HEAT FORMING A LENS-SHAPED RING

The projects in this book are designed to demonstrate principles of resin handling that are applicable to a variety of jewelry shapes. Since acrylics have excellent optical properties, this project demonstrates a simple technique, using no fancy equipment, with which to bring out these properties. You will learn:

How to make an acrylic lens shape, and fill it with acrylic syrup that is either colorless or colored with transparent pastes.

How to custom make additional acrylic shapes such as cylinders through heat forming by rolling up strips of acrylic sheet on a dowel stick.

How to imbed objects such as pewter in acrylic resins.

How to bond a piece of acrylic to the acrylic bezel (the collar which holds the "jewel") with HH 772 adhesive resin.

TOOLS AND MATERIALS

1. Jeweler's tools: saw and blades, files, a ring mandril or a piece of wood rounded off to the desired inner size of your ring.

2. Finishing tools: 180-grit to 400-grit wet-or-dry sandpaper, a buffer, 6″ muslin wheels, and buffing compounds.

3. An asbestos board or a piece of hard rubber, and asbestos gloves.

4. Any spherical piece of metal, wood, or stone, 1″ to 2″ in diameter, to form the lens, and a bottle with a mouth of similar diameter.

5. A dowel, slightly larger in diameter than the lens-forming tool, to form a bezel.

6. A heat-forming frame, which you can make yourself (see Project 1, Steps 1 and 2).

7. A heat-forming device, such as the top of your oven or a hot plate.

8. HH 572 soft modeling wax.

9. A piece of soapstone.

10. 1/16″ acrylic sheet. You should try to get scrap, which is the cheapest and is usually sold by the pound.

11. ⅛″ thick Plexiglas 70 to form the ring band. The manufacturer (Rohm and Haas) claims that this relatively new acrylic sheet is almost as strong as General Electric's polycarbonate, Lexan. Since the ring band should be strong, and at the moment I don't know how to glue Lexan securely to Plexiglas without the glue line showing, I selected Plexiglas 70.

12. 18-gauge pewter sheet or pewter ingot.

FORMULAS

ACRYLIC CASTING RESIN

HH 772 acrylic syrup	10 grams
HH 772 catalyst	9 drops (3%)
HH 772 bleach	9 drops (3%)
Color pastes	as needed

Use a dropper that gives 3 drops per gram to measure the catalyst and the bleach. Mix the resin, catalyst, and bleach for several minutes. Add needle-point amounts of transparent color paste and stir them well into the system. The mixture should be poured within 15 minutes.

RESIN ADHESIVE

HH 772 acrylic syrup	5 grams
HH 772 catalyst	5 drops (3%)
HH 772 bleach	5 drops (3%)

Mix well for several minutes.

CURING SOLUTION

Water	1 quart
Joy detergent	5 drops

Mix the detergent into the water and spray it onto the resin surface to exclude air.

---

13. Soft iron binding wire, used by silversmiths.

14. Joy detergent.

15. Polysciences HH 772 M/P acrylic syrup.

16. Polysciences HH 772 catalyst.

17. Polysciences HH 772 bleach.

18. Color pastes.

NOTES AND CAUTIONS

The procedure presented in this project can be used to fashion bracelets, tiaras, and other jewelry.

When the ring is completely finished, you can cure it harder by placing it in a heat box or in your oven, set absolutely no higher than 165° F. for about 5 hours. (Leave the oven door ajar to avoid vapor build-up.) Annealing assures that the poured resin is well cured and prevents it from developing stress cracks. (See *Finishing Your Jewelry*.)

Have excellent ventilation in your work area.

Don't smoke or light a flame while working with HH 772. This resin system is highly flammable and in closed areas its vapors can be explosive in the presence of sparks.

Wear polyethylene gloves and protective goggles while weighing and mixing the acrylic HH 772 system.

Step 1. Make a heat-forming frame (see Project 1, Steps 1 and 2) and clamp a 6″ square of 1/16″ acrylic sheet between the frames. Heat the sheet and immediately place it on top of a bottle mouth. Force the lens-forming device, here a wooden ball, into the mouth and hold it there for about 1 minute until the resin has cooled enough to retain its shape.

Step 2. Remove the wooden ball and take the form out of the bottle. The hollowed-out form will be the top of the ring.

Step 3. To make the bezel (the collar that holds the "jewel"), use a hand saw to cut a 1/16″ wide slot about ⅛″ deep into a dowel that has a diameter slightly larger than the lens-forming tool. With a jeweler's saw, cut a ½″ strip of 1/16″ Plexiglas about 4″ long, warm it over the hot plate, and wrap it around the dowel, pushing the end through the slot. Hold it there until cool.

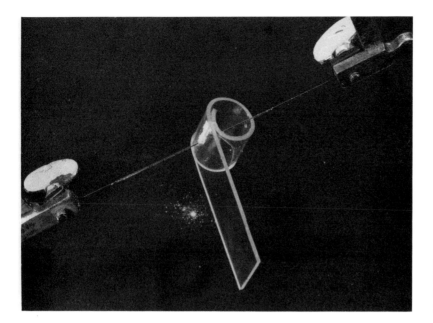

Step 4. With the jeweler's saw, cut through both overlapping resin strips at once, so that the edges of the bezel will fit together well.

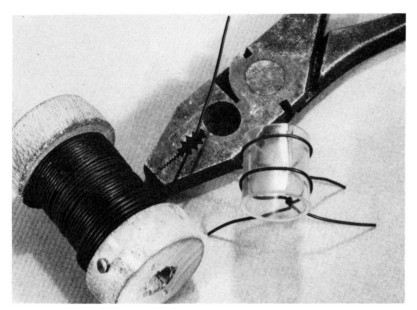

Step 5. Wrap soft iron binding wire tightly around the tube. Then gently heat the tube by turning it over the hot plate just long enough to soften the acrylic and to permit the edges to make contact.

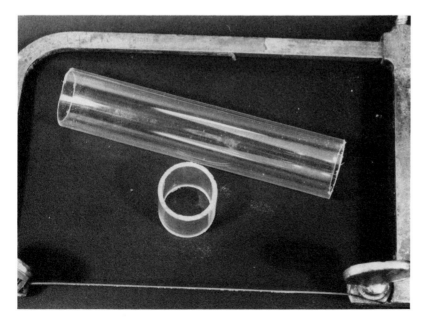

Step 6. If you can get a 1/16″ thick acrylic tube with a ¾″ outside diameter, you won't have to bother with tube-making; you can just saw off a piece of the tube to the correct width. However, if you want to make a bracelet with a ⅛″ tube and a 2¼″ diameter, you'll have to form the bezel as described above.

Step 7. Perch the bezel on top of the lens and secure it with HH 572 soft modeling wax. The wax also seals the edges of the bezel. Pour ⅛″ of the lightly tinted acrylic casting resin shown in "Formulas" for this project into the bezel and spray ¼″ of deterginated water over it. Cure the resin for 2 hours or more. When you can't penetrate the resin with a needle point, it's sufficiently cured. Pour off the water, mop up the excess moisture with a paper tissue, and dry the piece about 10″ away from an infrared heat lamp for ½ hour or more.

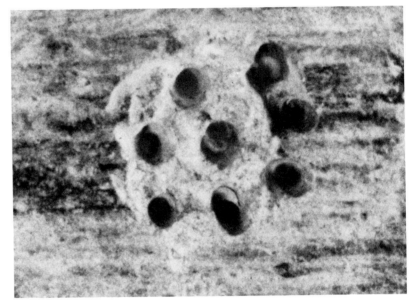

Step 8. With a 1/16″ bit, drill eight holes in a piece of soapstone. Gouge out the drill holes a bit more by twisting a nail in them.

Step 9. Melt about 50 grams of pewter in a tin can on a hot plate. The pewter has reached the proper pouring temperature when a paper taper dipped into the molten metal turns toasted-marshmallow brown. Pour the pewter into the soapstone, cover and flatten it with a piece of hard rubber or asbestos board.

Step 10. Let the pewter cool and remove it from the soap-stone. It needs no buffing or polishing.

Step 11. Mix up a small amount of fresh HH 772 resin and pour into the bezel to form a bed for the pewter. Place the pewter "jewel" face-down inside the bezel. Add more of the resin on top of the pewter to form a seal. Again spray the surface of the acrylic with deterginated water and let it cure. When the resin is hard, cut the bezel free from the original sheet with a jeweler's saw. File two opposite edges of the lens side of the bezel so that the ring band can be securely attached. Also saw off the unfilled part of the bezel tube.

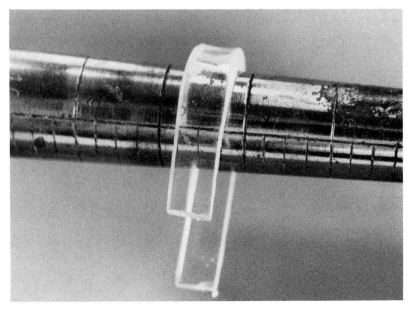

Step 12. Cut a ½″ x 3″ strip of ⅛″ Plexiglas 70 for the ring band. Soften the Plexiglas 70 over the hot plate, then wrap it around a ring mandril at the proper ring size. Wear a pair of asbestos gloves to avoid burning your fingers.

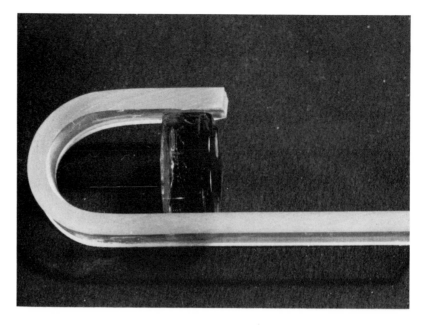

Step 13. File and sand the bezel to fit the bent Plexiglas 70. Experiment with the length of the band to see how the ring looks best.

Step 14. Saw the band off. Then clean and dry it and the sides of the bezel. Mix the resin adhesive shown in "Formulas" for this project, and apply it to the surfaces of the bezel and the inside surface of the Plexiglas 70 band. You can protect the exposed surfaces from drippings by wrapping them with Scotch tape, which can be removed after the resin is hard. Hold the ring together tightly with a rubber band for 3 or 4 hours until the acrylic has thoroughly cured.

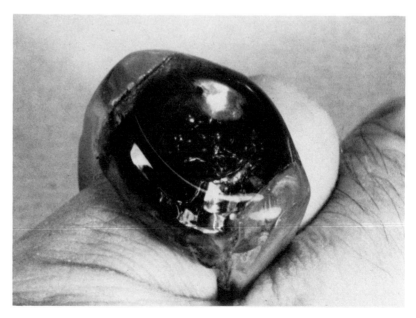

Step 15. Sand, polish, and anneal the ring (see *Finishing Your Jewelry*) to bring out the transparent brilliance of the acrylic resin.

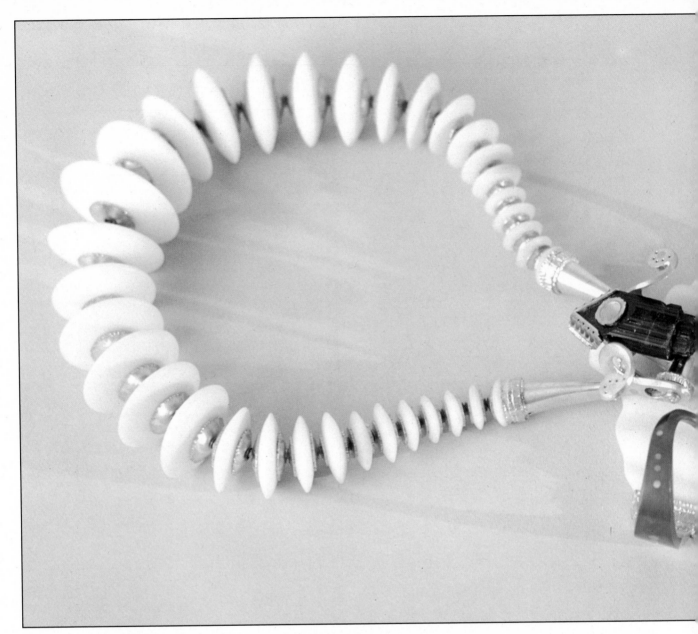

2. Neckpiece by Albert Paley, Rochester, New York.
Sterling silver, 14k gold, bronze with cameo, 4 pearls, and Delrin resin.
Photo courtesy of the artist.

3

4

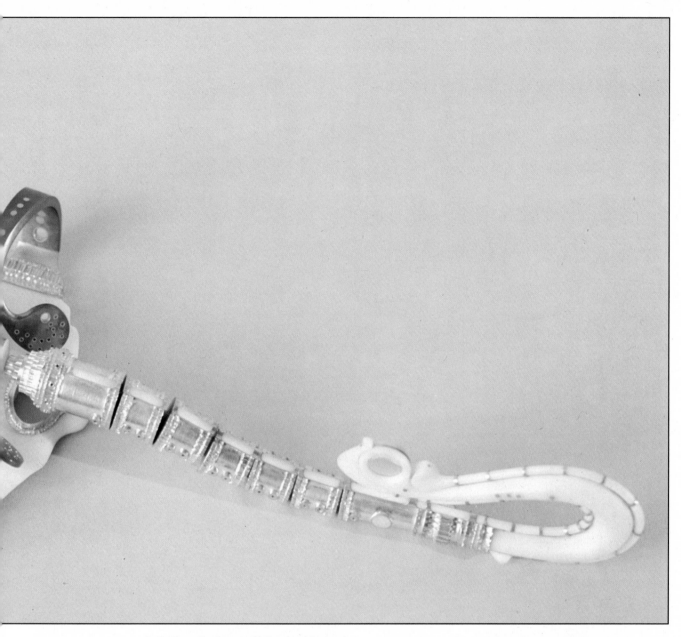

3–5. Rings by Joanne Hollander, Montreal.
Sterling silver and epoxy resin.
Photo by Astri Reusch.

6. Ring by Harold O'Conner, Calgary, Alberta.
18k gold and Plexiglas.
Photo courtesy of the artist.

5

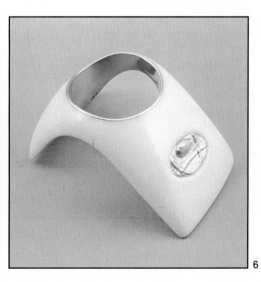

6

7. Brooch by Harold O'Conner, Calgary, Alberta.
18k gold, silver, Plexiglas, and paint.
Photo courtesy of the artist.

8. Necklace by the author.
Polyester resin, sterling silver, and pewter.
Project 16.

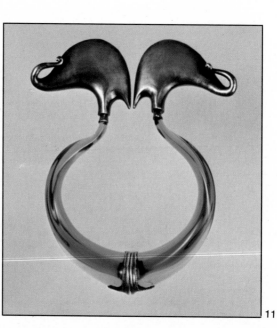

9–11. (Below) Torque neckpieces by Stanley Lechtzin,
Tyler School of Art.
Electroformed silver, gilt, and polyester resin.
Photos courtesy of the artist.

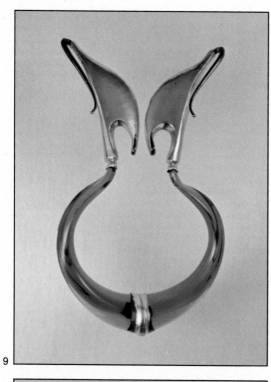

9

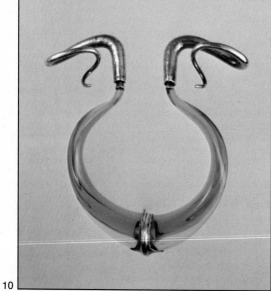

10

11

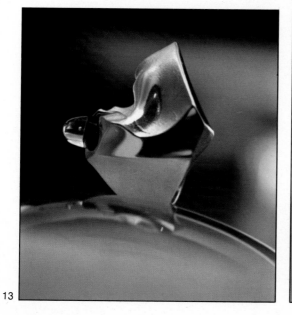

12. Pendant by Björn Weckström,
Lapponia Jewelry, Helsinki.
"Space Silver—Creature No. 5,"
silver and acrylic.
Photo by W. Zakowski.

13. Ring by Björn Weckström,
Lapponia Jewelry, Helsinki.
"Space Silver—Creature's Eye,"
silver and acrylic.
Photo by W. Zakowski.

14. Rings by Björn Weckström,
Lapponia Jewelry, Helsinki.
"Space Silver—Microns,"
silver and acrylic.
Photo by W. Zakowski.

12

13

14

PART TWO
EPOXY
RESINS

15. Sculpture and ring
by Marion Herbst Holland, Amsterdam.
Aluminum and Plexiglas, the sculpture.
Sterling silver and Plexiglas, the ring.
Photo by Hans Hoogland.

EPOXY RESINS

This part on epoxy resins will deal primarily with their use as "enamels" for jewelry. Since epoxy resin has now become a household word, like rubber cement, it isn't necessary to belabor the definition of an epoxy resin. All you really need to know is how much, by weight, of what epoxy resin must be combined with how much, by weight, of what hardener in order to convert these liquids into their non-melting (thermosetting) solid state. If you wish to obtain a little more background on this family of synthetic resins, consult my book, *Plastics for Artists and Craftsmen* (New York: Watson-Guptill Publications, 1972), pp. 39-100, or have a look at the *Handbook of Epoxy Resins* by Lee and Neville (New York: McGraw-Hill Publishing Company, 1967).

Epoxy resins are now being used successfully in jewelry in place of traditional vitreous enamels in combination with gold, silver, and copper. This has been done on a limited scale for the past 20 years. In jewelry, the use of epoxy resins is warranted when any or all of the following properties or conditions are needed:

When the "enamel" must have excellent adhesion to metals, precious and semi-precious stones, wood, natural fibers, and so on.

When the "enamel" must have abrasive resistance equal to or greater than that of gold, silver, copper, or pewter. Although epoxy resins aren't as abrasive as vitreous enamels, super-hard epoxy "enamels" are easily prepared when dry silica flour or sand is blended in with the resin. These are almost as abrasive resistant as the vitreous enamels.

When the "enamel" shouldn't crack, shatter, or break if the jewelry piece is accidentally dropped on a concrete floor.

When you don't have the permission, the availability, or the funds to use an electric kiln to fuse vitreous enamels.

When you want to enamel metals such as pewter or white metal, which melt about 500° F. below the fusing temperature of vitreous enamels.

When you are searching for an enameling procedure that is less time consuming, less expensive, and less complicated than that involving vitreous enamels.

When you want to repair a cracked or broken area of vitreous enamel in a jewelry piece, the epoxy resin "enamels" can be made to match any area exactly.

When you want to combine various media, such as "stones," wood, and metals in the same piece, epoxy resins, at the moment, are the only successful way.

When you want to enamel on materials other than metals, epoxy resin "enamels" adhere very well to "stones," plaster, wood, chipboard, slate, pumice, and so on.

When you want to re-enamel a particular area you don't fancy, you can soften the epoxy resin "enamel" while it's under an infrared heat lamp so that it may be completely picked out of the cloison with a sharp-pointed instrument. If care is used in this operation, the enameled object won't be hurt. It can be immediately cleaned with acetone and then re-enameled with more epoxy resin.

When you want to enamel large, non-brittle, plique-à-jour (see through) areas. This is easily accomplished by casting epoxy resin "enamels" into the jewelry piece, which is temporarily glued with rubber cement to Mylar sheet.

Epoxy resins are *not* usable:

When heat resistance above 500°F. is required.

When the great abrasive resistance of vitreous enamels is required.

EPOXY RESINS

An epoxy resin system is the combination of the epoxy resin with the proper hardener and the desired additives. Although there are many epoxy resins to choose from, when it comes to enameling jewelry I've selected one which has been on the market for about 25 years. This epoxy resin is called Araldite 502 and is, strictly speaking, a modified epoxy resin, manufactured by the CIBA-GEIGY Company. According to the *Handbook of Epoxy Resins*, Araldite 502 is a mixture of 83 parts by weight of Araldite epoxy resin 6010 (a straight epoxy) and 17 parts by weight of dibutyl phthalate (a plasticizer). This information is interesting only because dibutyl phthalate is a non-brittling agent which gives epoxy resin 502 some of its excellent nonfracturing properties. This kind of knowledge won't make you a chemist, but at least you know why I've picked CIBA-GEIGY's epoxy resin 502 as the base for epoxy resin "enameling."

Araldite epoxy resin 502 is one of the least skin-sensitizing epoxy resins. It's completely safe to breathe since it isn't volatile at room temperature, and it has practically no odor. Generally, however, I suggest that you work in a well-ventilated studio where the air is changed about six to ten times per hour. You shouldn't allow epoxy resins or epoxy hardeners (discussed below) to contact your skin, (see "Notes and Cautions" in *Your Studio and Basic Equipment*).

CURING AGENTS

Epoxy resin 502, a light, straw-colored liquid of medium viscosity, is converted to a solid resin or plastic by the careful addition and mixing in of a predetermined amount of a chemical called a curing agent, or hardener. There are many different kinds of curing agents on the market. I work with about five of these, which I'll call by the same names or numbers as those given by the manufacturers.

Before discussing this group of curing agents in some detail, I'd like to point out that you can do almost everything in "enameling" with curing agents N-001, B-003, or 956. If you pick N-001 which is a non-allergenic hardener manufactured by the Ajinomoto Company of Japan, it must always be heat cured under an infrared lamp, since it doesn't cure properly at room temperature. If you choose CIBA-GEIGY 956, although it's an excellent curing agent and is called a safety hardener (which means it has low volatility), it can still produce allergenic reactions after long periods of skin contact. Curing agent 956 is a very reactive heat-emitting hardener that offers no problem when used for 1/32" thick "enamels." This system also has to be heat cured because 956 is a moisture-absorbing curing agent which produces dull surfaces with room temperature cures. Infrared heat lamp curing gives bright and shiny surfaces.

Ordinarily, when the proper proportions of epoxy resin 502 and curing agent 956 are weighed out (100 grams of 502 to 20 grams of 956), mixed, and left in the container, they'll cure in about 20 to 30 minutes because of the high degree of heat emission (exotherm). If you can remove the heat while the resin is curing (polymerizing), you won't have problems such as yellowing and cracking.

I've developed the following method so that relatively thick castings can be made successfully using this combination of epoxy resin 502 and curing agent 956 to produce clear, transparent, non-brittle, hard enamels:

1. Weigh out in a small metal container, such as a cat-food can, 50 grams of epoxy resin 502 and 10 grams of curing agent 956.

2. Mix very well for about 2 minutes.

3. Secure the can and resin mixture in a large basin of water at 55°–60°F. Stir this resin mixture every 5 minutes for 45 minutes.

4. Use the epoxy resin system in its partially polymerized state for casting. (Castings which are ⅛" to ½" thick won't overheat.) This resin texture will keep a few hours in the cool-water bath.

5. Heat cure the resin system about 18" away from an infrared heat lamp.

Health-wise, the least objectionable hardener is one that gives off no smelly and noxious vapors. In addition, it shouldn't cause any skin allergies after frequent contacts. The following list should serve to acquaint you with the different hardeners available:

N-001 and B-003 are two of the series claimed by the manufacturer *not* to produce skin allergies. One allergy-prone student has used B-003 for the past three years with complete freedom from any ill effects. Vapors from B-003 and N-001 appear to be equally harmless.

RC-303 is very important in the realm of relatively non-allergy producing curing agents. It's a blend of two materials: DION-3-800 LC (DPM-3-800 LC) and DION EH-30 in the weight proportions of 9 to 1. (See *Suppliers and Manufacturers* for availability.) The RC-303, when added to epoxy resin 502 in the weight proportions of 1 to 2, effects a cure in 5 to 10 minutes. As you'll see in the projects, it's convenient to use under certain circumstances in enameling. RC-303 has a sulfurous, "stink-bombish" odor, but its vapors are non-toxic.

Araldite curing agent 956 is listed by CIBA-GEIGY as a safety hardener for use with 502 and other epoxy resins. I've used this product for many years safely and with good results. If you're careful not to have any skin contact with this curing agent, there's no cause for concern. However, it is water-soluble, so if some should get on you, wash it off right away with soap and water.

RC-125 is another curing agent that has been useful over the years. It cures in 20 to 30 minutes but is not a safety hardener. Good ventilation is a must. In addition to its fast-curing properties, RC-125 isn't moisture sensitive and usually gives good, clear surface effects with epoxy resin 502.

HH 1065B is a very low-viscosity, light-colored curing agent which I developed in 1965. It's being used by an increasing number of professional jewelry craftsmen with good success. This hardener does give off vapors which are considered toxic and great caution should therefore be exercised in its use. To get good results in enameling, you must heat cure the resin system. This heating further increases the vapor emission, so you must be sure to have good ventilation. Also be sure to keep the hardener off your hands by wearing polyethylene gloves when you work with it. Wear protective goggles when weighing!

HH 1065B is a mixture of equal amounts by weight of two curing agents: menthane diamine (manufactured by

TABLE OF EPOXY CURING AGENTS FOR JEWELRY ENAMELS AND PLIQUE-A-JOUR

Add the curing agents (hardeners) shown in this table to 100 grams of CIBA-GEIGY Araldite epoxy resin 502.

Thickness, backed or self-supporting	Curing agent	Amount in grams or PHR*	Approximate cure time at 70° F. (room temp.)
Thin enamels: 1/32" to 1/8"	956	20	2 hrs.**
	B-003	40	4 hrs. ††
	RC-125	25	1/2 hr.
Medium enamels: 1/8" to 1/4"	956 †	20	1 hr.**
	B-003	40	3 hrs. ††
	RC-303	50	5 minutes ††
	HH 1065B	25	must be heat cured ††
Heavy enamels: 1/4" to 1/2"	956 †	20	1 hr.**
	N-001	40	must be heat cured ††
	HH 1065B	25	must be heat cured ††

*Parts per hundred resin.

**Heat cure 18" away from an infrared heat lamp for several hours, depending on room temperature, if you want shiny surfaces.

† In this case the 956 is mixed and cooled with 502 as described above.

†† And/or held about 10" away from an infrared heat lamp, at 125° F. for about 4 hours. Generally speaking, a small amount of heat curing yields clearer enamels.

Rohm and Haas Company) and ZZL-0822 (manufactured by Union Carbide Corporation). This blend is available from the Resin Coatings or Polyproducts Corporation (see *Suppliers and Manufacturers*). HH 1065B is most useful as a curing agent with epoxy resin 502 since it cures very slowly with a low exotherm (heat emission) while curing (hardening) the resin. Furthermore, because of its very low viscosity, entrapped air bubbles easily float to the surface.

HY 837 is a new curing agent developed by CIBA-GEIGY. It cures in 20 to 30 minutes, is not moisture sensitive, and has a low exotherm (it cures without giving off much heat). My experiments using it in proportion by weight of 31 grams of HY 837 to 100 grams of epoxy resin 502 to cast ⅛″ thick enamels, yielded a brilliantly clear, almost color-less, bubble-free hard surface when cured at room temperature or 10″ away from an infrared lamp. CIBA-GEIGY claims that HY 837 is less affected by sunlight than many existing curing agents. Remember that it should be used with good ventilation and should not come in contact with your skin. This is still a new and experimental but very promising product.

ADDITIVES

Reactive diluents are viscosity-lowering thinners. They are usually smaller molecule epoxy chemicals. Reactive diluents don't evaporate as do solvents such as lacquer thinners. CIBA-GEIGY Epoxide 7 and 8, relatively non-toxic reactive diluents (Epoxide 8 is practically odorless), shouldn't be used in concentrations greater than 10%. Higher percentages could weaken the epoxy resin system.

If you find that the epoxy resin 502/curing agent 956 mixture shown in the table at left for heavy enamels (thick castings) is too viscous after 1 hour of water cooling, then the following formula variation will lower the viscosity:

Araldite epoxy resin 502	45 grams
Epoxide 7 or 8	5 grams
Curing agent 956	10 grams

Mix well, place in cool water, and handle as noted above for the 502/956 system.

Asbestos 244 and Cabosil, thixotropic or non-runny, inert materials, when used in proportions up to 5%, will make the resin system stay in place. The most satisfactory method for getting an almost clear, transparent, non-runny epoxy resin is to warm 100 grams of epoxy resin 502 to 250° F. in a coffee can placed 1″ away from an infrared heat lamp. Wearing a dust mask, carefully add 4 grams of Asbestos 244 to the hot resin. Using a paint mixer attached to a ¼″ drill, stir the mixture until it's uniform, without beating in excess air.

You may use this thixotropic epoxy resin 502/Asbestos 244 mixture with any of the curing agents above as if there were only 502 present. The small amount of Asbestos 244 won't throw off your calculations.

Metal powders in large quantities can be mixed with the following formula, used by the author for over 10 years to make a very fracture-proof and strong, relatively nonal-lergenic epoxy resin casting system.

Araldite epoxy resin 502	9 grams
Epoxide 7 or 8 (reactive diluent thinner)	1 gram
CIBA-GEIGY curing agent 840	5 grams
DION EH-30 or CIBA-GEIGY Acc.064	0.3 grams
Asbestos 244	0.2 grams

Mix all ingredients well in one container. Add 300-mesh metal powders slowly to the mixture until a heavy, flowing paste is made. You may also add 90 to 150 grams of copper or brass powder to this epoxy resin system. Cure the resin hard (preferably under an infrared heat lamp), then buff and polish the metalized epoxy resin to resemble a cast-metallic piece. Project 6 demonstrates what can be done with this system.

Color pastes, relatively lightfast, transparent, or opaque, are available from companies listed in *Suppliers and Man-ufacturers*. For jewelry purposes you'll have no fading troubles with the color you get *after* the curing of the resin. Transparent blue and green are the most lightfast, since they are phthalocyanine pigments. Transparent yellow and red are dyestuffs and aren't too good for extended outdoor exposure. Opaque colors, especially the earth colors, are the most lightfast.

Benzoflex 9-88 is a plasticizer which gives varying amounts of flexibility (non-brittleness). Do not use over 5% or you can weaken the resin system.

Dry fillers, such as various mesh sands, talcs, clays, pow-dered metals, sawdust, and so on, can be mixed with the epoxy resin systems. These additives often make the resins stronger.

DPM-3-800 LC (DION-3-800 LC), an accelerator manufac-tured by Diamond Shamrock Corporation, can be used in combination with 10% DION EH-30 to give a 5-minute cure with Araldite epoxy resin 502. (See formulas above.)

Remember, for those readers who scare easily when they read a lot of technical information, take heart. You can do everything in enameling, if you have to, with just epoxy resin 502 and curing agent 956. You merely order these two ingredients along with the color pastes.

Pendant by the author.
Epoxy-metal system and epoxy enamel.

PROJECT 6

CASTING A METALIZED PENDANT IN A WAX MOLD

Although this project describes how to make a specific pendant shape, the materials and techniques are applicable to almost any jewelry form. After finishing the pendant described here, you can provide additional "mystique" by pouring some transparent epoxy "enamel" into the center. Follow the directions for the epoxy "enamel" system listed under "Formulas."

In this project you will learn:

How to use two simple, safe, and inexpensive epoxy resin casting systems.

How to make a wax mold that is remeltable, high-temperature, medium-priced, and easily carved.

How to fill the wax mold with pourable, room-temperature-curing epoxy resin.

TOOLS AND MATERIALS

1. Drill and 1/16" bit.

2. Finishing tools: buffing compounds (Learok 765 and 884E), and buffing wheels.

3. Dividers and a mat knife.

4. Infrared heat lamp

5. Hot plate or stove top.

6. Vibrator (optional: this piece of jewelry-casting equipment is available from the jewelry-making suppliers listed in *Suppliers and Manufacturers*).

7. 20-mil cellulose acetate, acetone, and a syringe.

8. HH 572 soft modeling wax (Sun Oil Co.) 1290 Y microcrystalline wax, and green color paste to make the wax mold.

9. Woodcarving, linoleum-block cutting, or improvised tools to cut the wax.

10. Small sable brush.

11. Korax 1711 mold release spray. Although epoxy resins don't adhere to waxes, they're more easily separated from the mold if you spray the wax with an aerosol mold release agent.

12. 16-gauge sterling silver wire.

13. CIBA-GEIGY Araldite 502 epoxy resin.

14. CIBA-GEIGY Epoxide 7 or 8 reactive diluent. (Epoxide 8 is practically odorless.)

15. CIBA-GEIGY 840 or CIBA-GEIGY Lancast A, Diamond Shamrock DION EH-30, and Ajinomoto Ajicure B-003 curing agents.

16. 300-mesh tin powder.

17. Transparent color pastes.

FORMULAS

60/40 WAX

1290 Y microcrystalline wax	60 parts
HH 572 soft modeling wax	40 parts
Green color paste	1 part

1290 Y is a hard but carvable, high temperature (178° F. melting point) wax. HH 572 is an easily moldable, high-temperature wax which melts at the boiling point of water.

Weigh the waxes into a tin can along with a small quantity of green color paste to give the mixture an identifying color and place it about 5" away from an infrared heat lamp until the waxes are thoroughly melted. Stir well until the mixture is completely even and clear.

EPOXY METAL SYSTEM

Araldite epoxy resin 502	90 grams
Epoxide 7 or 8	10 grams
Curing Agent 840	50 grams
DION EH-30	2 grams

Mix well and add as much 300-mesh tin powder as you can to make a heavy paste—the more metal, the better the result will be.

EPOXY METAL SYSTEM VARIATION

Araldite epoxy resin 502	90 grams
Epoxide 7 or 8	10 grams
Lancast A	35 grams
DION EH-30	2 grams

Mix well and add 300-mesh tin powder as above. This is a low-viscosity mixture that will allow you to add more metal filler to make the resin system stronger.

EPOXY "ENAMEL" SYSTEM

Araldite epoxy resin 502	90 grams
Epoxide 7 or 8	10 grams
Ajinomoto Ajicure B-003	40 grams
Transparent color pastes	as needed

If you want to prepare epoxy resins effectively, you must use a scale or balance (such as the Ohaus 2610) (see *Your Studio and Basic Equipment*) that weighs accurately to 0.1 grams. Weigh the epoxy resin, the reactive diluent, and the hardeners into a plastic-coated paper cup, or virtually any container except Styrofoam. It doesn't matter which ingredients are added first, but be sure to put them into the same container. Stir the resin system very well for at least 2 minutes. Then add colors or powders, if you wish. There's little point in adding colors to powdered metal unless after buffing the piece there are depressions in which a colored effect is required. Adding carbon black powder is one way of achieving a black patina in the intaglio (depressed) areas.

The materials used in this project are available from the companies listed in *Suppliers and Manufacturers*.

Remember that epoxy metal pendants are not as strong as pure metal ones. They may be made stronger by sandwiching fiberglass cloth or filaments within the layers of liquid plastic (see Project 20).

If there are areas of the pendant which you want to "enamel," see the methods described in Projects 8 and 9.

You can use the finished pendant as a model for a series of similar pendants by making permanent molds of urethane or silicone rubber (see Project 8).

Remember that epoxy resin systems should be kept off your hands. Relatively safe formulas are given here, but there's always the risk of allergic reactions. If your hands come into contact with the liquid resin, wash them well with soap and water.

CASTING A METALIZED PENDANT IN A WAX MOLD

Step 1. Make a sketch for the pendant. You may vary the piece while working, but the sketch provides a definite starting point.

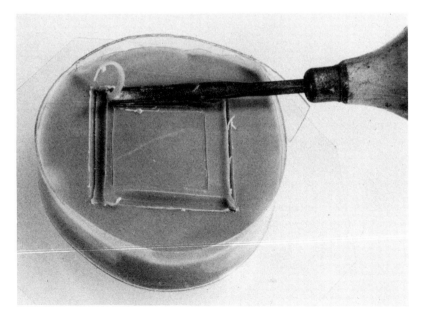

Step 2. Make a container for the wax mold from 20-mil cellulose acetate 1'' to 2'' deep with a diameter slightly larger than the pendant shape. Adhere it with acetone and place it on a flat piece of cellulose acetate. Mix the 60/40 wax shown in "Formulas" for this project, and pour it into the container. When the wax is cool, cut the design with woodcarving or linoleum-block cutting tools.

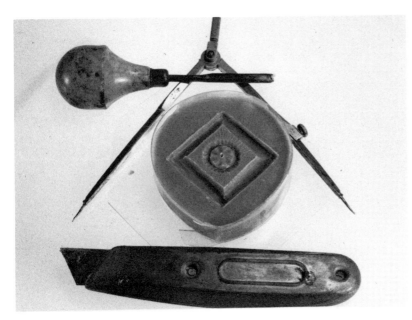

Step 3. Use dividers to help position the design in the wax, and a mat knife to trim up the cut surfaces.

Step 4. Just before applying the epoxy metal casting system, be sure to lightly spray the mold with a mold release (Korax 1711) to facilitate the later separation of the cured form from the wax.

Step 5. Make up the epoxy metal system described in "Formulas" for this project, taking about 20 grams of the well stirred epoxy resin and hardener and slowly stirring in the 300-mesh tin powder. The mixture should be pourable. To prevent air bubbles in the face of the casting, a good precaution is to lightly and carefully brush the entire surface of the wax mold with the epoxy metal mixture. Wash the paintbrush with soap and water when you are finished and it won't be effected by the uncured epoxy resin system.

Step 6. Carefully pour the rest of the epoxy metal mixture on top of the brushed-mold surface. To further remove air bubbles which could mar and weaken the casting, drop the container about a dozen times from a 4" height. You can also use a jewelry-casting vibrator to remove air bubbles. This movement acts to force more of the powdered metal toward the face of the casting. The more metal and the less resin in the front of the piece, the better the final results after polishing.

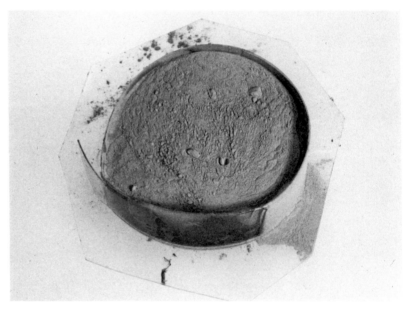

Step 7. The dropping or vibrating acts to separate the resin and the metal so that the upper surface (or back of the pin) contains more resin than anything else. Sift some 300-mesh tin powder on top of this resin surface to absorb the excess resin. Later, after the epoxy has cured out, you can remove the surplus tin dust by buffing.

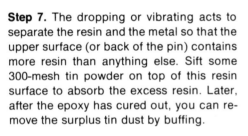

Step 8. Remove the fresh casting from the mold. The mold release adhering to it makes it shiny. This epoxy metal system will cure if left overnight at room temperature, but it's best to strengthen the piece by heat curing it about 12" away from an infrared heat lamp for 2 or 3 hours.

Step 9. Polish the back of the pendant with the greaseless buffing compound Learok 765 and then with Learok 884E. Apply each of these compounds to a 6″ muslin buffing wheel running at 1750 r.p.m. (see *Finishing Your Jewelry*).

Step 10. Also buff the front of the pendant. Be sure to buff lightly when you are buffing plastics which are clear or filled. Any heat will tend to soften the material and thereby mar the surface.

Step 11. Polish to a final gloss with Learok 336E, used on its own muslin finishing buffer (see *Finishing Your Jewelry* for the difference between regular and finishing buffers).

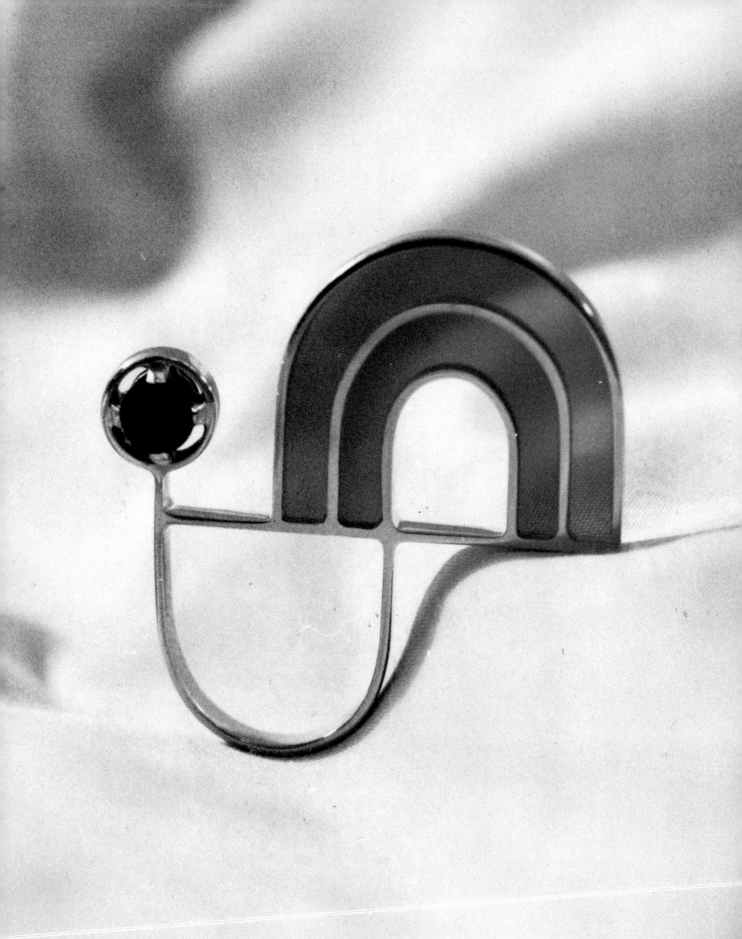

Ring by Arch Gregory, Knoxville, Tennessee.
Sterling silver and cast Araldite epoxy resin 502.
Photo by David Richer.

PLIQUE-A-JOUR ENAMELING A STERLING SILVER RING

Of all the projects in this book, this one is the only effort to show you in detail how to make a sterling silver ring containing a plique-à-jour (see-through) "enamel" of epoxy resin.

Methods of soldering silver are not covered in any detail in this book. For this type of jewelry information, see the jewelry-making books listed in the *Bibliography*.

Through the demonstration steps executed by Arch Gregory and photographed by David Richer, you will learn the following:

How to handle epoxy resins to make plique-à-jour enamels which are clear, permanent, unbreakable, and more abrasive resistant than the sterling silver itself. Vitreous enameling in plique-à-jour for a ring such as Arch has made would be almost impossible to achieve using traditional materials.

How to hand polish with Polysand sanding cloths.

How to improvise when working in unexplored territory.

TOOLS AND MATERIALS

1. Jewelry tools: saw and blades, pliers, files, a ring mandril, and a rawhide mallet.

2. Infrared heat lamp.

3. Acetylene, propane, or butane gas torch.

4. 20-gauge sheet of sterling silver.

5. "Easy" and "medium" silver solder and silver-solder flux.

6. Tweezers and a needle.

7. Isolant for silver (rubber cement).

8. 220-grit, 400-grit, and 600-grit wet-or-dry sandpaper.

9. Polysand TR-34 Sanding Cloth Kit, manufactured by Micro-Surface Finishing Products. These cloths go down to 8000 grit.

10. CIBA-GEIGY Araldite epoxy resin 502.

11. CIBA-GEIGY Epoxide 8 reactive diluent.

12. RC-303 and HH 1065B curing agent.

FORMULAS

EPOXY RESIN ADHESIVE

Araldite epoxy resin 502	2 parts
Curing agent RC-303	1 part

Mix the ingredients well and use a toothpick to drop small amounts on the inner and outer silver ring bands.

EPOXY RESIN SYSTEM

Araldite epoxy resin 502	90 grams
Epoxide 7 or 8	10 grams
Curing agent HH 1065B	25 grams

Weigh all the ingredients into the same container (a tin can) and stir them slowly and thoroughly until the mixture appears completely clear throughout.

NOTES AND CAUTIONS

Most of the epoxy resin enameling which is now being done in quality jewelry is combined with gold and silver. In this book, I urge you to delve into jewelry-making, using resins, such as epoxies, which can be married to precious metals and stones or gems.

Resin materials, color pastes, and jewelry supplies can be obtained from the companies listed in *Suppliers and Manufacturers*. Your local hardware store and craft shop will fill in the balance.

Remember that the curing agent, HH 1065B, is a volatile, toxic material until it's cured into the epoxy resin system. Use it with great care.

Have excellent ventilation and wear disposable polyethylene gloves and goggles while weighing and mixing the resin system.

**PLIQUE-A-JOUR ENAMELING
A STERLING SILVER RING**

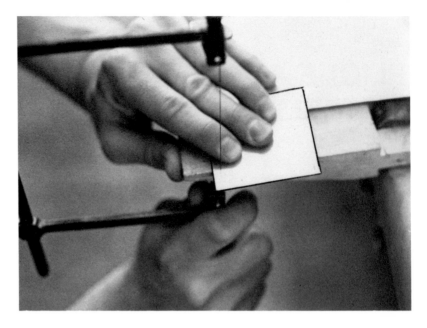

Step 1. With a jeweler's saw, cut a piece of 20-gauge sterling silver sheet into two ⅝" strips to form the ring. Determine the circumference of the ring band by measuring the circumference of the chosen ring-mandril size. Cut the inner strip about ¼" longer than necessary. The original design should indicate the length of the outer silver band.

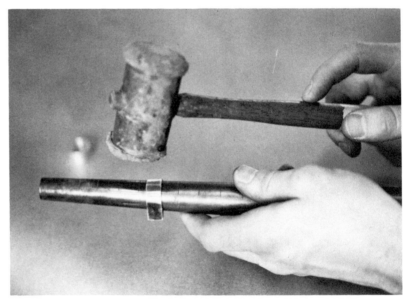

Step 2. Form the sterling silver band and the outer section of the ring over the metal mandril, using a rawhide mallet, which won't scratch the silver. Bend the band to overlap, then saw through both ends at the same time (see Project 3, Steps 3 and 4) to get a perfect fitting of the ends.

Step 3. Place tiny snippings (paillons) of silver solder and silver solder flux on the joint and flux them with an air-acetylene torch. Consult any of the numerous excellent books on jewelry-making listed in the *Bibliography* for details on soldering silver. If you don't need strength in the solder joint, you can use soft tin/lead solder and pewter flux (see Project 9, Steps 5 through 8). After soldering the ring, remove excess solder with a needle file.

Step 4. Sand the entire inside of the band in one direction with 220-grit wet-or-dry sandpaper to make a good surface on which to bond the resin adhesive. Buff the inner band of the ring on a 6″ muslin wheel running at about 3000 r.p.m. with Lerok 765 greaseless tripoli compound to remove all scratches. After buffing, wash the sterling silver pieces with detergent and water and dry them with tissue paper. Subsequently, only handle them with tweezers because any soil will keep the resin system from adhering well.

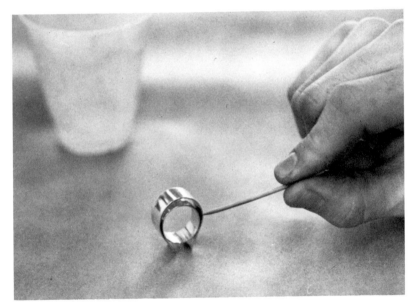

Step 5. "Tack" the outer sterling silver band to the inner ring with epoxy resin adhesive shown in "Formulas" for this project.

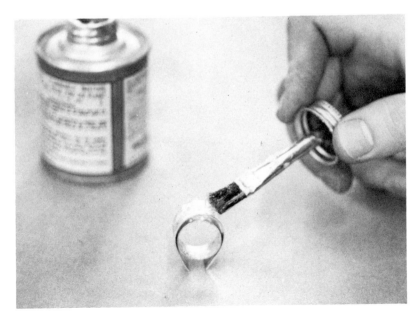

Step 6. Brush the exterior of the ring with rubber cement. This is an excellent self-releasing material which prevents epoxy resin from adhering to a substrate (the foundation or mold on which it's placed).

Step 7. Weigh out the epoxy enameling system shown in "Formulas" for this project and mix in the desired color paste.

Step 8. Place the sterling silver ring in a plastic-coated cup and pour in the resin system. If you want to waste less of the epoxy resin, make a tight-fitting cellulose acetate form, glued with acetone, to contain the epoxy and the ring (see Project 6, Step 2). Place the casting about 12" away from an infrared heat lamp. Agitate the resin with a needle to make sure that there are no air bubbles clinging to the silver. A spray of acetone will also help to rid the resin surface of any bubbles. Cure the epoxy in this manner until it has set. Then lower the heat lamp to about 9" from the resin surface and cure it for another 2 hours. The resin is well cured when, upon cooling, you can't indent it with your fingernail.

Step 9. When the resin is completely cured, carefully saw away and file the excess from the exterior areas of the ring.

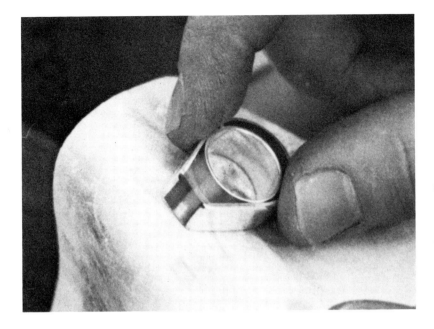

Step 10. Finish the ring using only sandpapers of grits from 220 to 600. Polish it with Polysand sanding cloths described in ''Tools and Materials'' for this project. These cloths go down to 8000-grit which will yield a surface with the shine of a piece of Plexiglas. The only drawback to this procedure is its expense and the time it takes. The finished ring is shown below.

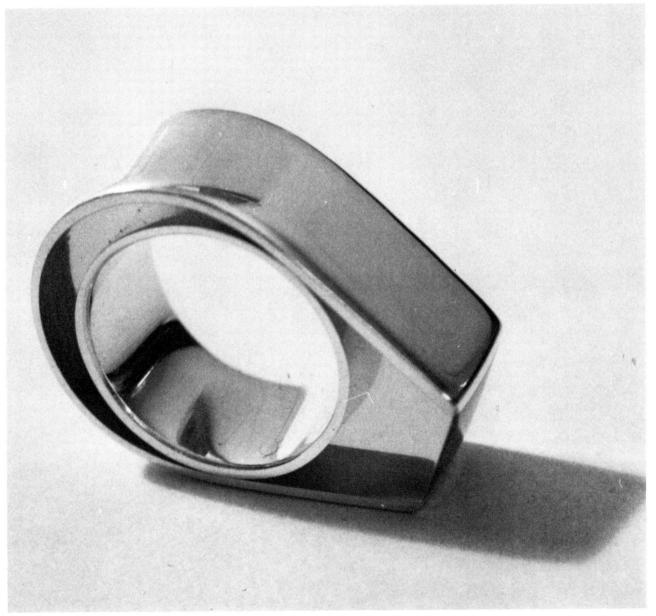

Pendant by the author.
Pewter and epoxy enamel.
Photo by Mike Yarrow.

PROJECT 8

ENAMELING A PEWTER BAS-RELIEF PENDANT

The procedure used for making this bas-relief pendant can be applied to many kinds of jewelry. Here is what you will learn in this project:

How to prepare a wax mold.

How to prepare a silicone rubber mold for casting.

How to modify pewter.

How to prepare pewter for epoxy resin "enamels."

TOOLS AND MATERIALS

1. Linoleum-block cutting tools for carving the wax mold. (Wax modeling tools, wood-cutting tools, or dental tools may also be used.)
2. Jeweler's tools: saw, drill and 1/16" bit, and pliers.
3. Finishing tools: 180-grit to 320-grit wet-or-dry sandpaper, buffing and polishing compounds, and wheels.
4. A piece of asbestos board.

FORMULAS

60/40 Wax

1290 Y microcrystalline wax	60 parts
HH 572 soft modeling wax	40 parts
Green color paste	1 part

Melt the two waxes together under an infrared heat lamp held about 4" from the metal container. Mix the ingredients until clear and then pour them into mold-released pans (pans sprayed with Korax 1711) or teflon-lined containers. Add green color paste to color-code the mixture so that you can recognize it after storage.

Mold-Making Rubber

Silastic A rubber	100 grams
Silastic F catalyst	10 grams

Mix the ingredients slowly and well. If a degassing vacuum is available, you can use it to eliminate all the air bubbles trapped in the mixing of the Silastic A. Use a vacuum of 29.5" of mercury for 5 minutes, a mix the Silastic A and catalyst in a large container so that when it is put under the vacuum, the moisture won't overflow. If you don't have access to a vacuum, you should still have no problem with air bubbles if you mix the rubber very carefully.

I'm using Silastic A here for its resistance to air bubbles and its insensitivity to moisture and sulphur. As compared with Silastic E, for example, Silastic A doesn't have a high tear resistance. On the other hand, Silastic E has a tendency not to cure in the presence of moisture and free sulphur. A third product, Silastic G, has both the strength of Silastic E and the moisture insensitivity of Silastic A, but G's drawbacks are its high viscosity which generates air bubbles, and the inability of heat to accelerate the cure.

Your resin supplier can give you further information on these rubber molds. Both Dow Corning and General Electric make silicone rubber mold-making materials. Their literature is excellent, but don't bother them for samples!

Epoxy Resin "Enamel": Low-Viscosity, Slow Cure

Araldite epoxy resin 502	100 grams
HH 1065B	25 grams
Color pastes	as needed

Mix resin and hardener well. Add small amounts of color pastes to portions divided into plastic-coated cups.

Epoxy Resin "Enamel": Medium Viscosity, Medium-Speed Cure

Araldite epoxy resin 502	90 grams
Epoxide 7 or 8	10 grams
Curing agent 956	20 grams
Color pastes	as needed

Mix the three main ingredients well for several minutes until uniform. Then immerse the container in 60-65° F. water for 1 hour. Keep the mixture at 60-65° F.; it may be used as long as it is pourable. (See *Epoxy Resins* for more details.) Add colors just before use.

Pewter

Tin	90–95%
Antimony	4–8%
Copper	1–2%

The craftsman today could make his own casting pewter, giving it the properties he wants. Increasing antimony makes the pewter harder. The adition of bismuth, silver, or cadmium can also change the characteristics of the pewter.

If you're ambitious enough to make your own pewter, here is a method suggested by Alcan Metal Powders:

Step 1. Melt the copper pellets in an iron crucible.

Step 2. Add a small amount of the 100-mesh tin powder, making a low-melting alloy.

Step 3. Next add the 100-mesh antimony powder and mix until melted.

Step 4. Add the remainder of the tin powder. Do not overheat, since this will oxidize the metals.

5. A sable brush.

6. 18-gauge sterling silver wire.

7. 20-mil cellulose acetate container, acetone, and a syringe.

8. Korax 1711 mold-release spray. Although epoxy resins don't adhere to waxes, they are more easily separated from the mold if you spray the wax with an aerosol mold release.

9. Sun Oil Company 1290 Y microcrystalline wax, HH572 soft modeling wax, and green color paste.

10. Infrared heat lamp.

11. Dow Corning Silastic A silicone mold-making rubber and Silastic F catalyst.

12. Graphite powder.

13. Degassing vacuum (optional).

14. Sheet pewter or ingot. You can make your own pewter from tin, antimony, and copper. (For instructions, see "Formulas" for this project).

15. CIBA-GEIGY Araldite 502 epoxy resin.

16. HH 1065B or CIBA-GEIGY 965 curing agents.

17. CIBA-GEIGY Epoxide 7 or 8 reactive diluent.

NOTES AND CAUTIONS

You can get waxes, Silastic A, epoxy systems, and color pastes from the companies listed in *Suppliers and Manufacturers*, pewter sheet and ingot from C. R. Hill Company, and powders to make pewter from Alcan Metal Powders.

For instructions on finishing your piece, study *Finishing Your Jewelry*.

To vary the transparent epoxy enamel, you can underfill the cloisons to create texture, blow materials such as metal glitter or mica flakes onto the surface, or add thin coatings of opaque epoxy resins. Cure these resin systems and pour a coating of clear epoxy enamel on top of them.

Silastic A with catalyst F has one main drawback. It tears quite easily. If you need a pourable silicone rubber which has a high tear strength without moisture and sulfur inhibition, Dow Corning suggests Silastic G. After testing it, I found that it takes about 24 hours to cure, but works well in the presence of both moisture in wet clay and sulfur in the 60/40 wax.

Do not allow epoxy resin systems to touch your skin!

Do not place pewter pieces too near the infrared heat lamp, as the heat could melt the metal

Pendants by the author. Pewter and cast Araldite epoxy resin 502.

Step 1. You can make your own high-temperature, semi-rigid modeling and engraving wax, which is shown in "Formulas" for this project, since it's not easy to find one ready-made.

Step 2. Melt the mixture about 4″ away from an infrared heat lamp. Keep an eye on this cooking, since heat lamps held so near are hotter than red peppers in the desert. After both waxes are melted (1290 Y melts at about 178° F. while HH 572 melts at about 210° F.), thoroughly mix in the green color paste. Pour it into mold-released pans (pans sprayed with a mold-release agent such as Korax 1711) to make slabs of any desired thickness.

Step 3. As in Project 6, carve the 60/40 wax with linoleum-block cutting tools and small, sharp blades. After "sculpting" the wax, make a 20-mil cellulose acetate collar, glued together with acetone, to fit it (see Project 6, Step 2). Glue a flat sheet of acetate underneath the collar and use a little melted 60/40 wax to seal the bottom of the wax form to the bottom of the collar.

Step 4. Mix up the mold-making rubber shown in "Formulas" for this project.

Step 5. To eliminate any possible formation of air bubbles at the surfaces where wax contacts rubber, lightly and quickly brush the silicone rubber mixture all over the face of the model. Since this silicone rubber preparation has a pot life of only about 5 to 10 minutes, you should do your pouring no later than 3 minutes after mixing. If you want to proceed less hysterically, then make up two batches, one for brushing and the other for pouring. As soon as the brushed coat becomes tacky, pour the next batch.

Step 6. Separate the Silastic A rubber mold from the wax after 15 to 30 minutes.

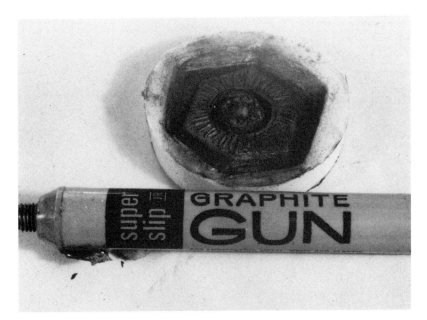

Step 7. To obtain the most accurate pewter casting the manufacturer suggests lightly dusting or brushing the inside of the mold with graphite powder before pouring in the molten metal. Silicone rubber molds will stand temperatures of over 500° F. for short periods of time.

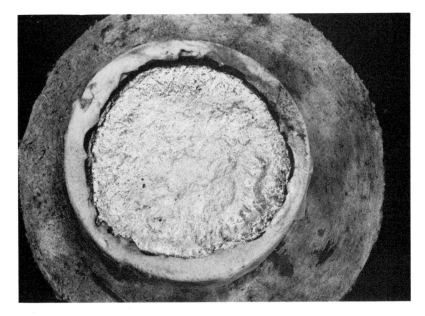

Step 8. Melt the pewter in a tin can placed on a hot plate (see Project 5, Step 10). To obtain the proper temperature for the pouring, heat the metal until a rolled-up paper taper turns marshmallow-brown when dipped into the liquid pewter. After pouring the pewter, place a piece of asbestos board on top of the molten metal and push down firmly yet lightly. Hold the board in this position for a few seconds until the metal is no longer liquid.

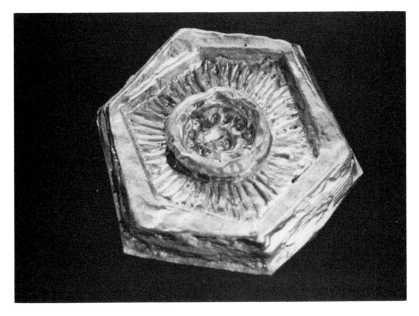

Step 9. Separate the pewter casting from the rubber mold and cut the balance of the pewter from the cast form with a jeweler's saw. Lightly buff the piece with greaseless buffing compound Learok 765. Clean it with acetone and facial tissues.

Step 10. Weigh out the epoxy resin system shown in "Formulas" for this project and let it cure for 1 hour. Add needle-point amounts of color pastes and mix very well in order not to have any color lumps. Place the piece on a level surface about 10" away from an infrared heat lamp. Carefully pour the resin into the two different areas until they're brim full. You'll notice that the heat lowers the viscosity of the resin and any air bubbles will float to the surface. Lightly spray with acetone to assist in ridding the epoxy resin enamel of air bubbles. Once the resin surface is hard, lower the infrared heat lamp to about 8" away for several hours or until the resin has cured.

Step 11. Wet-sand the piece with 180-grit and 320-grit wet-or-dry sandpaper to evenly level the pewter and the epoxy enamel surfaces.

Step 12. Buff the pendant with Learok 765 applied to a 6" muslin buffer running at 1750 r.p.m. Change the buffing wheel and polish with Learok 884E.

Step 13. Finish polish with Learok 339E. Then drill two holes with a 1/16″ bit through one corner. Bend a strand of 18-gauge sterling silver wire through these holes and polish it to make the hanger for the pendant.

Pendant by Gretchen Anderson, Honolulu.
Sterling silver and epoxy resin enamel.
Photo courtesy of the artist.

PROJECT 9

SOLDERING AND ENAMELING
A WIRE-CLOISONNE PEWTER PIN

In this project you will learn how to fashion a pin from three thicknesses of pewter which are all soldered together. Soldering pewter with tin and lead solder requires practice, since the melting point of the solder is less than 100° F. lower than that of pewter, which melts at about 425° F. If you can successfully solder pewter, there will be few new problems to conquer when it comes to silver-soldering copper, brass, and silver. This project will also show you:

How to use the portable Ronson Varaflame torch. This will be of great help to you in learning how to solder pewter.

How to incise the pewter area which is to be epoxy "enameled." This type of surface abrasion gives interesting effects when seen through the enamel.

How to mix epoxy "enamel" using CIBA-GEIGY epoxy resin 502, Epoxide 7 or 8, and curing agent 956. The basis of this system has been used for many years, but the method of preparation as described below is *new*, and will give trouble-free, thick castings for jewelry.

How to fashion a cloisonné star from a ⅜″ strip of 18-gauge pewter.

How to finish the pin by grinding down the epoxy enamels so that the cloisonné metal is exposed.

TOOLS AND MATERIALS

1. Jeweler's tools: saw and blades, drill and bits, bench pin, pliers, files, cutting tool or burr, and soft iron binding wire, used by silversmiths.
2. Finishing tools: buffing wheel or hand buffer and polishing compounds, wet-or-dry sandpaper, and a grinding stone.
3. Ronson Varaflame butane-fuel torch (see *Your Studio and Basic Equipment*).
4. Tweezers, a dental tool (optional, any sharp pointed tool, such as a nail) and a toothpick.
5. A piece of carbon paper.
6. Acetone spray.
7. MirrorGlaze wax.
8. A jeweler's coiled asbestos plate.
9. Fine (pure), silver cloisonné wire to dress up the piece, or if you want thicker cloisons you can cut ⅛″ strips from an 18-gauge pewter sheet.
10. 18-gauge pewter sheet.
11. 1/16″ pewter soldering wire (60% tin/40% lead) with a melting point of 375° F.

FORMULAS

EPOXY RESIN QUICK CURE ADHESIVE

Araldite epoxy resin 502	2 parts
Curing agent RC-303	1 part

Mix well in a plastic-coated cup and apply with a toothpick.

EPOXY ENAMEL

Araldite epoxy resin 502	45 grams
Epoxide 7 or 8	5 grams
Curing agent 956	10 grams
Color pastes	as needed

Weigh all the ingredients into the same container (a tin can) and stir them slowly and thoroughly until the mixture appears completely clear throughout. Place the container in cool water 60°–65° F. for 1 hour to reduce reaction heat, or you'll have problems in heat curing the epoxy. Stir occasionally. Pour small portions into plastic-coated paper cups and add desired needle-point amounts of color pastes.

EPOXY ENAMEL VARIATION

Araldite epoxy resin 502	50 grams
HH 1065B	12.5 grams

This resin mixture has a lower viscosity, but it has a little more color and takes longer to heat cure. Place the resin surface about 10″ away from an infrared heat lamp for 5 hours at 140° F. The resin is cured when, upon cooling, it is fingernail hard.

---

12. Pewter flux. You can buy ready-made flux or you can make your own by adding 10 drops of muriatic (hydrochloric diluted, to chemists) acid to 1 oz. of glycerin.
13. CIBA-GEIGY Araldite 502 epoxy resin.
14. CIBA-GEIGY RC-303, 956, and/or HH 1065B curing agents.
15. CIBA-GEIGY Epoxide 7 or 8 reactive diluent.

NOTES AND CAUTIONS

If you want to use epoxy resins, you should invest in a scale or balance, such as the Ohaus 2610 scale (see *Your Studio and Basic Equipment*), which weighs accurately to 0.1 grams.

Remember that epoxy resins may cause skin irritation. Keep these products off your hands.

Good ventilation is very important!

SOLDERING AND ENAMELING A WIRE
CLOISONNE PEWTER PIN

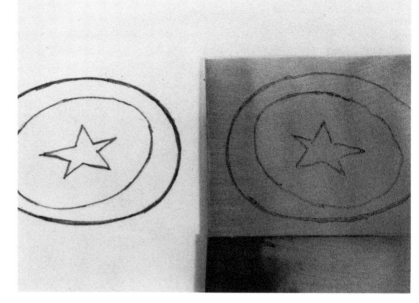

Step 1. Sketch your design on paper. For this demonstration, I'm making the pewter shapes of a large and small star, a large and small doughnut, and an oval base. Sand a sheet of 18-gauge pewter with 320-grit wet, wet-or-dry, sandpaper or buff it lightly with Lea Abrasive Compound C. After dulling the surface, transfer the design to the pewter using carbon paper.

Step 2. Since the carbon-paper markings can be rubbed off easily, engrave the design into the pewter with a sharp-pointed tool. Then drill a hole in the metal sheet so that a jeweler's saw can be inserted. Saw out the star and doughnut shapes.

Step 3. After sawing, grind the pewter pieces smooth with a half round file.

Step 4. Use a rectangular piece of pewter, (Britannia metal) for the base of the pin. Place the larger, bottom doughnut in the center of the three pewter sections. Place the smaller star under the larger star in the center of the doughnuts. This will create the illusion of floating. In designing and making jewelry for the first time, it doesn't hurt to keep reassembling the pieces as you make them. In this way you may find that you want to make necessary changes. Here, the star seems too small for the pin.

Step 5. Flatten a 1″ to 2″ length of 60/40 tin/lead solder wire with a pair of jeweler's pliers. Use scissors to cut the solder into small snippings or "paillons" which you'll apply with a pair of tweezers (see *Your Studio and Basic Equipment*). Use the same solder throughout this project. Place the pieces of solder on the pewter shapes ⅛″ to ¼″ apart and then cover them with the pewter flux. Arrange the pewter sections on a jeweler's coiled asbestos plate.

Step 6. Adjust the Varaflame torch to extend the blue part of the flame about ¼″ from the nozzle. Gently fan the pewter flux and the solder from a height of 2″ to 3″ with a pendulum-like swing taking 1 second to go in each direction. A dentist tool is helpful to keep the solder snippings in place. When you first heat it, the solder tends to dance about wildly. You should remember that solder melts at about 375° F. while pewter melts at the relatively low temperature of 425° F. Be sure to first practice soldering on scrap pieces of pewter. The flame of the butane torch must be kept continually in motion and should be slowly wafted over the pewter and the solder very much as the slave might have fanned the sultan: not too close, but steady and even. As soon as an area of solder becomes liquid and spreads out, remove flame and fan adjacent area.

SOLDERING AND ENAMELING A WIRE CLOISONNE PEWTER PIN

Step 7. After all the solder has been melted and cooled in this manner on both plates, lightly reflux the soldered areas and stack the three pewter plates as you want them arranged for your pin. "Sweat solder" the pieces of pewter together by relighting your torch, making the flame about ¼" longer, because you are now melting a larger volume of metal. Carefully fan the pieces in the same way as before until all the solder is melted. Usually you can see a thin, bright, shiny line of molten solder between each pewter plate. When this happens, remove the flame and let the mass cool. Attach the three large pieces of pewter to the asbestos plate with soft iron binding wire. This anchoring will prevent the pieces from accidentally moving if they are jarred.

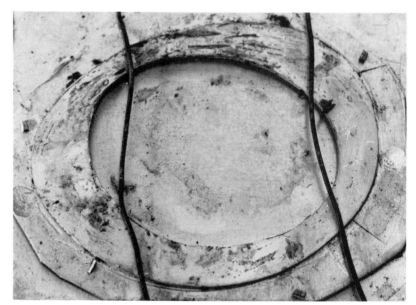

Step 8. Melt new pieces of solder to fill in the voids. It's often helpful in this method of soldering, where you can't tell exactly when the solder has begun to melt, to have a few morsels of solder lying in the path of the torch to act as a temperature guide.

Step 9. Saw the pin free from the balance of the pewter base plate. Wash the pewter shell clean with detergent and running water in preparation for enameling.

Step 10. Upon reconsidering the design of the pin, I decided to make a larger star as a decorative center. To make this star, mark off a ⅜″ strip of 18-gauge pewter with dividers and then lightly engrave the outline with a sharp pointed tool. This will assist in the accurate bending of the strip to form a star.

Step 11. Shape the star by bending the pewter strip with toothless jeweler's pliers. Do this forming on the side away from the engraving. Overlap the two ends which form the fifth star point. With a thin saw blade, vertically cut through the center of the "X" at the overlap to be able to join the star point perfectly. Now solder the ends together using the same techniques as described above.

Step 12. To clean the pewter shell, apply Lea Abrasive Compound C to a small muslin buffer which you attach to a flexible-shaft drill. Brightboy rubber abrasive disks are helpful in removing blemishes (see *Your Studio and Basic Equipment*). Buff the piece with Learok 765 using both the large 6″, 1750 r.p.m. buffing wheel and a small, clean muslin buffer attached to the flexible-shaft drill, to obtain a semi-matte finish. In order to brighten up the area to be epoxy enameled, lightly abrade the inner surface of the pin with a cutting tool or burr. Remove the star shape during the burring.

Step 13. Mix the 5-minute epoxy-resin adhesive shown in "Formulas" for this project. Apply a very thin coat of this mixture with a toothpick all over the inner base of the pin. This quick-curing epoxy acts as a seal for the cloison area inside the star, and being quite flexible, it acts as a shock-absorber against temperature changes and grinding.

Step 14. Just before enameling with the epoxy resin system shown in "Formulas" for this project, brush the top surface of the pewter pin lightly with a protective coating of MirrorGlaze wax. Since MirrorGlaze is an excellent releasing agent, any drippings of epoxy resin can be easily removed after curing. If you forget this step, you may mar the piece when you try to buff off the excess epoxy from the metal. You should remember that cured epoxy resins are much more abrasive resistant than pewter or even sterling silver. Age the epoxy resin system for 1 hour in water at about 60-65° F. and then color it with needle-point amounts of color paste. Stir well for a few minutes to be sure that *all* of the color is dispersed. Now carefully drop, with a coffee stirrer or dropper, or pour, the desired shade of epoxy enamel into the star area. Immediately place the pin about 18" away from an infrared heat lamp. Spray with acetone to get rid of air bubbles.

Step 15. Cure the "star attraction" under the heat lamp for 1 to 3 hours. Then apply a little MirrorGlaze wax to the resin surface to prevent any further resin drippings from adhering. Using the same process, enamel and cure the section around the exterior of the star. When this area has also cured hard, move the heat lamp about 2″ closer and cure both the resin enamels for about 2 hours more. Cool the pin to room temperature. If you find that you can't indent or mar the surface of the resin with your fingernail, you can stop the curing operation, but if the resin is still soft, then continue to heat cure for another hour. Glue a well-cleaned and sanded store-bought pin-back (see *Finishing Your Jewelry*) with the epoxy-resin quick-cure adhesive described in "Formulas" for this project, to which has been added a generous amount of 300-mesh tin powder, to the back of the pin. Be sure to cover the top of the pin-back with the adhesive. Heat curing will yield a quicker cure and firmer adhesive. (Make a bend in the pin with needle-nose pliers if you want the pin to be hung as a pendant.) Finally, fill the center of the star with colorless epoxy enamel. Following the complete heat curing of the resin system, carefully wet-sand the star surface with 320-grit wet-or-dry sandpaper. After sanding the resin flush with the metal surface, buff the entire pin first with Learok 765 and then with Learok 339E (see *Finishing Your Jewelry*).

Pendant by Robert Stoetzer, Miami.
Copper and plique-à-jour epoxy resin enamel.
Photo by Mike Yarrow.

PROJECT 10

CARVING A SOAPSTONE MOLD FOR A PEWTER PLIQUE-A-JOUR PENDANT

Soapstone is such fun to carve, pewter is so simple to melt, and epoxy resin enamels are so controllable, that a project involving the use of all three materials is a must! So, here's what will be demonstrated in this project:

How to work with soapstone, a material used by the Eskimos for years, which is not only very easy to carve, but also releases beautifully from molten pewter.

How to mix several epoxy resin formulas to give excellent results when casting into pewter which has been cut out for plique-à-jour.

How to use rubber cement as a sealing device so that the epoxy resin enamel won't run under the open pewter shapes.

TOOLS AND MATERIALS

1. Jeweler's tools: saw and blades, files, drill and 1/16" bit, pliers, and a rawhide mallet.

2. Finishing tools: 180-grit to 400-grit wet-or-dry sandpaper, buffing wheels, and compounds.

3. Woodcarving, linoleum-block cutting, or dental tool, or any sharp tool to gouge out the soapstone.

4. Rubber cement.

5. Dividers and a compass.

6. An asbestos board or a piece of stiff rubber.

7. A piece of white cardboard.

8. A block of soapstone, 3" x 3" x 1½".

9. Pewter, scrap or ingot and a 18-gauge sheet for making ¼" strips.

10. Acetone and a Preval aerosol sprayer, available from your local hardware store.

11. 16-gauge or 18-gauge sterling silver wire.

12. A small sheet of 1/16" Plexiglas.

13. CIBA-GEIGY Araldite 502 epoxy resin.

14. CIBA-GEIGY Epoxide 7 or 8 reactive diluent.

15. RC-303; RC-125 or HH 1065B curing agents.

16. Additives: color pastes, Asbestos 244 thickener, and pearlescence (optional).

NOTES AND CAUTIONS

All of the resins system materials and the Mylar are available from suppliers listed in *Suppliers and Manufacturers*. The remaining items can usually be purchased from your local hardware or hobby store.

If you use a very light, clear enamel, such as the formula based on HH 1065B, you might be interested in the variation of having a negative-space design on the back of

---

FORMULAS

EPOXY ENAMEL SYSTEM, 5-MINUTE CURE

Araldite epoxy resin 502	20 grams
Curing agent RC-303	10 grams
Color pastes	as needed

Because this system has such a short cure time, you must work rapidly yet carefully. First, add the color pastes to the epoxy resin. Remember that the enamel casting will be quite thick, so you should make the color shade somewhat lighter than you want it to be in the finished piece. Then weigh out the RC-303 and mix it in slowly to avoid air bubbles. However, mix as well as possible for no more than 1 minute since there are only 3 minutes remaining of pot life. Now pour the enamel into the enclosed area. If you see any unwanted surface air bubbles, spray lightly with acetone in a Preval aerosol sprayer. You can do this a few times before the resin hardens. (To reduce the amount of air bubbles, weigh out 18 grams of Araldite 502 and 2 grams of Epoxide 7 or 8 and stir until they are well mixed.) Then add color pastes and continue mixing as above.)

You can add interest to this system by stirring the resin while it's hardening to make a textured surface. Heat cure the resin system at about 150° F. for 3 or 4 hours until it's fingernail hard. This enamel has good shock resistance, since it has a built-in flexibility provided by both the epoxy resin 502 and the RC-303 curing agent.

EPOXY ENAMEL SYSTEM, 30-MINUTE CURE

Araldite epoxy resin	20 grams
Curing agent RC-125	5 grams
Color pastes	as needed

This curing system gives you 20 to 30 minutes to work, depending upon the room temperature. Be sure that you wear polyethylene gloves if there's a risk of getting the resin on your hands. Add color pastes and mix well for several minutes. Pour the resin system into the enclosed area. If you want a textured surface, begin about 15 minutes after the pour and keep stirring until the resin has set. This system doesn't require post curing. (The formula above produces a lot of air bubbles, giving an antique-glass effect. If you want lower viscosity and less air bubbles, weigh out 18 grams of Araldite 502, 2 grams of Epoxide 7 or 8, and 5 grams of RC-125.)

EPOXY ENAMEL SYSTEM, 3-HOUR CURE

Araldite epoxy resin 502	20 grams
Curing agent HH 1065B	5 grams
Color pastes	as needed

This formula will give you the clearest bubble-free enamel in the epoxy resin range. To get the best results, mix the Araldite 502, the HH 1065B (no reactive diluent is necessary), and the desired color pastes and pour immediately. Heat cure at 150° F. for 3 to 4 hours to get a good fingernail hard surface.

your epoxy enamel plique-à-jour. You can do this by placing a microcrystalline wax design in relief on top of the rubber-cement coating on the Plexiglas. Carefully paint the wax with a little silicone oil, such as GE RTV 910. This will make the wax separate very easily from the cured epoxy resin system.

Wear disposable polyethylene gloves (which, by the way, burn like paper and are of no ecological consequence), even though, according to the Diamond Sharmrock Corporation, DPM-3-800 LC (DION-3-800 LC) the major ingredient of the RC-303, is non-sensitizing to the skin. Of the epoxy resins in wide-spread use, it's my understanding that Araldite epoxy resin 502 is one of the least allergenic. However, this is not an invitation for you to be careless when using this and other materials mentioned in this book.

When using HH 1065B, be sure to have good ventilation by changing the air in your studio at least ten times per hour.

CARVING A SOAPSTONE MOLD FOR A PEWTER PLIQUE-A-JOUR PENDANT

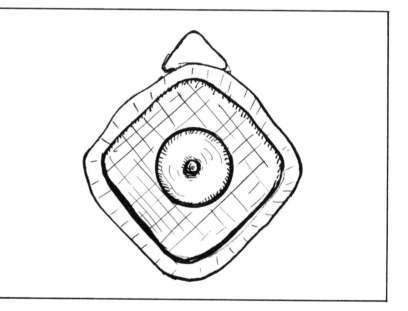

Step 1. A simple sketch is all you need to begin making this jewelry piece. Using soapstone as a one-piece mold, you can modify the pewter form either by the way you pour and cool the molten metal or by the way you saw or file the piece after casting.

Step 2. Carve the soapstone with wood carving tools, sharp-pointed instruments, or old dentist tools. Since nothing adheres well to soapstone, the best method of design transfer is to work from the original sketch, marking reference points with dividers and compass. Remember that the high part of your design will be the low part of the pewter, which you'll eventually cut out to make the plique-à-jour. To allow more flexibility in the design, cut this center circle out after coating the pewter. Don't make any undercuts or you'll break the mold when trying to remove the pewter.

Step 3. Pour the molten pewter (see Project 5, Step 10 for instructions on melting pewter) into the mold. Immediately after pouring, cover the liquid metal with a flat, nonmetallic material (an asbestos sheet or a piece of rubber). Do this so that the metal won't cool too quickly resulting in a very thick back for the pendant.

Step 4. Remove the pewter casting from the mold. The thickness of the pendant back can also be controlled through the temperature of the mold: the warmer the mold, the thinner the pendant back.

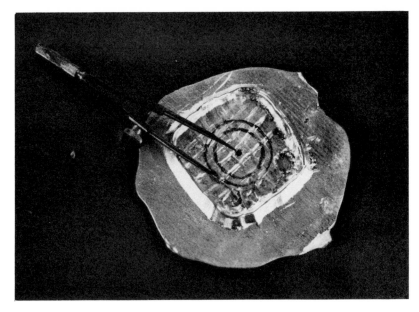

Step 5. Drill a small, 1/16″ hole in the center of the pewter casting and mark out the center circle with a pair of dividers. I decide to cut out the larger circle.

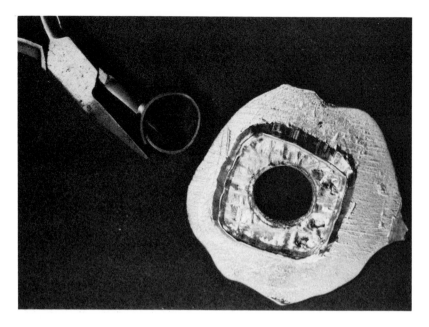

Step 6. Thread a jeweler's saw through the 1/16" center hold and cut out the circle. Shape a ¼" wide strip of 18-gauge pewter to fit the circle with a pair of jeweler's pliers having both a flat and a rounded jaw. The length of the pewter strip, for the math majors in the crowd, may be calculated by the formula for the circumference of a circle: circumference equals diameter of the circle by π (the ratio of the circumference of any circle to its diameter) which is about 3.14. Or you can make the pewter band, like most of us, by trial and error. You can get a very close fit using a jeweler's saw and thin files or sandpaper.

Step 7. Fit the pewter ring to the opening as snugly as possible, so that the non-soldered joint won't be too unsightly. A rawhide mallet, which doesn't mar the pewter surface, is usually helpful to use as a persuader.

Step 8. Make a small cylinder to be placed in the center of the circle from a ¼" strip of 18-gauge pewter. Shape the cylinder with a pair of small, round-nose pliers. Then saw it off the strip with a jeweler's saw. The finer the saw blade you use, the less adjusting will have to be done to bring the ends of the pewter together. Carefully squeeze the ends together with toothless jeweler's pliers.

Step 9. Temporarily place the little cylinder on top of a piece of white cardboard to see how the pendant will look when finished.

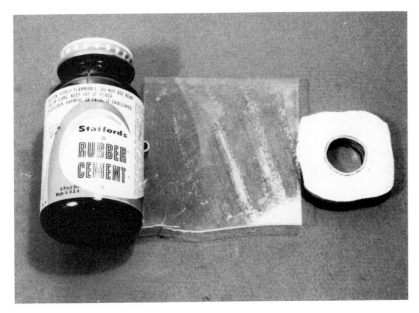

Step 10. To make a convenient form into which to pour the epoxy enamel, paint a small piece of 1/16″ Plexiglas with rubber cement. Saw the pewter form away from the balance of the pewter casting and coat the back of it with rubber cement also. After both surfaces are dry, put them together to adhere there.

Step 11. Paint the outside contacting edges with more rubber cement, so that the container for the plique-à-jour epoxy resin enamel won't leak.

CARVING A SOAPSTONE MOLD FOR A PEWTER PLIQUE-A-JOUR PENDANT

Step 12. Mix up the epoxy resin enamel, given in "Formulas" for this project and pour it into the plique-à-jour area, not up to the brim. Then make up another batch of different-colored enamel to fill the circle. Later, if the shade of color is deep enough, you can add transparent resin to fill these areas. Also apply resin enamel of the desired color to the outer chamber.

Step 13. After placing all the epoxy enamel where you want it, put the piece about 14" away from an infrared heat lamp. This is a greater distance then I ordinarily suggest. The reason for using a heat lamp with a curing agent which cures in 20 to 30 minutes at room temperature is to make certain that there will be no moisture blemishes. Such blemishes usually happen during room-temperature curing in the absence of high humidity. Heat overcomes this problem.

Step 14. After the resin has been well cured (when, upon cooling, it's fingernail hard), remove the pewter epoxy pendant from the Plexiglas.

Step 15. Buff and polish the pewter epoxy pendant using three different muslin buffers all running at about 1750 r.p.m. (see *Finishing Your Jewelry*).

Step 16. There are many ways to attach a hanging device to the pendant. One way is to drill the piece with a 1/16″ bit through one corner so that the hanger won't mar the front surface of the pendant (see *Finishing Your Jewelry*). Bend a piece of 16-gauge or 18-gauge sterling silver wire into an equilateral triangle for the hanger.

Pendant by the author;
macramé necklace by Marie Clark,
Bradenton, Florida.
Slate, cast pewter,
and Araldite epoxy resin 502.

FASHIONING A SLATE AND PEWTER PENDANT

Age-old slate, a hard, fine-grained rock that cleaves naturally into thin, smooth-surfaced layers, is an excellent material for jewelry. It can be rendered abrasive resistant with resins; sets of cufflinks I made out of slate impregnated with epoxy resins fifteen years ago still don't show the effects of wear. In this project you will learn:

How to impregnate slate, while hot, with a low-viscosity epoxy resin to make it abrasive resistant.

How to combine slate, which is highly heat-resistant, with molten pewter.

How to easily saw, cut, file, drill, and sand slate using jeweler's tools.

TOOLS AND MATERIALS

1. Jeweler's tools: saw and blades or coping saw, drill and bits, files, and vise-like pliers.

2. Finishing tools: 180-grit to 320-grit wet-or-dry sandpaper, buffing wheels, and buffing compounds.

3. Infrared heat lamp.

4. Hot plate or stove burner.

5. An asbestos board.

6. Newspapers.

7. Hammer, chisel, and any sharp tool such as a sharpened nail.

8. A piece of slate. Roofing material made of slate, obtainable from any building-supply company, is ideal.

9. Ingot and 18-gauge sheet pewter, available from C. R. Hill Company.

10. CIBA-GEIGY Araldite epoxy resin 502.

11. CIBA-GEIGY Epoxide 7 or 8 reactive diluent.

12. CIBA-GEIGY 956 curing agent.

13. Additives: color pastes, Asbestos 244, talc, and carbon black powder.

NOTES AND CAUTIONS

All resin materials are available from the companies listed in *Suppliers and Manufacturers*.

Impregnated slate has the appearance of ebony. In addition to the epoxy enamel that is combined with slate in this project, precious metals such as gold and silver, as well as precious stones, look wonderful with slate.

Remember that curing agent 956, although it's called a safety hardener, must not be in continuous contact with your skin. If you permit repeated skin contact with these epoxy resin systems, you risk becoming sensitized and coming down with poison-ivy-like skin allergies.

FORMULAS

SLATE IMPREGNATION

Araldite epoxy resin 502	9 grams
Epoxide 7 or 8	1 gram
Curing agent 956	2 grams

Mix well for 2 or 3 minutes and apply.

SLATE-REINFORCING MIXTURE

Araldite epoxy resin 502	45 grams
Epoxide 7 or 8	5 grams
Curing agent 956	10 grams
Asbestos 244	1 gram
Talc	25 grams (approx.)
Carbon black powder	3 grams (approx.)

Mix all the resin system liquids for about 2 minutes and then thoroughly stir in the Asbestos 244. Finally, add the carbon black powder and the talc to make a self-leveling, non-flowing paste.

EPOXY ENAMEL

Araldite epoxy resin 502	45 grams
Epoxide 7 or 8	5 grams
Curing agent 956	10 grams
Color pastes	as needed

These very important directions for preparing this enamel must be carefully followed to get good results: Mix all the ingredients in a small tin can until the liquid appears completely uniform. Place the can in a basin surrounded with 60°–65° F. water. Stir the resin mixture slowly for a few seconds every 5 minutes for 1 hour. The preparation is then ready to use. Keep the part you don't need initially in the cool water. In this way, it will be usable for several hours, although it will eventually become completely hard. Add colors just before applying the resin mixture.

RESIN ADHESIVE

Araldite epoxy resin 502	10 grams
Curing agent 956	2 grams
Carbon black powder	0.5 grams (approx.)

Mix very well and apply to either or both surfaces.

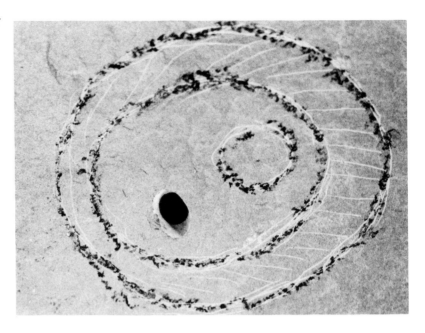

Step 1. Slice a piece of slate about 3/16" thick with a hammer and chisel and make a pencil sketch on it. If you want the slate to be thinner, you can sand or file it down. Scratch over the pencil sketch with a sharp metal point. Drill a ⅛" hole, through which to fit the saw blade.

Step 2. Although a jeweler's saw will cut through the slate piece, a coping saw works very well. Be sure to take your time during this sawing operation so that you won't shatter the slate or break your saw blades.

Step 3. Use a half round file to trim the piece. You can saw, file, and sand slate almost as easily as soapstone. At this stage, be sure not to drop the piece on a hard floor. It could shatter!

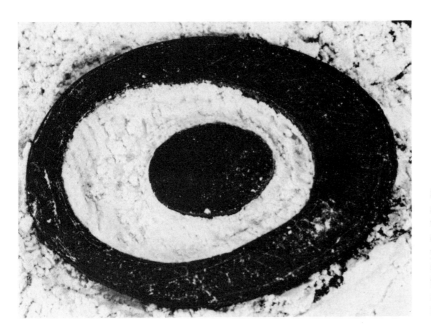

Step 4. Make up a slurry of Asbestos 244 and water. Be sure to wear a dust mask while working with asbestos powder because it's a dangerous material to get into your lungs. Spread the mixture out on a flat surface of absorbent newspaper and place the slate pieces face down on top of it. This makes a heat-resistant container for pouring the molten pewter.

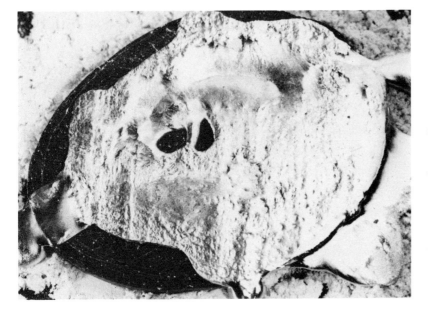

Step 5. Melt pewter scrap or ingot in a tin can directly on a burner. Keep heating the molten pewter until a newspaper taper, when dipped into it, turns marshmallow brown (see Project 5, Step 10). Then, with a pair of vise-like pliers which lock closed, latch onto one side of the can, and pour the molten pewter into the asbestos-lined enclosure. Right after pouring the pewter press an asbestos board into the molten metal until it's flush with the slate. Hold the board there until the metal has solidified.

Step 6. When the piece has cooled down, turn it over to check the pour. If you're not satisfied with it, melt and pour the pewter again.

Step 7. Saw, file, and sand away the excess pewter until the metal surface is flush with the slate. Carefully mix up the slate-reinforcing system listed in "Formulas" for this project. Turn the pendant face down and "butter" the mixture evenly all over the back to a thickness of 1/16" to ⅛". Then place the pendant about 12" away from an infrared heat lamp. When the resin system has hardened, sand it smooth using wet, 180-grit and 320-grit wet-or-dry sandpaper.

Step 8. Again turn the piece over onto its back and place it about 9" away from the infrared heat lamp. While the pendant is warming, make up the slate-impregnating mixture shown in "Formulas" for this project. Stir well and spread the mixture all over the exposed surfaces of the slate. Allow the epoxy resin mixture to remain on the slate surface about 3 minutes and then, wearing polyethylene gloves, wipe off the excess. Leave the pendant under the heat lamp until the resin has cured. Enamel the pewter with the epoxy enamel given in "Formulas" for this project, following the directions very carefully. Unless you follow the cooling procedure, you could run into trouble because an unfilled system of Araldite 502, Epoxide 7 or 8, and curing agent 956 ordinarily gives off a lot of heat while curing. Thick castings can froth, yellow, and crack unless they're heat controlled. After applying all of the enamel, place the resin surface about 12" away from an infrared heat lamp for about 2 hours until cured.

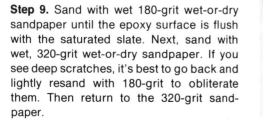

Step 9. Sand with wet 180-grit wet-or-dry sandpaper until the epoxy surface is flush with the saturated slate. Next, sand with wet, 320-grit wet-or-dry sandpaper. If you see deep scratches, it's best to go back and lightly resand with 180-grit to obliterate them. Then return to the 320-grit sandpaper.

Step 10. To finish the pendant, buff with Learok 884E and 339E greaseless buffing compounds applied to separate muslin buffing wheels running at 1750 r.p.m.

Step 11. To make the hanger for the pendant, cut a ¼″ strip of 18-gauge pewter and shape it with jeweler's pliers. With a sharpened nail, scratch the opposite side of the pewter and thoroughly clean it to remove any grease or oil that might effect the adhesive properties of the epoxy resin. Mix up the resin adhesive shown in "Formulas" for this project and use it to glue the pewter strip to the pendant. After the resin system becomes "leather hard", cut free the excess epoxy. Be sure to cure well, either 24 hours at room temperature or 2 hours about 10″ away from a heat lamp.

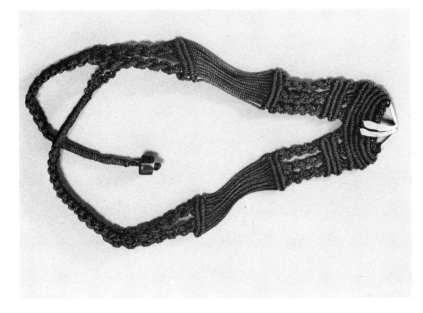

Step 12. Make a "necklace," such as this one done in macramé by Marie Clark of Bradenton, Florida, for your pendant. This one has a detachable hook so that it can be attached to other pieces.

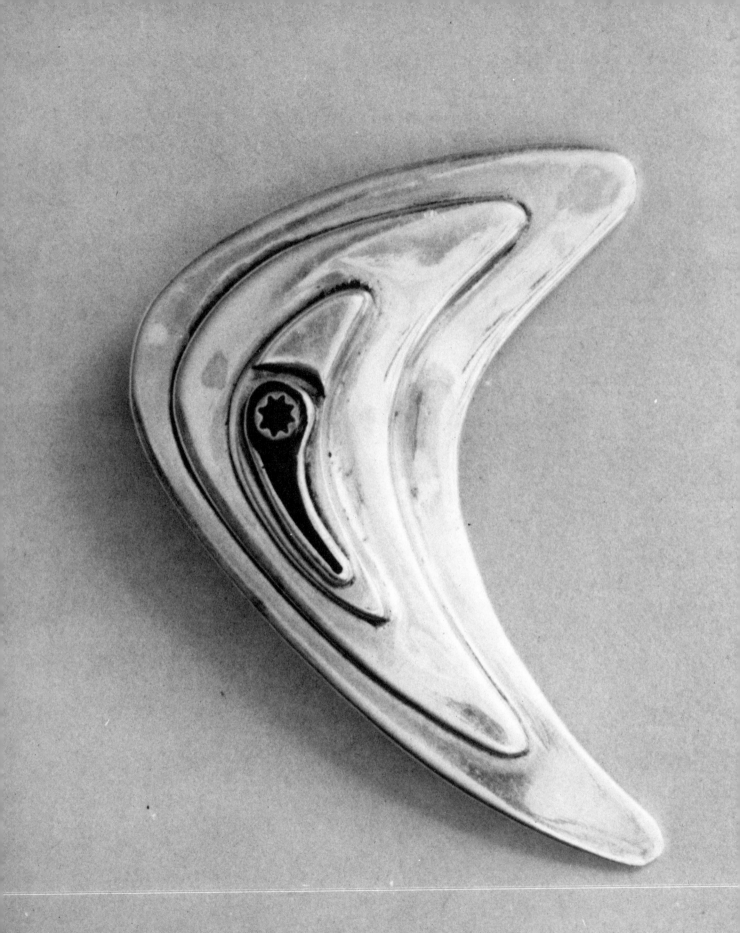

Pin by the author, Penland School of Crafts.
Sterling silver and mille fiori glass chip
embedded in epoxy resin enamel.
Photo by Mike Yarrow.

ENAMELING WOOD PLIQUE-A-JOUR EARRINGS

Wood has esthetic characteristics that are not easy to copy. From the artist/craftsman's viewpoint, there are many hardwoods such as ebony, lignum vitae, coca-bola, walnut, and rosewood that are ideal for jewelry projects. Combining wood with epoxy resin has a number of advantages. This project will demonstrate:

How to seal wood from changes caused by humidity and temperature by saturating it with a low-viscosity epoxy resin system.

How to use epoxy resins for adhesion and strength to make excellent "enamels" on top of the wood and transparent "windows" inside the wood.

How to combine wood with other media. In this project I combine mille fiore glass chips in the epoxy resin.

TOOLS AND MATERIALS

1. Jeweler's tools: saw and blades, pliers, files, and a drill and bits.

2. Finishing tools: 220-grit wet-or-dry sandpaper, buffing compounds (Learok 765, 884E, and 339E), and 6" muslin buffing wheels.

3. Infrared heat lamp.

4. A toothbrush and a sable brush.

5. A medium-sized watertight container.

6. Wood, ⅛" or thicker, available from your local lumberyard or from companies such as C.R. Hill (see *Suppliers and Manufacturers*).

7. 18-gauge sterling silver wire.

8. Earring parts: wires and findings.

9. Mille fiore glass chips, which are available from Leo Popper and Co. (see *Suppliers and Manufacturers*).

10. Mold-release agent, Korax 1711 aerosol spray.

11. A sheet of Mylar or any releasing surface.

12. Sun Oil Company 1290 Y microcrystalline wax, HH 572 soft modeling wax, and green color paste.

13. CIBA-GEIGY Araldite epoxy resin 502.

14. CIBA-GEIGY Epoxide 7 or 8 reactive diluent.

15. CIBA-GEIGY 956 curing agent.

16. Color pastes.

NOTES AND CAUTIONS

All resinous materials, color pastes, and waxes are available from the companies listed in *Suppliers and Manufacturers*. You can find the other products at local stores. Wood is lighter than metal or stones, but when well saturated with epoxy resin, it will have greater abrasive resist-

---

FORMULAS

EPOXY RESIN WOOD PRIMER

Araldite epoxy resin 502	9 grams
Epoxide 7 or 8	1 gram
Curing agent 956	2 grams

Mix well for several minutes and use.

60/40 MODELING WAX

1290 Y microcrystalline wax	60 parts
HH 572 soft modeling wax	40 parts
Green color paste	1 part

Melt together in a tin can (see Project 8, Steps 1 and 2). Add green color paste for later identification.

EPOXY "ENAMEL" AND PLIQUE-A-JOUR RESIN

Araldite epoxy resin 502	9 grams
Epoxide 7 or 8	1 gram
Curing agent 956	2 grams
Color pastes	as needed

In order to obtain heavy enamels and thick plique-à-jour windows, follow this simple procedure for "aging" the epoxy resin system. Mix the epoxy enamel system well in an empty, clean, 6 oz. tin can (a coffee can). I usually mix up about five times the amount of the basic formula. Place the can in a larger container and surround it with 60°-65° F. water. Stir the resin mixture gently and frequently for an hour before use. The system is usable for about 2 hours if kept in the cool-water bath. Add color pastes just before use.

After applying the resin, heat the piece about 12" to 18" away from an infrared heat lamp. The viscosity will decrease appreciably and all air bubbles will come to the surface. You can also spray the surface with acetone to eliminate air bubbles. You should try a few experiments with this system before risking an important piece.

---

ance than sterling silver. You can experiment with inlaying different kinds of wood into cloisons in a wooden panel or mixing wood flour, made from ebony or other hardwood, with epoxy resin to use as an "enamel."

Be sure to prevent curing agent 956 from contacting your hands and skin.

Wear goggles and disposable polyethylene gloves when you weigh and mix resins. If you should get these materials in your eyes or mouth, rinse with cold running water for 15 minutes and then obtain medical attention. Make it a point to tell the nurse or doctor that 956 is a highly *alkaline* nitrogen compound. Don't panic—I've used 956 for well over 14 years with no problems. *But I am extremely careful.*

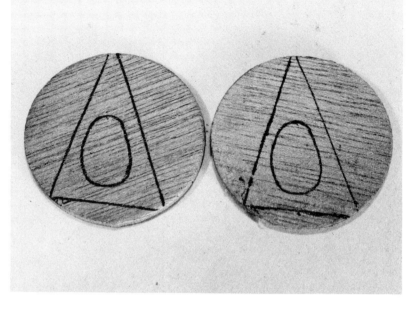

Step 1. Mark out very simple designs on circles of ⅛″ wood. Drill 1/16″ holes in the center of each piece so that a jeweler's saw can be inserted to cut out the center pieces.

Step 2. Saw out the pieces. Save all the odd pieces to use in exploring other combinations, such as wood inlays in metal, for jewelry. It's most important to first prime the wood pieces with low-viscosity epoxy resin to seal all the pores. If you don't do this before you put on the heavy enamel, there's a good chance that air bubbles will seep out of the wood while the resin is curing and mar the resin surface. Mix up the epoxy resin wood primer shown in "Formulas" for this project and brush it all over the pieces.

Step 3. Sand the earrings with dry, 220-grit wet-or-dry sandpaper to remove all wooden "whiskers," which seem to grow after wood surfaces are first primed. Coat the pieces with the uncolored epoxy enamel shown in "Formulas" for this project. Place the pieces on a piece of waxed and polished Mylar or any releasing surface about 10″ away from an infrared heat lamp for 1 hour. After the resin has cured hard, turn the pieces over, coat the backs with resin, and heat cure as before. Sand lightly to remove any imperfections. If you want a higher polish and decide to buff the resin surfaces, be sure to heat cure the resin for several more hours to guarantee a very hard surface.

Step 4. To make a secure place for mille fiore glass chips during the resin pouring, mix the 60/40 modeling wax shown in "Formulas" for this project and spray it with Korax 1711 mold release. Put the glass chips on the wax and push them in slightly so that they'll protrude through the other side of the resin pour. Also push the wood pieces into the wax to make a leak-proof container for the epoxy resin system.

Step 5. Mix up the epoxy resin plique-à-jour system described in "Formulas" for this project and pour it into the openings. Place an infrared heat lamp about 10" away from the resin surface for 1 to 2 hours to cure it out. Once the epoxy has cured, remove the pieces from the wax and use a toothbrush dipped in water and detergent to clean them. After drying with tissues, wipe quickly with acetone to cleanse and slightly tenderize the surface.

Step 6. With a brush, apply a very thin coat of the plique-à-jour enamel and let it cure as in Step 7. Sand the earring findings with dry 220-grit, wet-or-dry sandpaper. Then mix up the epoxy enamel, add the desired color, and apply it to the findings as decorative "jewels" (see Project 2, Step 10). Heat one end of the 18-gauge sterling silver wire with a butane torch until it forms a round ball, then polish it on a buffing wheel. Drill a hole in the top of each earring piece with a 1/16" bit. Pull the wire through and shape it with needle-nose jeweler's pliers. Saw away the excess wire with a jeweler's saw. File the edge of the wire smooth with needle files and then buff with Learok 765 buffing compound (see *Finishing Your Jewelry*).

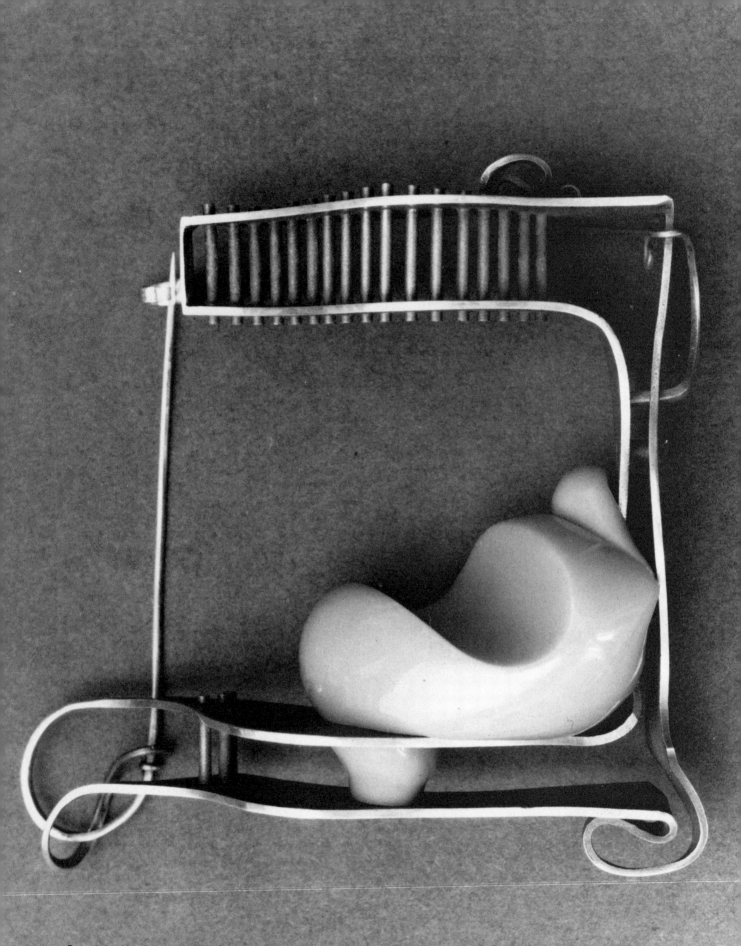

Brooch by Amy Buckingham, Philadelphia.
Precious metal and cast epoxy resin.
Photo courtesy of the artist.

PROJECT 13

WINDING A FIBERGLASS FILAMENT REINFORCED RING

You can apply the procedure shown in this project to making many other things, such as bracelets and buckles, which should be strong. In this project you will learn:

How to make a mandril of cellulose acetate for shaping an epoxy resin ring.

How to wind on the fiberglass-filament reinforcement.

How to make pewter and epoxy resin "jewels" for the ring.

TOOLS AND MATERIALS

1. Jeweler's tools: saw and blades, pliers, drill and bits, and files.
2. Finishing tools: 320-grit wet-or-dry sandpaper, buffing compounds, and buffing wheels.
3. A ring to determine size.
4. Staple gun.
5. Tie tack or similar shiny piece to make the "jewel."
6. 10-mil sheet of cellulose acetate, acetone, and a syringe.
7. A strip of 8 oz. fiberglass cloth, 3" x 50".
8. Korax 1711 mold-release spray or MirrorGlaze wax.
9. 1/8" metal rod, such as a paint stirrer for rotating the mandril.
10. Scrap piece of wood and used saw blades to make a frame.
11. Polyethylene bag (Baggie).
12. 18-gauge sheet of pewter.
13. CIBA-GEIGY Araldite epoxy resin 502.
14. RC-125 and RC-303 curing agents.
15. Additives: color pastes and Asbestos 244.

NOTES AND CAUTIONS

The convenience of using curing agent RC-125 is that it cures hard in 1/2 to 1 hour. If you want to metalize any part of the ring, try using the epoxy metal system described in Project 6 under "Formulas." For this system, sift into the resin mixture as much 300-mesh metal powder as possible while stirring. Let this combination stand for about 2 hours to allow it to become less runny and easier to model. If it's still to difficult to work, let it rest another hour.

FORMULAS

INSIDE RING COATING

Araldite epoxy resin 502	10 grams
Asbestos 244	0.2 grams
Curing agent RC-125	2.5 grams

A transparent thickening agent such as Asbestos 244 dispersed in epoxy resin 502 is so handy that I always keep prepared mixtures on hand and ready to use. (When mixed with a hardener, this makes a good glue for household repairs.) A 2% or 4% concentration of Asbestos 244 in 502 keeps forever.

Warm 100 grams of Araldite epoxy resin 502 to 250° to 300° F. by placing an infrared heat lamp about 2" from the top of the can. Weigh out 4 grams of Asbestos 244 carefully (dustlessly) for mixing into the hot 502. Stir the Asbestos 244 into the hot resin with a coffee stirrer or paint mixer. Let the resin mixture cool slowly and then add the hardener. (Hardener proportions aren't altered by this small percentage of Asbestos 244.)

RESIN BINDER FOR THE FIBERGLASS FILAMENT (ALSO EPOXY ENAMEL)

Araldite epoxy resin 502	10 grams
Curing agent RC-125	2.5 grams
Color pastes	as needed

Mix well and add color paste as desired.

EPOXY ADHESIVE 5-MINUTE CURE

Araldite epoxy resin 502	1 gram
Curing agent RC-303	0.5 gram

Mix well and use immediately.

You can also add pearlescent paste to the epoxy resin non-filled systems to achieve a mother-of-pearl appearance. Carbon black and burnt umber color paste will simulate ebony. Sand or flint powder when mixed into an epoxy resin system, will make it extremely hard.

Be sure to wear gloves when you handle the fiberglass filament. Also don't handle curing agent RC-125 with your bare hands. It can sensitize your skin to poison-ivy-like allergies.

Wear a dust mask when working with powdered Asbestos 244.

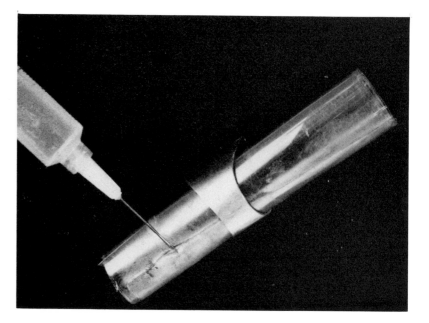

Step 1. Roll up a 6″ x 4″ piece of 10-mil cellulose acetate. Fit this tube into a ring of the desired size and then seal it at the outer edge with acetone applied with a syringe. Massage the tube as you apply the acetone to get an evenly spread, closed seam.

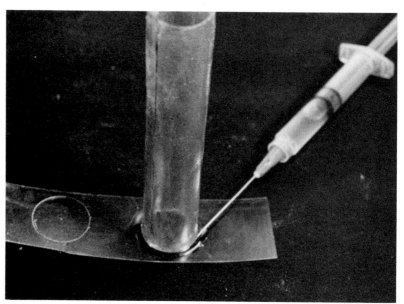

Step 2. To construct the mandril to be used for "spinning" the ring, drill a ⅛″ hole in the center of two pieces of cellulose acetate and use acetone to glue one piece to each end of the main tube.

Step 3. Construct an impromptu wooden frame to support the mandril. Staple a broken saw blade at each end to act as a friction bearing during the spinning. (Such improvising saves time and money.) Insert a ⅛″ metal shaft through the holes in the cellulose acetate ends of the tube so that you can rotate the mandril. (I use a ⅛″ rod that was part of a paint mixer.) Secure the rod beneath the saw blade at each end.

Step 4. Mix up the inside ring coating shown in "Formulas" for this project. You can stir the Asbestos 244 into the hot resin more quickly by using a paint mixer attached to a ¼" bit of an electric drill. Stir very slowly so that you won't beat in air bubbles until the Asbestos is evenly dispersed.

Step 5. Spray the tube with mold-release spray or coat with MirrorGlaze wax. With a coffee stirrer, evenly coat the tube with the asbestos resin system so that there will be a layer of this system between the fiberglass and the finger upon which the ring is worn.

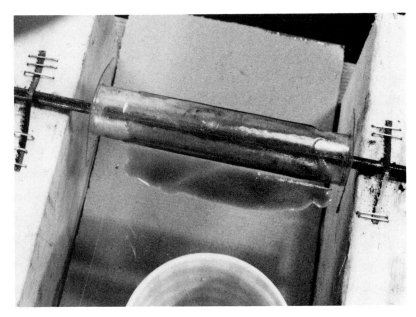

Step 6. Slowly rotate the resin-covered mandril while using a 20-mil piece of cellulose acetate to spread the resin system evenly. This epoxy resin system cures in ½ to 1 hour at room temperature (70° F.).

Step 7. Place an empty polyethylene Baggie under the reinforcing operation to catch drippings. Mix a fresh amount of the resin system *without the asbestos* and apply a thin coat to the resin-covered mandril. Unravel a fiberglass filament from a 50″ piece of 8 oz. fiberglass cloth, and begin to wind it onto the resin. (100″ of fiberglass filament reinforces a ⅜″ epoxy resin ring.)

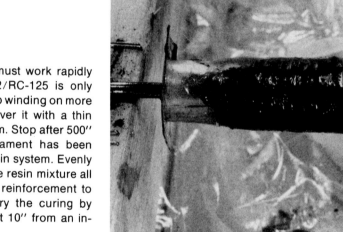

Step 8. Remember you must work rapidly since the pot-life of 502/RC-125 is only about ½ hour. As you keep winding on more fiberglass, be sure to cover it with a thin coating of the resin system. Stop after 500″ to 600″ of fiberglass filament has been evenly wound into the resin system. Evenly apply a thin coating of the resin mixture all over the tube. Allow the reinforcement to cure hard. You can hurry the curing by placing the mandril about 10″ from an infrared heap lamp.

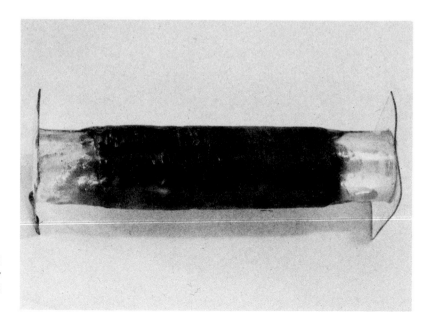

Step 9. File or sand smooth the hardened surface of the fiberglass-reinforced epoxy resin in preparation for decorating the band and finishing the ring.

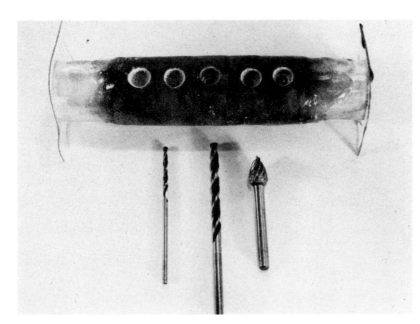

Step 10. To make the "jewel bed" holes, use various bits attached to a drill. Unfortunately, I've drilled through the acetate tube, and it will therefore be difficult to fill these holes.

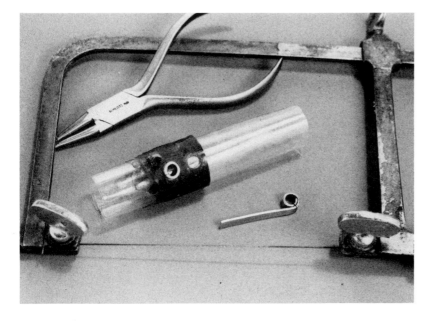

Step 11. Saw the ends off the tube. Because I drilled through the tube, I insert another tube of acetate to block up the hole. Coil up a strip of 18-gauge pewter, sawing through the overlap to make a good fit, and insert this circle into the hole drilled in the ring tube.

Step 12. To achieve a little more brilliance in the "jewel," I need a shiny ball of metal to place in the tube. I find just the thing in the end of a tie tack, which I cut off and polish with Learok 339E.

Step 13. Glue the shiny, gold-plated ball (or whatever ornament you're using) into the base of the pewter circle on the tube, using a few drops of 5-minute curing epoxy adhesive shown in "Formulas" for this project. Use the epoxy enamel system, which is the same as the resin binder under "Formulas" for this project, to fill in the pewter circle. To get a hard surface, cure the epoxy enamel about 8" from an infrared heat lamp for 1 or 2 hours.

Step 14. Cut the rings apart with a jeweler's saw. You can pull the loose acetate in the center right out. Then sand the surfaces of the epoxy and pewter with wet 320-grit, wet-or-dry sandpaper.

Step 15. Buff and polish the ring and "jewel" with Learok 884E and then with Learok 339E. (See *Finishing Your Jewelry* for additional information.)

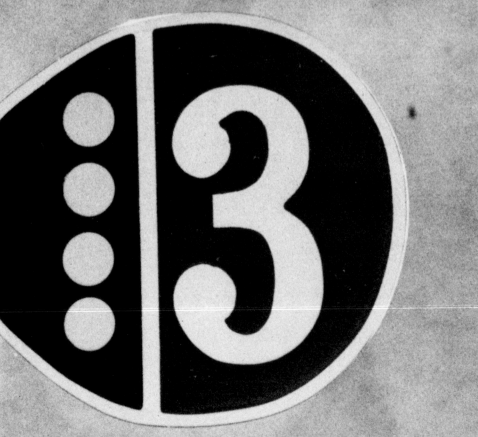

Rings by Walter Schluep, Montreal.
Precious metals and epoxy enamel.
Photo courtesy of the artist.

PROJECT 14

INLAYING PEWTER IN AN ENAMELED, SILVER-BANDED RING

Pewter has many of the attributes of sterling silver, although it's about ten times cheaper than this precious metal. Today's pewter is an excellent candidate for inclusion in jewelry making. The "new" pewter is called Britannia metal and contains no lead. Its formula is approximately 92% tin, 7½% antimony, and 1½% copper (see Project 8, "Formulas" for instructions on making pewter). One of the great assets of this alloy is that it doesn't tarnish. Pewter is easy to engrave, saw, melt, cast, buff, and polish. It's relatively soft and therefore cannot be successfully used alone in pieces such as rings or bracelet bands, where rigidity and springiness are needed. Rings I've made with pure pewter bands haven't held up well. This project shows a way to use pewter in a ring and yet not have the wear problems.

Each of the three materials, epoxy resin, pewter, and sterling silver, used in this project has certain characteristics which give it validity in the ring. You will learn:

How to use sterling silver as a band to give the ring physical strength, rigidity, and the value associated with a precious metal.

How to easily cast pewter in a silicone rubber mold.

How to adhere pewter to sterling silver with an epoxy resin.

How to use epoxy resins as transparent, hard, abrasive-resistant jewelry enamels.

TOOLS AND MATERIALS

1. Jeweler's tools: coping saw and blades, files, rawhide mallet, and a ring mandril.
2. Finishing tools: wet-or-dry sandpaper, buffing compounds, and buffing wheels.
3. Graphite.
4. Korax 1711 mold-release spray.
5. Scotch or masking tape.
6. Rubber cement.
7. Silly putty.
8. C-clamp.
9. 20-gauge sterling silver strip.
10. Scrap piece of pewter or ingot.
11. Cellulose acetate, acetone, and a syringe.
12. Sun Oil Company 1290 Y microcrystalline wax, HH 572 soft modeling wax, and green color paste.
13. Dow Corning Silastic A silicone mold-making rubber and Silastic F catalyst.
14. CIBA-GEIGY Araldite epoxy resin 502.
15. HH 1065B, CIBA-GEIGY 840, and DION EH-30.
16. Additives: color pastes, Asbestos 244.

FORMULAS

1290 Y microcrystalline wax	60 parts
HH 572 soft modeling wax	40 parts
Green color paste	1 part

Melt the two waxes together in a tin can about 4" away from an infrared heat lamp (see Project 8, Step 1 for detailed instructions).

MOLD-MAKING RUBBER

Silastic A rubber	50 grams
Silastic F catalyst	5 grams

Mix the ingredients slowly and well (see Project 8, "Formulas" for detailed instructions).

RING-PROPPING MIXTURE

Silly putty	100 grams
Asbestos 244	as needed

Mix some asbestos into the silly putty and knead it with your hand until the putty is stiff. To make the mixing easier, warm the silly putty and the asbestos.

EPOXY ADHESIVE

Araldite epoxy resin 502	10 grams
Asbestos 244	0.4 grams
Curing agent 840	5 grams
DION EH-30	0.2 grams (3 drops approx.)

Mix the ingredients together in a plastic-coated cup and apply with a toothpick.

EPOXY ENAMEL

Araldite epoxy resin 502	20 grams
Curing agent HH 1065B	5 grams

Weigh the ingredients into a tin can and stir slowly and thoroughly until the mixture is completely clear throughout, then use it.

NOTES AND CAUTIONS

All the resin systems used here can be purchased from the companies listed in *Suppliers and Manufacturers*.

Precious stones can be included in this type of ring. Be sure the gem is well cleaned before gluing it into the resin.

When handling the epoxy resin system, which contains HH 1065B, remember that this hardener is very corrosive and should not be allowed to get on your skin. If this should happen, wash your hands or the affected area well with soap and lots of running water. Eye contamination requires immediate medical attention, after you've rinsed out the eye with cold running water for 15 minutes.

Good ventilation is a must when using HH 1065B.

INLAYING PEWTER IN AN ENAMELED, SILVER-BANDED RING

Step 1. Sketch a simple ring band design on a piece of paper. To check for size you can cut the pattern from 10-mil cellulose acetate and wrap it around a ring mandril. With rubber cement, glue the paper with the design to a piece of well cleaned 20-gauge sterling silver. Cut the sterling silver band with a jeweler's saw rubbed with a little wax to facilitate the cutting. You'll find sawing sterling silver a bit harder than sawing pewter. With a rawhide mallet, hammer the band to form a U over the proper size on a ring mandril (see *Your Studio and Basic Equipment*). Hold the mandril firmly in a vise while striking the silver with the mallet. (See the *Bibliography* for books on jewelry-making, which will provide more details.)

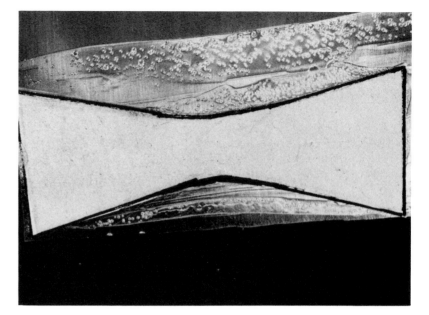

Step 2. Make a wax mold from the 60/40 wax shown in "Formulas" for this project (and in Project 8, Steps 1 and 2). Cut the wax design, following the procedure described in Project 6, Steps 2 and 3. Make a rubber mold on the wax, as in Project 8, Steps 4 and 5. Quickly brush the rubber mixture over the face of the wax to be sure there won't be air bubbles, then pour on the balance of the rubber and allow it to cure. Silastic A is a silicone RTV (room-temperature-vulcanizing or curing) rubber that cures to its rubber form in about ½ hour when its speedy catalyst Silastic F is added. Slower catalysts are also available.

Step 3. Brush graphite powder lightly into the silicone rubber mold. The graphite will allow the gases to escape as you pour in the molten pewter.

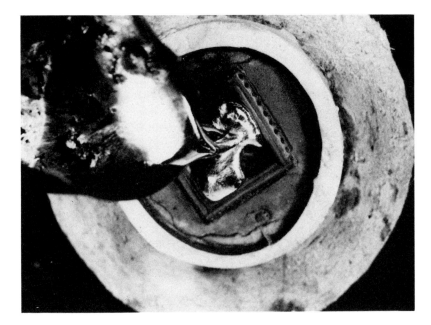

Step 4. A Silastic RTV rubber mold is used here because its melting point is around 500° F., thereby permitting the pouring of molten pewter, which melts at around 425° F. Heat the pewter (see Project 5, Step 10) to 700° F. to 900° F. (this overheating prevents the liquid pewter from freezing when it hits the mold), and pour it into only the center portion of the mold. This mold, which I used for another piece, has a center design that can be used as a pewter "jewel." (To protect the surface you're working on, you may want to put the mold on an asbestos block before you pour the metal.)

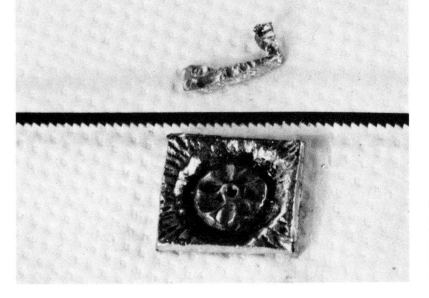

Step 5. Remove the pewter "jewel" from the rubber mold and trim it with a coping saw. To give the pewter casting a higher shine, buff it with Learok 884E and with Learok 339E applied to separate muslin buffing wheels.

Step 6. Sand the sides of the pewter "jewel" to make them parallel. Clean and rough the area of the sterling silver and the edges of the pewter where the gluing is to be done.

INLAYING PEWTER IN AN ENAMELED, SILVER-BANDED RING

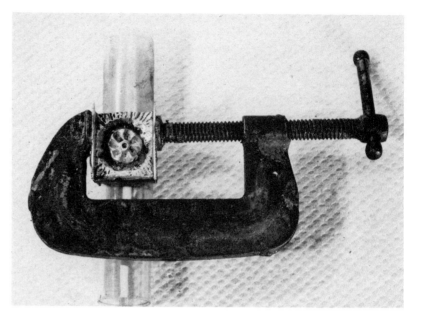

Step 7. Glue the pewter "jewel" to the sterling silver band with the epoxy adhesive shown in "Formulas" for this project. Use a C-clamp to hold the band in place. Be sure that the sterling silver surface is protected from clamp marks by covering it with Scotch or masking tape. Allow the ring to set about 10" away from a heat lamp for 2 to 4 hours.

Step 8. Wrap masking tape tightly around the sterling silver band and the pewter "jewel" to prepare the piece for the epoxy enamel. You can prop up the ring in the mixture of silly putty and asbestos described in "Formulas" for this project. Then mix the epoxy resin enamel and pour it over the pewter. Place the ring about 10" away from an infrared heat lamp for at least 2 hours. Make sure that the surface is fingernail hard when the resin has cooled down. If it isn't, heat the resin for another hour.

Step 9. After the resin enamel is well cured, remove the tape. Sand the surface with wet, 180-grit wet-or-dry sandpaper to make it flush with the sterling silver edge. Sand lightly with a circular motion, trying to minimize scratches. Sand the silver band in a similar manner, switching to wet, 320-grit wet-or-dry sandpaper, until you're sure that there are no deep scratch marks. Wash and dry the surface frequently so that you can check for marks. When you have a uniform matte surface, start buffing with Learok 765. A light, even buffing produces a matte surface. Follow this with Learok 884E, and finally, buff with Learok 336E for the high-gloss finish. I prefer a Swedish-type matte finish (see *Finishing Your Jewelry*) on the band because bright finishes on sterling silver are easily marred.

1. Ring by Arch Gregory, Knoxville.
Sterling silver and Araldite epoxy resin 502.
Photo by David Richer.

2. Necklace by the author.
Pewter and acrylic resin.
Project 3.

3. Bracelet by the author. Fiberglass-
reinforced polyester resin, epoxy, and
pewter. Project 20.

4. Pendant by Peter Prip, Pearson Studio,
Deer Isle, Maine. Sterling silver and epoxy.
Photo courtesy of the artist.

5. Earrings by the author.
Pewter and polyester resin.
Project 18.

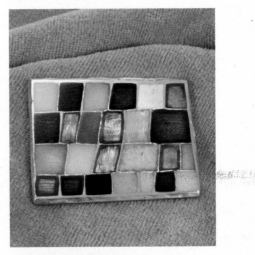

6. Pendant by Nadine Rutledge, Truro.
Cast pewter and epoxy enamel.
Photo by Mike Yarrow.

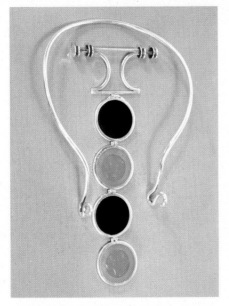

7. Neckpiece by Deborah Johnston, Ontario.
Forged and constructed silver and Araldite
epoxy resin 502. Photo by Harry Hollander.

8. Necklace by the author. Polyester resin,
sterling silver wire, and raku beads.
Project 17.

9. Pendant by Walter Schluep, Montreal.
Sterling silver, epoxy enamel, and a ruby.
Photo by Mike Yarrow.

10–13. Brooches by Claus Bury,
Hanau, Germany.
Plexiglas acrylic.
Photos by Werner Kumpf.

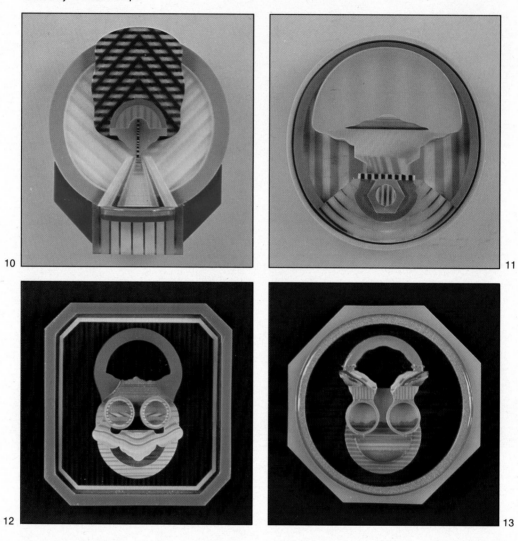

10

11

12

13

14. Pendant by Bob Natalini, Philadelphia.
Sterling silver, 14k gold,
copper, ivory, and Plexiglas.
Photo courtesy of the artist.

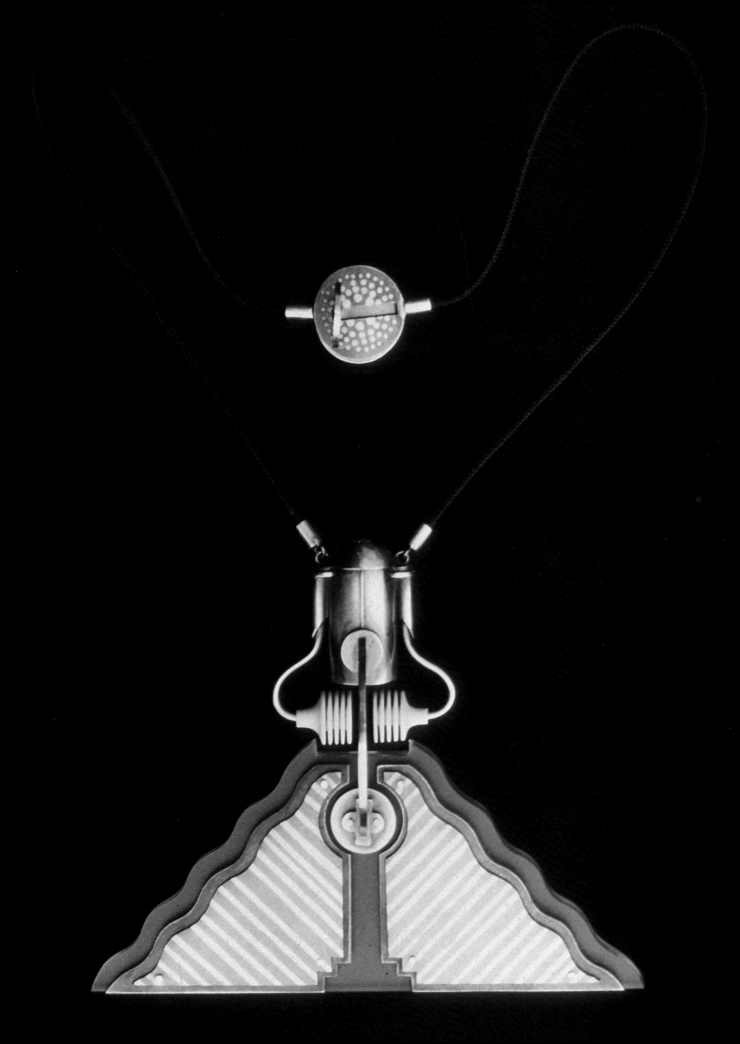

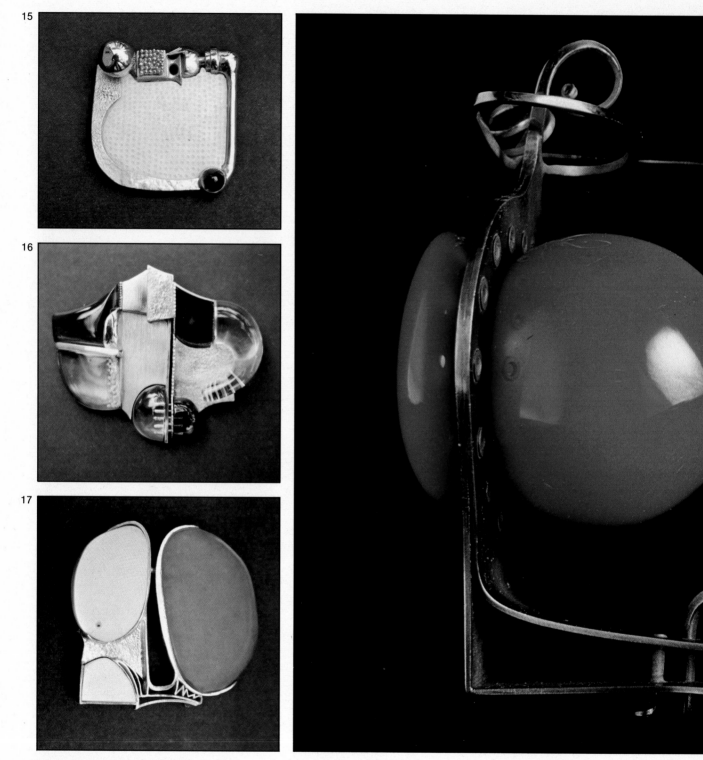

15–17. Brooches by Toni Goessler-Snyder,
Audubon, Pennsylvania.
18k gold, fiberglass-reinforced polyester,
denture plastic, Tourmalin, ivory, and Lucite.
Photo courtesy of the artist.

19. Brooch by Stanley Lechtzin, Tyler School of Art.
Electroformed silver, gilt,
amethyst crystals, and purple polyester.
Photo courtesy of the artist.

18. Brooch by Amy Buckingham, Philadelphia.
14k gold, sterling silver, sculpted
and cast epoxy resin (high polish finish).
Photo courtesy of the artist.

20. Brooch by Harold O'Conner, Calgary, Alberta.
18k gold, silver, Plexiglas, and paint.
Photo courtesy of the artist.

21–23. Rings by Claus Bury,
Hanau, Germany.
Gold and acrylic.
Photos by Werner Kumpf.

21

22

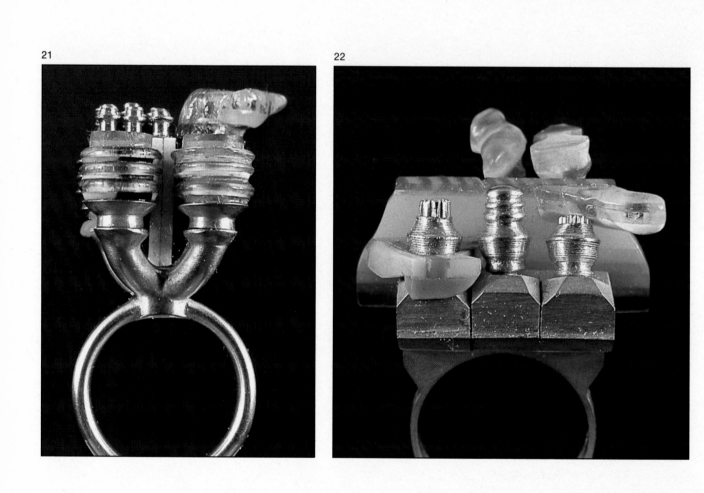

23

PART THREE
POLYESTER
RESINS

24. Pendant by Bob Natalini, Philadelphia.
Sterling silver, 14k gold, copper, turquoise,
Plexiglas tubing, and two hand-formed Plexiglas domes
(one of which is inlayed with white pigmented epoxy);
the catch is silver inlayed with gold.
Photo courtesy of the artist.

POLYESTER RESINS

Water-clear polyester casting resins are relatively inexpensive, fluid synthetic (man-made) organic carbon-containing materials. They contain 60% solid polyester chemical compounds mixed with 40% liquid combinations of styrene and methyl methacrylate. Any polyester resin can be thinned down with styrene (used to make Styrofoam) or methyl methacrylate (the basis of Plexiglas, Lucite, and Perspex). Adding methyl methacrylate will also make the polyester resin more resistant to the ultraviolet rays of the sun.

CASTING RESINS

Water-clear casting resins, such as the Polylite 32-032 polyester resin manufactured by Reichhold Chemicals, and similar ones manufactured by Koppers and by Rohm and Haas, have the following properties when they're cured into hardened plastics:

They're almost as water clear and transparent as acrylic resins such as Plexiglas, Lucite, and Perspex.

They're more stable, to date, when exposed to sunlight than are epoxy resins, yet they yellow more readily than acrylic resins. Keep polyester resin 32-032 in an amber or opaque container to prevent it from curing in sunlight.

They're cheaper than epoxy or acrylic resins.

They don't adhere at all well to metals or nonporous surfaces such as glass and ceramics. They do adhere to one another.

They shrink in volume on curing (hardening) about twice as much as epoxy resins, which shrink about 3% to 5%. The 7½% shrinkage of polyester resins is about half that of acrylic resins such as HH 772. This high shrinkage rate prevents the use of polyester resins for enameling directly on metals.

They aren't as mechanically strong as acrylic resins. When strength is required, they can be used with fiberglass reinforcement. Such reinforcement reduces transparency.

They're air-inhibited at their surfaces while curing at room temperature. This problem is overcome in "general-purpose" polyester resin by the presence in the resin of a small amount of dissolved paraffin. The inclusion of the wax in the polyester resin causes a dulling and clouding of the resin surface upon curing. They tend to be somewhat brittle in casting without the addition of plasticizers (flexibilizing agents).

They may harden in the can if they aren't kept at temperatures below 65° F. If you buy any casting resin in a hobby shop, be sure to shake the can and *hear* the liquid slosh about on the inside. Resin that isn't completely liquid is valueless!

MEK PEROXIDE (MEK-Px)

This organic chemical, manufactured by Reichhold Chemicals, is not the same as the peroxide you buy in a drugstore. The polymerization process brought about by mixing the MEK-Px thoroughly into the water-clear, colorless Polylite 32-032 polyester resin occurs in the following way. The system increases in viscosity, creating lumps which become increasingly larger. Then the resin becomes "leather hard" and can be easily and cleanly cut with a sharp knife. This leather-hard stage will last several hours if the resin hasn't been too highly catalyzed (if you haven't added too much MEK-Px). Gradually the resin hardens so that it can't be cut with a knife, but it can still be bent easily.

In the next state, the resin is hard and unbendable at room temperature but can be shaped somewhat if warmed in a heat box or oven set at 125° F. After shaping, it will retain this position if held until it cools down to room temperature. The cured 32-032 polyester resin will be more resistant to future distortion if it's annealed (post-cured) in a heat box or oven for several hours at 150° F. Then the resin casting may be sawed, drilled, filed, sanded, and polished as you would any hardwood or metal.

The most notable result of the addition of the MEK-Px is the emission of heat called exotherm. This generated heat, which you can often feel, makes the polymerization process move more rapidly. The more MEK-Px added to the Polylite 32-032, the more heat will be developed.

Since thin coatings or castings of 32-032 permit the heat generated by peroxide addition to readily escape, larger quantities of MEK-Px can be added initially to set the polymerizing mechanism in motion. For thick castings, on the other hand, you should cut the MEK-Px way down. The simple table below lists the quantities of MEK-Px needed to cure out different thicknesses of 32-032 water-clear polyester casting resin.

TABLE OF CATALYST MEK-PX FOR CURING POLYESTER RESIN CASTINGS

Add the MEK-Px shown in this table to 100 grams of Polylite 32-032 polyester resin and 5 grams of Benzoflex 9-88 (a flexibilizer which acts to make resin less brittle).

Thickness of resin casting	MEK-Px in Grams or PHR*
1/64" to ⅛"	2
⅛" to ¼"	1 to .75
¼" to ½"	.50 to .25
1" to 3"	.25 to .10

*Parts per hundred resin

ADDITIVES

Antioxidants such as Irganox 1010 or Irganox 1076 used in conjunction with the ultraviolet absorbers can markedly improve the properties of 32-032. Consult a resin supplier for information.

Benzoflex 9-88 is a flexibilizer (plasticizer) which when added to polyester resin will prevent impact chipping without noticeably softening the resin surface. I use about 5% (5 grams per 100 grams of 32-032) Benzoflex 9-88. I've found that 32-032 tends to be somewhat brittle when cast into ⅛" transparent sheets without reinforcement.

Colors are used in this book to decorate the resin systems. For convenience and economy, transparent or opaque color pastes are the best buys. Liquid colors are expensive and probably not as lightfast as those in paste form. For the color systems which are the most lightfast, try the Microliths manufactured by CIBA-GEIGY. You can make your own color pastes quite easily from these pigments.

Fiberglass filaments, cloths, and mats are the most common reinforcements for polyester resins. These are available from resin suppliers. Other reinforcing materials, which aren't as strong, are cotton gauze, dacron, and rayon. Try out different materials and see which you prefer. Often you don't need the great strength provided by fiberglass. Don't use more resin than necessary with these reinforcements; it won't increase the strength and will simply be a waste of material. Also be sure to roll out any air bubbles formed in the application of the polyester to the reinforcing material. A roller-type vegetable slicer like the one shown in Project 19, Step 8 yields a stronger and more translucent panel.

HH 371 Quik-Gel is a relatively new accelerator for polyester resins. This mixture of 10 grams of DION-3-800 LC and 90 grams of styrene has the magical property of making the 32-032 polyester resin gel very rapidly. This saves valuable time; once a resin casting has gelled, you can add more resin to it even though it hasn't cured out. Amounts of HH 371 can be varied from ½% to 2% based on the amount of 32-032 polyester resin. Depending on the quantity of HH 371 used, gelling will occur in 15 seconds to 5 minutes. The complete hardening process still takes time, although not quite as much as it would without the use of the accelerator. When using the HH 371 Quik-Gel, I usually cut the MEK-Px quantity in half.

Internal releases can be added directly into the resin system to prevent the polyester resin from adhering to metallic and nonporous surfaces such as glass. The one I use is manufactured by Axel Plastic Research Laboratories of

Long Island City, New York. It's called Internal Release 54 and is available from the suppliers listed in *Suppliers and Manufacturers*. Use no more than ¼ gram of Internal Release 54 to 100 grams of 32-032 polyester resin. You can measure conveniently with a calibrated dropper; 6 drops will be approximately ¼ gram.

Methyl methacrylate monomer can be used as a reactive diluent and does provide protection from the ultraviolet rays of the sun. Since 32-032 already contains about 10% MMA (methyl methacrylate) and the Rohm and Haas Company suggest 20% MMA for the maximum light resistance for polyester resins, you should add an additional 10% MMA to thin down the 32-032 if it's too viscous.

Nonburning additives are not of major importance here because the amounts of polyester resin used in jewelry are so small that you needn't be concerned with flammability. However, for the sake of completeness, you should know that you can obtain fire-resistant polyester resins from resin suppliers. Polyester resin 32-032 is in no way resistant to burning unless you add large amounts of special additives. If you want to make murals or large sculpture, be sure to get information on fire-resistant resins.

Opacifiers and fillers include inert materials such as talc, bentonite, calcium carbonates, and wood flour. They're all inexpensive products which can be added in relatively large quantities to the 32-032 polyester resin. Be sure to mix the MEK-Px well into the polyester resin before adding these fillers. Remember that the resin won't cure evenly if the MEK-Px is not evenly distributed. Certain fillers can cause the catalyst to become less reactive; you may notice that you need to add more MEK-Px. Only trial and error can tell you the correct amounts to use. Metal powders such as 300-mesh aluminum, copper, brass, and bronze can be added to 32-032 in large quantities, although these resin-metal combinations won't have the adhesive strength of those formulated with epoxy resin binders.

A solution of paraffin wax and styrene, which you can get from a resin supplier, will act as an air-drying additive to aid in curing the 32-032 polyester resin at room temperature. Add 1 oz. per gallon of 32-032. When paraffin is used, the resin ceases to have a nice water-clear surface. To improve the surface, you can sand, buff, and polish it after curing or, even better, either exclude air or use an infrared heat lamp while curing the resin.

Pearlescence, which is manufactured by the Mearl Corporation of New York City and can be obtained from any resin supplier, makes resin look like mother-of-pearl (most shirt buttons are made from polyester resins and pearlescence). Use only transparent color pastes with pearles-

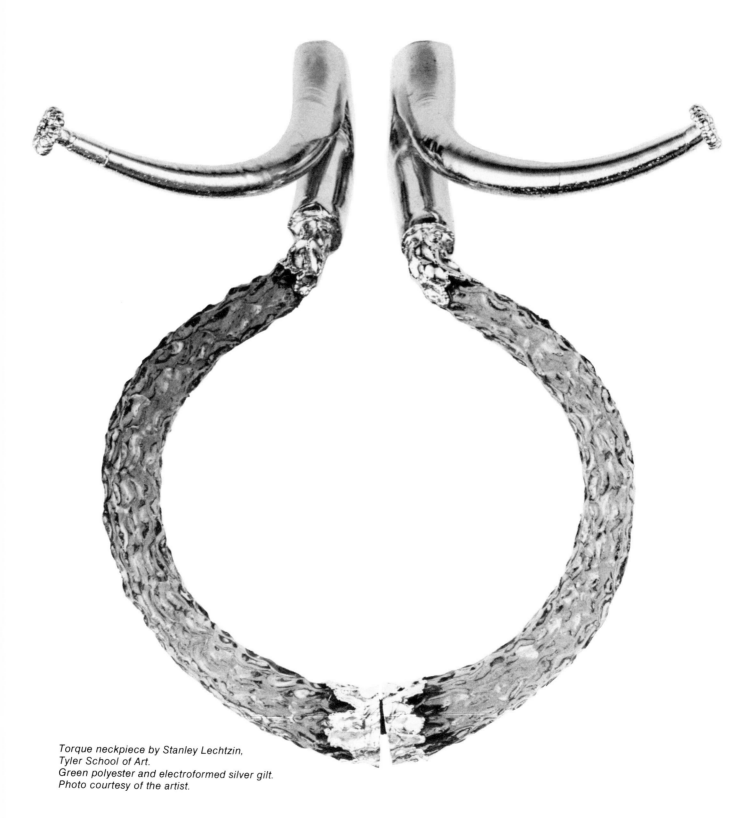

Torque neckpiece by Stanley Lechtzin,
Tyler School of Art.
Green polyester and electroformed silver gilt.
Photo courtesy of the artist.

cence. In Projects 19 and 20 in this book, pearlescence is added to the colored resin system.

Styrene is the most common reactive diluent (nonvolatile reacting thinner) for use with 32-032 polyester resin. Use about 10% (10 grams per 100 grams of 32-032) styrene to thin the resin. Styrene doesn't provide protection against the ultraviolet rays of the sun.

Thixotropic agents , such as Asbestos 244 manufactured by Union Carbide Corporation, are the most transparent of the materials that can be added to polyester resin in small quantities to make it non-runny. Between 2% and 4% Asbestos 244, based on the amount of 32-032, will yield a clear to translucent, nonflowing resin system. Because asbestos is inert, it doesn't react with the resin or any of its additives. If you don't have Asbestos 244, you can substitute Cabosil (M5), which is specially formed pyrogenic (heat-produced) silica sand (SiO_2). It isn't quite as transparent as the 244.

Ultraviolet absorbers tend to delay the yellowing of polyester 32-032 in sunlight. Dyestuff colorants are also more lightfast in the presence of 1% to 2% U-V absorbers such as Tinuvin P or Tinuvin 328 manufactured by CIBA-GEIGY. American Cyanamid's Cyanabsorber UV 9 is also worth considering. Consult these resin suppliers for more information.

NOTES AND CAUTIONS

Curing times for polyester resin castings vary according to factors such as room temperature, amount of catalyst used, and additives. In your particular working area, you'll learn curing times by experience.

Pay attention to safety precautions, which will make your use of the synthetic polymers far less hazardous and much more pleasant:

Be sure to have good ventilation. If you can't work near an open window or outdoors, be sure that the air in your studio is changed at least six to ten times every hour.

Don't smoke around any of the resin systems. Not only are many of them, such as the acrylic syrups, very flammable, but when you put your resin-contaminated fingers up to your mouth you could develop an allergic reaction.

Be sure to wear disposable gloves when weighing and mixing resins. And please wear safety goggles.

When cutting fiberglass, wear polyethylene gloves and a dust mask. Only the careless will breathe in the fiberglass needles, which are released into the air when the cloth or mat is cut.

Wear a dust mask when weighing and mixing Asbestos 244 and Cabosil. The former is now considered to be carcinogenic; the latter can produce silicosis. Once these materials are wet with resin, this hazard is diminished.

Do not use any more MEK-Px than necessary. Using amounts above those recommended in the table nearby is wasteful and could ruin the casting through overheating. Remember that organic peroxides, such as MEK-Px, are very flammable and should be handled with great caution. Any spillage should be wiped up immediately with a paper towel and flushed down the toilet.

MEK-Px can explode when mixed with certain accelerators. To play safe, only add the MEK-Px directly to the resin.

Be sure to mix the polyester resin and all the required ingredients very well. If you don't do this, you may have unsatisfactory results.

Keep all the polyester resin and catalysts in a cool place in opaque containers. Don't store the 32-032 at temperatures above 65° F. if you want to keep it longer than six months.

Put lids back on tightly. If air gets to the resin, a brown formation will occur around the inside of the lid and the resin will become foggy and useless.

Cufflink by the author.
Fiberglass-reinforced polyester
resin with pewter inlays.

MOLDING AND REINFORCING CUFFLINKS

Since polyester resins are a very important class of resinous materials for the jeweler, the projects in this part will focus on characteristics of the materials that shouldn't be overlooked. These projects will also demonstrate methods of handling these polymers that will allow you to make jewelry more easily from them. In this project you will learn:

How to use polyester resins.

How to strengthen water-clear polyester resin 32-032, a good transparent casting resin, by filling it with substantial amounts of aggregate.

How to mix media in jewelry containing resins to get more interesting results than those achieved solely with plastics.

TOOLS AND MATERIALS

1. Jeweler's tools: saw and blades, and pliers.
2. Finishing tools: 180-grit to 320-grit wet-or-dry sandpaper, buffing compounds, and buffing wheels.
3. Vacuum or vibrating table (optional).
4. A roller-type vegetable slicer.
5. Infrared heat lamp.
6. Hot plate or your stove.
7. Sable brush.
8. X-Acto knife.
9. Metal can cover.
10. Sun Oil Company 1290 Y microcrystalline wax, HH 572 soft modeling wax, and green color paste.
11. 20-mil cellulose acetate, acetone, and a syringe.
12. Dow Corning Silastic A silicone mold-making rubber and Silastic F catalyst.
13. Korax 1711 mold-release spray and Joy detergent.
14. Scrap pieces and ⅛" square rod of pewter.
15. Cufflink findings.
16. Reichhold Chemicals Polylite 32-032 polyester resin.
17. Reichhold Chemicals MEK Peroxide (MEK-Px) catalyst.
18. A small piece of 8 oz. fiberglass cloth.
19. Additives: talc, color pastes, Benzoflex 9-88 (optional).

NOTES AND CAUTIONS

You can get resinous materials from the resin suppliers in *Suppliers and Manufacturers.* Modeling wax HH 572 is available only from Resco. Pewter can be obtained from C. R. Hill Company. Cufflink findings can usually be obtained from your local hobby store.

To give your cufflinks more value, you can add small pieces of either gold or sterling silver or inlay tiny precious

---

FORMULAS

60/40 Wax

1290 Y microcrystalline wax	60 parts
HH 572 soft modeling wax	40 parts
Green color paste	1 part

Melt the two waxes and the color paste together as described in Project 8, "Formulas" and pour them ¼" deep into a metal pan lightly coated with Joy detergent.

Cufflink Shell Mixture

Polylite 32-032 polyester resin	100 grams
MEK-Px catalyst	1 gram
Talc	50 grams (approx.)
Black color paste or carbon black powder	2 grams

Stir the MEK-Px into the polyester resin and add just enough talc so you'll still have a pourable but heavy, cream-like liquid.

Cufflink "Enamel"

Polylite 32-032 polyester resin	10 grams
MEK-Px catalyst	0.2 grams (4 drops)
White color paste	2 drops (approx.)
Transparent color paste (blue or other color)	as needed

Mix the resin and catalyst together well and add color pastes sparingly.

Cufflink Deep Glaze

Polylite 32-032 polyester resin	10 grams
MEK-Px catalyst	0.2 grams (4 drops)

Mix the resin and catalyst together well. If you want the mixture to be less brittle or hard, you can add 5% Benzoflex 9-88 to the resin.

---

stones. My dentist gave me some small gold fillings that work splendidly.

Each time you finish using a mold, be sure to spray it with mold release to protect it.

If you find silicone rubber (Silastic A and Catalyst F) too expensive or too difficult to obtain, you can use a urethane, mold-making rubber system such as TU-80 or TU-50, which is softer. Both of these are cheaper. The polyester resin system is, of course, useful for making any kind of jewelry. The mold you make for this project can also be used for plique à jour. You can use it to cast more of the same forms and then place the forms on 60/40 wax lightly coated with mold-release spray and pour clear polyester resin into the interstices. These pieces can then be used for earrings or pieces in a necklace.

The curing time of polyester resins varies widely depending on many factors including the room temperature, the quantity of the mixture, the amount of catalyst, the thickness of the resin pour, and the use of additives. Curing time will therefore be gauged by your particular working area and specifications.

Have very good ventilation. Work outdoors, open all of the windows, or make sure that you have an exhaust fan which will force a change of air six times per hour. Vapors from polyester resins are considered hazardous to breathe if they are greater than 100 parts per million in the air.

Polyester resin may be removed from your skin or clothing with lacquer thinner. Be sure to wash immediately with soap and water and apply a little lanolin to your hands to replace natural skin oils.

MOLDING AND REINFORCING CUFFLINKS

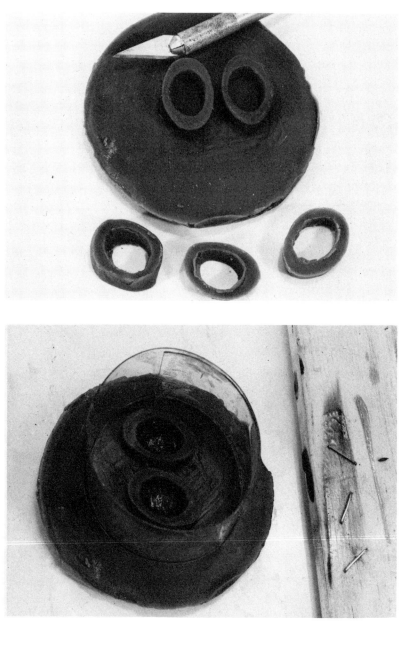

Step 1. Melt the 60/40 wax as demonstrated in Project 8, Steps 1 and 2, and pour it out to make a slab about ⅜″ thick. Then cut out the shapes, or models, for the cufflinks and shape the remaining part of the slab to make a base. The wax mixture, which melts at about 190° F., can be carved nicely with a sharp X-Acto knife. Adhere the cufflink models to the wax base with a drop or two of the same melted 60/40 wax.

Step 2. Make a container to hold the pourable, silicone rubber mold from a collar of 20-mil cellulose acetate. Glue it together with acetone and push it into the wax base. Leave a space of about ½″ between the acetate wall and the cufflinks.

Step 3. Mix the Silastic A mold-making rubber with 10% of the catalyst F as described in Project 8 "Formulas", and brush a thin coat of it on the wax models. This will insure that there won't be air bubbles trapped on the finished mold surface. (Exposure to a high vacuum will also eliminate this problem.) Then pour the remaining rubber over the wax models.

Step 4. Cure the silicone rubber mold for about ½ hour. Although catalyst F cures Silastic A quickly at room temperature, the mold can be made somewhat more chemical resistant if the cured silicone rubber is heated for approximately an hour about 8" from an infrared heat lamp. Remove the wax models from the rubber. All silicone rubber molds are attacked somewhat by the liquid resins described in this book. Even though these Silastic rubber molds are self-releasing, the manufacturer suggests using a protective coating. You can spray a mold-release, such as Korax 1711, onto the rubber to give it slight protection (consult your resin supplier for other suggestions).

Step 5. Mix up the cufflink shell mixture given in "Formulas" for this project. To make sure that there will be no air bubbles trapped on the mold surface, brush the resin mixture, which should be of a very heavy but fluid consistency, over the entire mold surface. Next pour the balance of the resin mixture to fill the mold and cover its top surface. If you have access to a vacuum, use it to remove all the air bubbles in the resin pour. If not, the next best thing is to place the piece on a vibrating table. Here the air bubbles come floating to the surface. If you don't have either of these pieces of equipment, you can loosen most of the air bubbles by carefully dropping the mold several times on a hard horizontal surface from a height of about 6".

Step 6. Place a small piece of 8 oz. fiberglass cloth on the surface of the wet polyester resin mixture in the rubber mold. With a roller-type vegetable slicer force the resin into the fiberglass cloth. Continue rolling until the material is well saturated. Such fiberglass reinforcement gives strength to the polyester resin. For small items such as cufflinks, the strength obtained might not be as necessary as for larger items such as belt buckles. Be sure to clean the metal roller and brushes with lacquer thinner as soon as you've used them. Hardened resin is very difficult to remove.

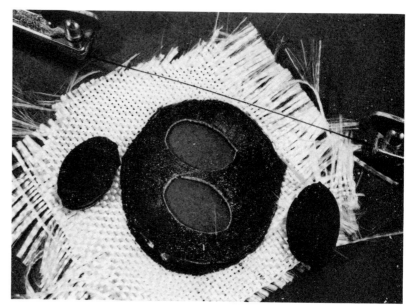

Step 7. Once the polyester resin has cured hard, cut the cufflink shells free from the fiberglass cloth with a jeweler's saw. Sand the cufflink shells with wet, 320-grit wet-or-dry sandpaper.

Step 8. If you wish to modify these original polyester resin castings and then make more of the modified version, you can make a new silicone-rubber mold using the modified shells as your models. Place the sanded, modified shells in a metal can cover and surround them with a cellulose acetate collar. Seal the edge of the collar with HH 572 soft modeling wax, mix up more of the silicone-rubber mixture, and follow Steps 3–5 of this project to make your new mold.

Step 9. To give the pewter cubes a good reflecting background, mix up a small amount of the cufflink enamel described in "Formulas" for this project. Brush this mixture lightly into the base of the cufflink shell cavity and allow it to cure. Place the pewter cubes on the blue-white background and pour the cufflink deep glaze given in "Formulas" for this project into them. Fill the "chamber" to the brim and then allow the resin to cure very well about 10" away from an infrared heat lamp.

Step 10. To decorate the inside of the cufflink shells, saw a few pewter cubes from a piece of ⅛" square pewter rod. Sand the cubes with wet, 180-grit to 320-grit, wet-or-dry sandpaper. Then buff them with Learok buffing compound 765 followed by 339E. Give the cubes a very high polish so that they'll appear "jewel-like."

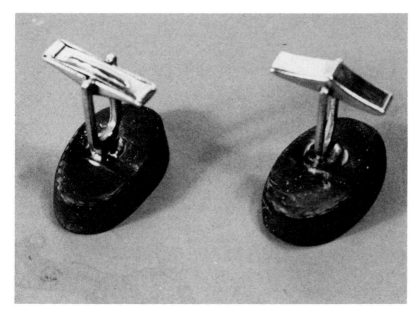

Step 11. Make another batch of the cufflink shell mixture, brush it on the back of the cufflinks, and imbed the cufflink attachments in it. Allow the resin to cure. The cufflink attachments provide something to hold onto while finishing. Sand and polish the cufflinks on successive buffing wheels running at 1750 r.p.m. with Learok 886E and 339E (see *Finishing Your Jewelry*).

Necklace by the author.
Pewter and cast polyester resin.

CASTING A WEDGE FOR A PENDANT

This project will help you understand the intriguing nature of water-clear casting polyester resins, with which you should be able to make some exciting jewelry. This project will emphasize:

How to use a relatively new method for quick-gelling polyester resin which enables you to quickly and easily cure the resin "on demand" and to give it a textured or curved surface while it's hardening.

How to use glass as an excellent mold surface, taking advantage of the fact that polyester resins do not adhere well to nonporous materials.

How to emboss and incise a waxed layer on a glass mold in order to obtain a more interesting polyester resin surface.

TOOLS AND MATERIALS

1. Jeweler's tools: saw and blades, and pliers.
2. Finishing tools: 180-grit to 320-grit wet-or-dry sandpaper, 100-grit garnet sandpaper, 6″ muslin buffing wheels and compounds, or for hand buffing, cotton flannel stapled around a wooden paint-mixing stick and a slurry of tin oxide powder and water.
3. Infrared heat lamp.
4. Woodcarving tools, linoleum-block cutters, and/or X-Acto knife.
5. Scotch tape.
6. Two pieces of double-strength window glass, 7″ x 2½″.
7. Some pieces of cardboard.
8. A sharp tool such as a nail.
9. Sun Oil Company 1290 Y microcrystalline wax, HH 572 soft modeling wax, and green color paste.
10. Korax 1711 mold-release spray and Internal release 54.
11. Reichhold Chemicals Polylite 32-032 polyester resin.
12. Reichhold Chemicals MEK-Peroxide (MEK-Px) catalyst.
13. Additives: HH 371 Quik-Gel, color pastes, and styrene.
14. 18-gauge sterling silver wire and ⅛″ square pewter or sterling silver bar.

NOTES AND CAUTIONS

All resin system materials and waxes can be purchased from the companies listed in *Suppliers and Manufacturers.* Metals can be obtained from C. R. Hill Company. Other products can usually be bought at your local hardware or hobby store.

FORMULAS

60/40 Wax

1290 Y microcrystalline wax	60 parts
HH 572 soft modeling wax	40 parts
Green color paste	1 part

Heat and mix all ingredients well while liquid as shown in Project 8, Steps 1 and 2. Add color paste to identify the mixture. Cool and use whenever you wish.

Polyester Casting Resin

Polylite 32-032 polyester resin	25 grams
Internal release 54	2 drops
MEK-Px catalyst	10 drops
Color pastes	as needed
HH 371 Quik-Gel	6 to 12 drops

Mix the 32-032, the MEK-Px, the internal release, and the color pastes as well. To increase the speed of the cure, use HH 371 Quik-Gel (a mixture of 10 parts DION 3-800 LC and 90 parts styrene). Use half (.5%) of the MEK-Px and no more than .5% to 1% of the Quik-Gel. This mixture will gel in 1 to 5 minutes. To further decrease the speed of the resin cure, cut the HH 371 to ¼ gram (.25%). Without the Quik-Gel, the gelling of the polyester resin can take 30 to 40 minutes.

Polyester Adhesive

Polylite 32-032 polyester resin	9 grams
Styrene diluent	1 gram
MEK-Px catalyst	5 drops

Mix well and use at once.

Don't cut the cast polyester triangles too thin or they may break. I usually saw off the thin edge of the triangle until I have an edge which is a little thicker than 1/16″. Try samples of different thickness of resin to determine the strength you want.

Pieces of Plexiglas, metal, or wood may be imbedded in the resin before you saw the pieces for the pendant assembly.

Have excellent ventilation when using styrene. Do not get the resin system on your skin. If you get resin in your eye, let someone remove it with a handkerchief corner and then wash your eye out for 15 minutes in cold running water. Be sure to see a doctor immediately.

CASTING A WEDGE FOR A PENDANT

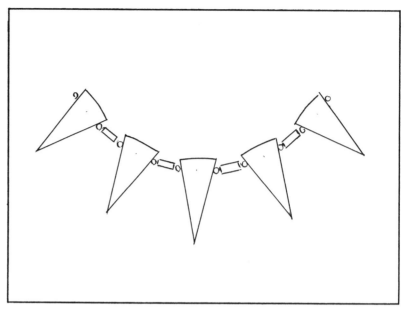

Step 1. The design for this necklace made of polyester resin is merely five isoceles triangles, each 2'' high with bases of ⅞'' to 1''. Make a sketch of your design on a piece of cardboard.

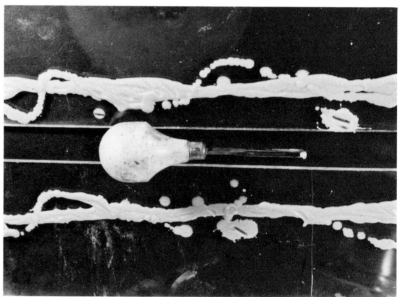

Step 2. Cut two 7'' x 2½'' pieces of double-strength glass. Lightly sand all sharp edges. Melt some 1290 Y microcrystalline wax under an infrared heat lamp and pour it freely over the glass in a loose design. With wood-carving tools, engrave the surface of the wax or cut a hard-edged design with an X-Acto knife to give an additional intaglio texture. Then spray both the glass and the 1290 Y wax *lightly* (as you would apply perfume) with Korax 1711 mold-release spray, so that it can be easily released from the polyester resin casting.

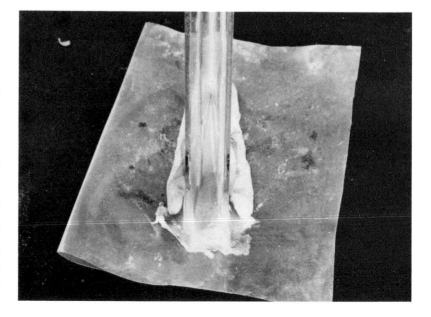

Step 3. Scotch tape the sheets of glass together along one of the sides. Then fold them together with the waxed sides in. Position the sheets on end on a polyethylene square and secure them at the desired angle by surrounding the base with 60/40 wax mixture described under "Formulas" for this project. One way to do this is to pour some of the softened wax over an area of the polyethylene square and, as the wax cools, push one end of the glass V into it. Seal the other end in the same manner. Remove the polyethylene squares; the wax won't adhere to them, and they should lift right off.

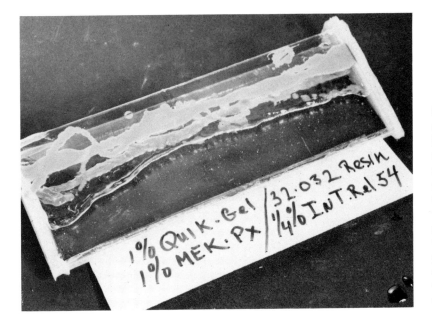

Step 4. Mix up the polyester casting resin according to "Formulas" for this project. Pour the mixture into the glass wedge and rock it gently from side to side while the resin is curing. The polyester resin will gel in a matter of minutes, forming a pleasant, wave-like pattern. Remember to add the Internal Release 54 to the resin system as an extra measure to insure easy release from the glass. As soon as the resin system gels, you can add another batch of resin mixed with whatever color pastes you wish. Continue this procedure until the glass wedge is filled up.

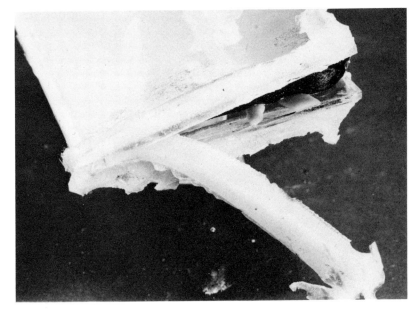

Step 5. Remove all the 60/40 wax from the glass wedge. The wax is semi-rigid and should easily release from the mold.

Step 6. Open the wedge with a wooden stick or another plastic wedge being careful not to break the glass. If everything has been according to the above steps, there will be no trouble!

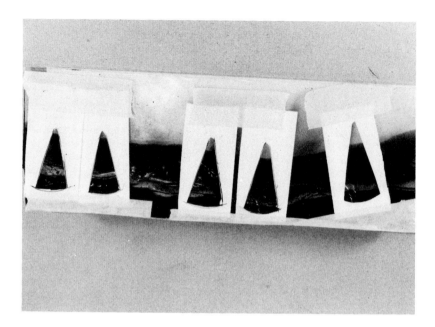

Step 7. Carefully position and tape the cardboard templates on top of the resin wedge. Place the templates so that the triangles for the necklace will have a design relationship. With a sharp tool, scratch the outline of the triangles into the resin surface.

Step 8. Cut out the polyester resin triangles with a jeweler's saw. Roughly shape the triangles with 100-grit garnet sandpaper. Then wet sand the pieces by rubbing them on both 180-grit and 400-grit wet-or-dry sandpaper placed flat on a tabletop. (Glass works well as a sandpaper support if the back of the sandpaper is also wet. Several sheets of wet sandpaper are even better; placed one on top of the other, they give a slight cushioning effect.) Then buff and polish the pieces successively with Learok 884E and 339E. During the polishing operation, you can saw off the sharp ends of the triangles, sand, and polish the stubs.

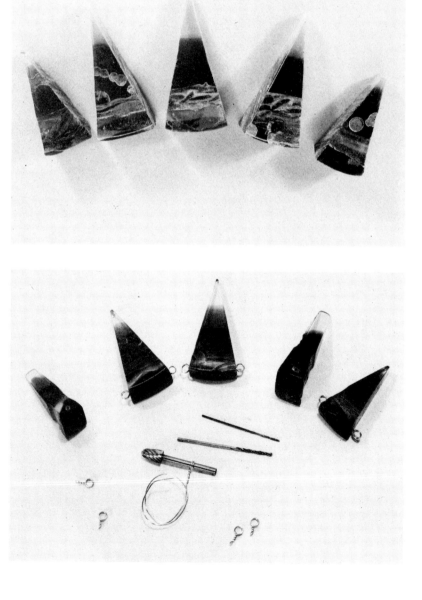

Step 9. Fashion hangers for the triangles from 18-gauge sterling silver wire. Drill holes into the sides of the plastic with a 1/32" bit followed by a 1/16" bit. Glue the ends of the hangers into the holes with fresh polyester resin described in "Formulas" for this project. Be sure to allow the adhesive resin to cure very well for 1 to 2 hours about 10" away from an infrared heat lamp.

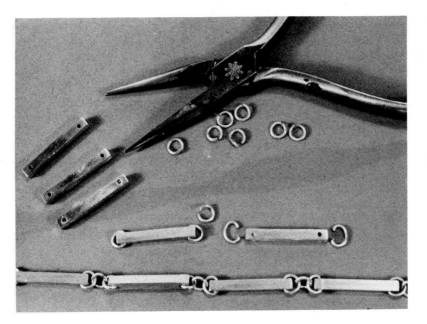

Step 10. Make links for the chain from ⅛″ square pewter or sterling silver bar. Make jump rings from the 18-gauge sterling silver wire, drill 1/16″ holes in the bars, and bend the jump rings through them. Use more jump rings to attach the links to one another.

Step 11. Use jump rings to attach the polyester resin triangles to the links.

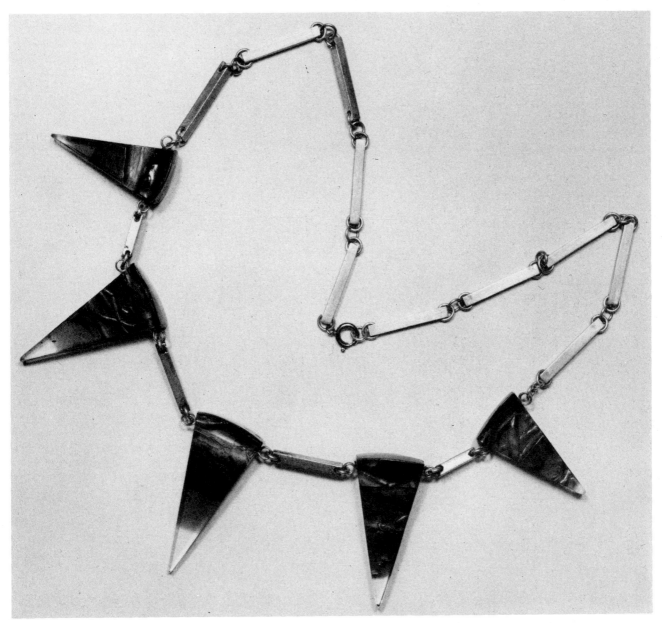

Torque neckpiece by Stanley Lechtzin,
Tyler School of Art.
Opalescent polyester resin
and electroformed silver gilt.
Photo courtesy of the artist

PROJECT 17

POURING AND SWIRLING A NECKLACE

In this project, as in the others in this book I'll try to inspire you to create jewelry designs and finished pieces that are your own. I think that taking an idea from another person is fine as long as you modify it so that it reflects you.

The technique of rotational casting used in this project is applicable to making many kinds of jewelry. The plastics industry does a lot of rotational casting in machines that cost thousands of dollars. In this project you will learn:

How to cast polyester resin in a container rotated by hand or attached to an electric rotisserie such as that used for turning meat.

How to form the cone-shaped container using 7½-mil or 10-mil cellulose acetate sheet.

How to make nonrepetitive pieces by a simple and repeatable process.

How to use the principle of the "sliced pickle" as a simple way to make necklace pieces or other shapes of varying sizes.

How to combine polyester resin pieces, pottery, cord, and silver wire in the necklace so that the natural and synthetic materials complement one another.

TOOLS AND MATERIALS

1. Jeweler's tools: saw and blades or band saw, drill and bits, files, pliers, and a butane torch.
2. Finishing tools: 180-grit to 400-grit wet-or-dry sandpaper, buffing compounds, and buffing wheels.
3. MirrorGlaze wax.
4. Infrared heat lamp.
5. Raku pottery beads and fishnet cord.
6. A barbecue spit which turns electrically (optional).
7. 7½-mil to 10-mil cellulose acetate sheet, 20'' x 50'', acetone, and a syringe.
8. A sharp knife such as an X-Acto knife.
9. Reichhold Chemicals Polylite 32-032 polyester resin.
10. Reichhold Chemicals MEK Peroxide (MEK-Px) catalyst.
11. Additives: color pastes, HH 371 Quik-Gel (optional), and Benzoflex 9-88.
12. CIBA-GEIGY Araldite epoxy resin 502.
13. RC-125 epoxy curing agent.
14. 18-gauge and 24-gauge sterling silver wire or chain.

NOTES AND CAUTIONS

All of the resin, additives, and buffing equipment are available from the companies listed in *Suppliers and Manufac-*

FORMULAS

COLORLESS RESIN

Polylite 32-032 polyester resin	100 grams
Benzoflex 9-88	2.5 grams
MEK-Px catalyst	1 gram

Mix the polyester resin and benzoflex together and then thoroughly stir in the peroxide catalyst for several minutes. For the first resin pour, you'll probably need 50 grams of the 32-032 resin.

COLORED INTERNAL RESIN

Polylite 32-032 polyester resin	100 grams
Benzoflex 9-88	5 grams
MEK-Px catalyst	1 gram
Color pastes	as needed
HH 371 Quik-Gel (optional)	as needed

Mix ingredients well as above, then stir in color pastes. (See Project 16, "Formulas" for instructions on using the Quik-Gel.) Quik-Gel should be added to the resin system *after* you've adjusted the mixture to the desired color.

EPOXY ADHESIVE

Araldite epoxy resin 502	5 grams
Curing agent RC-125	1.25 grams

Mix together well and apply immediately.

---

turers. Other materials can be obtained from your local hardware and hobby stores.

If you want to use polyester rather than raku beads to separate the polyester resin pieces, you can fashion them from the same polyester resin mixture you use to make the necklace pieces. To make the beads, add about 125% to 150% talc and a small amount of color paste to the resin mixture. Put on polyethylene gloves and knead the sticky resin mixture into the loose talc on a polyethylene sheet. Form the bead around a mold-release-sprayed polyethylene toothpick or drill through it after curing to make the holes.

Before using the accelerator HH 371 Quik-Gel on a valuable piece, you should test it in another acetate form to familiarize yourself with its properties. When you've learned how to use it properly, you can add it even after you've poured the resin into the forming mold.

Have good ventilation when you work with polyester resins. Change the air at least six times per hour. Work outside if you're lucky enough to be in a warm climate, or work near an exhaust fan. Styrene vapors from the polyester resin 32-032 are hazardous to breathe in large quantities.

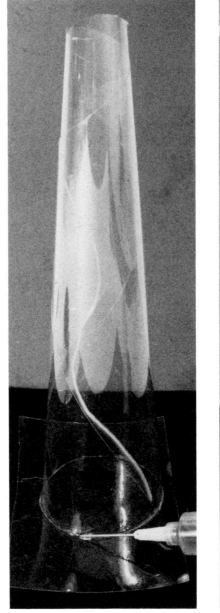

Step 1. Here is one project in which it would be impossible to follow a sketch exactly. Only after the polyester resin pieces have been sliced, sanded, and polished can you plan how to assemble them. Once they're finished, the "surprise" you'll have created will dictate in part how they'll look best together. Form a piece of 7½-mil to 10-mil acetate into a truncated cone about 8″ high with top and bottom diameters of 1″ and 3″ respectively, and glue it together with acetone ejected from a syringe. If you use a lot of acetone in this step, the cone will somewhat distort, resulting in more irregular shapes in the sliced pieces. Also use acetone to glue a 10-mil piece of acetate to the wide base of the cone. (Acetone works as a glue by temporarily dissolving the cellulose acetate surfaces so that they bond together.) Remember that acetone is *very flammable*!

Step 2. Glue another piece of 10-mil acetate onto the narrow end of the forming mold.

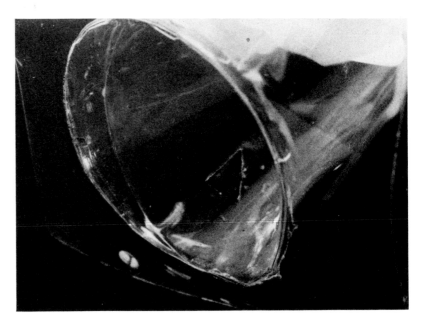

Step 3. Use a sharp knife to cut a triangular opening in the base of the cellulose acetate form as a filling port.

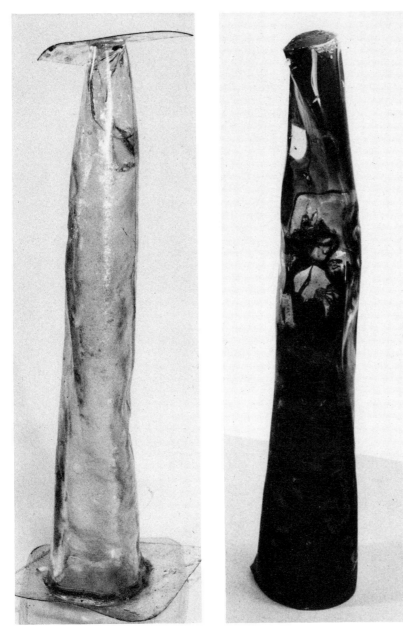

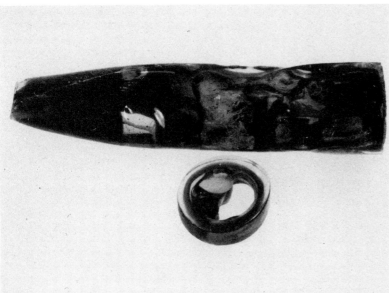

Step 4. Mix the colorless resin and additives shown in "Formulas" for this project. Partially fill the cone with about 50 grams of the resin mixture. Close the triangular hole with a piece of masking tape. You must rotate the cone-like cylinder for about ½ hour until the resin gels and becomes non-runny. This is the only way to put a thin coat of resin on all of the internal surfaces at the same time. If you feel that this process takes too long, you can add HH 371 Quik-Gel (see Project 16 "Formulas" for instructions on using Quik-Gel). After the 50 gram batch of resin has gelled, remove the masking tape, cut into the gelled resin that covers the hole, and add another batch of the same resin mixture. Keep adding the resin mixture in this manner until all the walls of the mold have a ⅛" to ¼" thick coating. Mix up another batch of resin and color pastes. Be sure to keep the initial colors very light so that you can see what you are doing as you rotate the tube during subsequent additions. Pour in and rotate several resin batches of different colors. By this time you probably realize that it's possible to somewhat direct where the polyester resin will gel. Also, each time you reopen the filling hole, you can check to get an idea of about how much more resin filling is needed. If the mold isn't completely filled with resin the necklace pieces will contain interesting internal spaces.

Step 5. When you think the mold is full enough, let it set for at least 5 to 7 hours, or for a quicker curing place it 14" from an infrared heat lamp for about 2 hours. Remove the acetate skin from the casting. To protect the surface, rub a protective paste wax such as MirrorGlaze wax all over the form and polish it right away.

Step 6. To get an idea of how the largest necklace "dangle" will look, slice off the base and another ⅜" piece with a jeweler's saw. Sand and polish the latter.

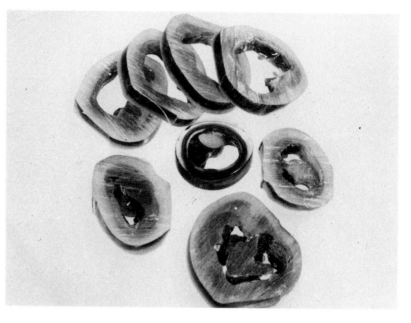

Step 7. With a jeweler's saw (or a band saw if you have access to one), slice off as many more pieces as you can so that you'll have a good selection to choose from for the assemblage.

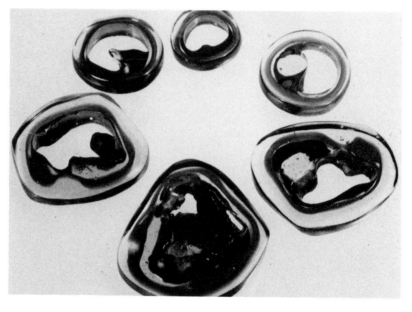

Step 8. Sand the pieces with wet, 180-grit to 400-grit wet-or-dry sandpaper. Then buff them with a series of three different buffing compounds—Lea Abrasive Compound C, Learok 884E, and Learok 339E—each applied to separate 6″ muslin buffers running at about 1750 r.p.m. You can cut down the sharp edges of the slice somewhat to make a more gently shaped unit. Assemble the major necklace pieces to decide how they'll be put together.

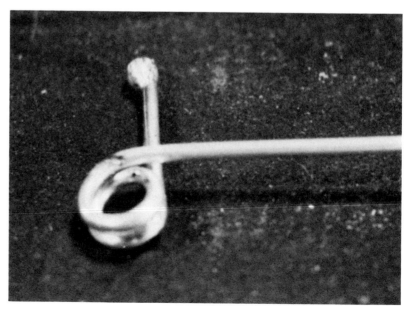

Step 9. Form a ball at the ends of 18-gauge wire lengths with a Ronson butane torch. Polish the ball with any buffing compound.

Step 10. Drill holes in the polyester resin pieces where you want to attach the beads and pass the open end of each length of silver wire through one of the holes. Use pliers to make a loop at the free end of each length of wire. Thread a length of fishnet cord through each bead and then thread one end of each cord length through one silver wire loop. Tuck the ends of the cord into the hole in the bead it runs through, and use a few drops of the epoxy resin listed in "Formulas" for this project to glue the ends in place. This tough adhesive cures in about ½ hour.

Pendant by Albert Paley, Rochester, New York.
Copper forged and fabricated with Delrin,
glass, and 14k gold inlay;
copper and Delrin neckpiece.
Photo courtesy of the artist.

PROJECT 18

LAMINATING EARRINGS WITH PEWTER

The design for the earrings in this project evolved from a desire to "marry" two dissimilar materials, polyester resin and pewter. The water-clear polyester casting resins are very transparent, can be polished like gem stones, and for jewelry purposes they are physically and chemically stable. Pewter although softer than sterling silver, has visual warmth when polished and doesn't tarnish.

The shape of these earrings was taken from a cone-shaped piece of sculpture I made at the Penland School of Crafts during the summer of 1971. Just visualize one of these earring cones 2' high. Marion Herbst Holland of Amsterdam has also made both a ring and a piece of sculpture based on one design which is shown in the color plate section.

Making jewelry successfully from thermosetting resins such as the polyesters depends in part on how well you, the craftsman, understand the character of the material with which you are working. To assist you in learning some of these characteristics, I will emphasize in this project:

How to use epoxy resins to securely fasten pewter to polyester resin, since polyester resins don't adhere well to metal surfaces.

How to make clear, inexpensive, transparent molds for polyester resins using cellulose acetate glued together with acetone.

How to use a semi-flexible mold such as cellulose acetate so that the 7½% shrinkage of the polyester resin is not a problem.

TOOLS AND MATERIALS

1. Jeweler's tools: saw and 0 or 1 blades (for fine work, use 2/0 or 3/0), drill and 1/16" to ⅛" bits, files, and pliers.
2. Finishing tools: 180-grit to 400-grit wet-or-dry sandpaper, 6" muslin buffing wheels, Lea Compound C, Learok 339E, or for hand buffing, a mixture of tin oxide powder and water rubbed on a cotton flannel wheel.
3. A sheet of carbon paper.
4. Any sharp pointed tool such as a nail.
5. C-clamp.
6. Silly putty.
7. Korax 1711 mold-release spray.
8. 7½-mil to 10-mil cellulose acetate, acetone, and a syringe.
9. 16-gauge sterling silver or 18-gauge pewter.
10. 16-gauge or 18-gauge lead sheet used by plumbers and available from a hardware store, 6" x 12".
11. Soft iron binding wire.
12. 18-gauge to 20-gauge sterling silver wire.

FORMULAS

CLEAR CASTING RESIN

Polylite 32-032 polyester resin	100 grams
MEK-Px catalyst	.75 grams
HH 371 Quik-Gel (optional)	1 to 2 grams
Benzoflex 9-88 (optional)	5 grams
Color pastes	as needed

Stir the MEK-Px well into the polyester resin. Mix in color pastes. Then, if desire, add the Quik-Gel and/or the Benzoflex.

EPOXY RESIN ADHESIVE

Araldite epoxy resin 502	10 grams
Curing agent RC-125	2.5 grams

This curing system allows 20 to 30 minutes for you to work, depending on the room temperature. Be sure to wear polyethylene gloves if there's a risk of getting the resin system on your hands. Mix the ingredients well for several minutes and use.

---

13. Reichhold Chemicals Polylite 32-032 polyester resin.
14. Reichhold Chemicals MEK Peroxide (MEK-Px) catalyst.
15. Additives: HH 371 Quik-Gel (optional), Benzoflex 9-88 (an optional flexibilizer or non-brittling agent), and Asbestos 244.
16. CIBA-GEIGY Araldite epoxy resin 502.
17. RC-125 epoxy curing agent.
18. Silver earring findings or ear wires.

NOTES AND CAUTIONS

All the resinous materials, sheet acetate, color pastes, and so on are available from the resin suppliers listed in *Suppliers and Manufacturers*. Your local hardware or hobby store will probably have the remaining materials.

You can also easily inlay metal wire or metal strips in the original pouring of the polyester resin. Be sure, however, that the strips are imbedded in the resin; if they lie only on the surface they may easily drop off.

It's not necessary to always use transparent colors; interspersing opaque layers can be quite effective.

Have good ventilation when using polyester resins. Styrene vapor should not be inhaled in concentrations greater than 100 PPM (parts per million) of air. One of the main drawbacks to the home use of polyester resins is the very penetrating smell of styrene.

Keep your hands out of the resin. It's not good for your skin.

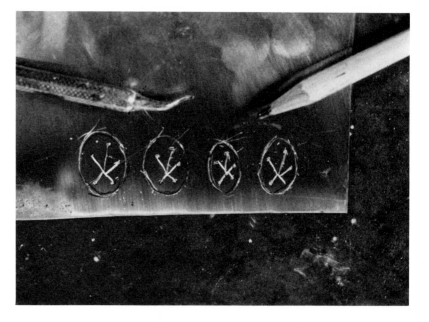

Step 1. Make a simple sketch of your design and use carbon paper to transfer it onto a sanded (matte-finished) pewter sheet. Engrave the design into the sheet with a sharp-pointed tool.

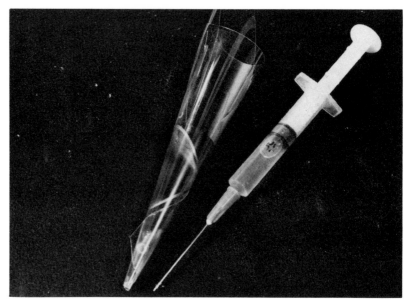

Step 2. Roll a sheet of 10-mil cellulose acetate to form a cone of the desired width. Here, I wrap the acetate around an existing earring so that I can duplicate its size and shape. Use a syringe to squirt acetone sparingly along the acetate seam and massage carefully along the edge until the ends adhere smoothly.

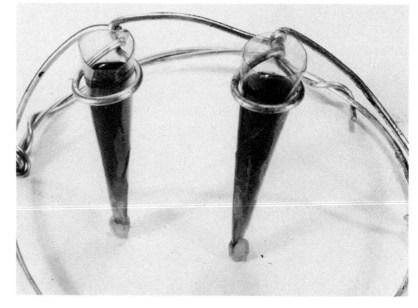

Step 3. Seal the bases of the acetate cones with HH 572 soft modeling wax and stand them upright in an iron binding wire frame. Mix up the water-clear polyester casting resin shown in "Formulas" for this project and pour it into the cones. If you want to preserve the cellulose acetone molds, spray them with a mold release such as Korax 1711 before pouring the polyester resin. Allow the resin to cure at room temperature overnight. For a faster cure, place the pieces 10" away from an infrared heat lamp for several hours (remember that heat curing causes greater shrinkage).

Step 4. Remove the castings from their molds.

Step 5. In preparation for laminating the pewter into the earring pieces, cut a strip from one edge of the 6″ x 12″ lead sheet, and position a cone along the indentation. Scratch a mark on the sheet and continue the line onto the cone at the point where you want to laminate the pewter. Use a jeweler's saw to cut the cone along this guideline. Cut the other cones by positioning them in the indentation and sawing along the same guideline.

Step 6. Cut another section of each cone in the same manner, at the point where you want to laminate a second pewter form. The illustration of the finished earring shows how the lamination will look.

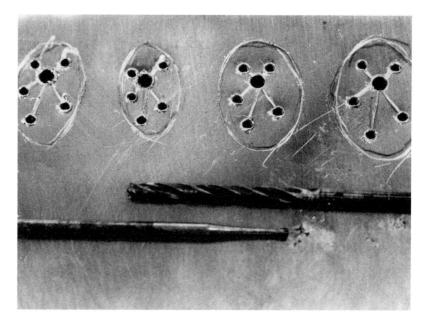

Step 7. Drill designs in the pewter with a 1/32″ or 1/16″ bit and then with a larger ⅛″ bit. Saw out the pieces with a jeweler's saw.

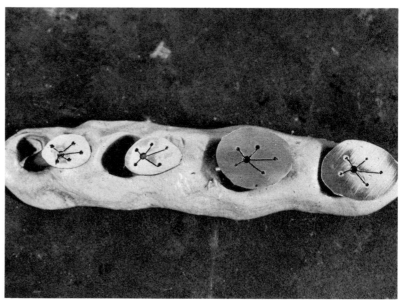

Step 8. Sand the pewter pieces with wet 320-grit wet-or-dry sandpaper. This cleans the metal and gives a rough gluing surface. Position the top and bottom cone sections in a mixture of silly putty with 8% Asbestos 244 as described in Project 14, "Formulas" to prepare for gluing the pewter to the polyester resin.

Step 9. Glue a pewter piece to each polyester resin section with the epoxy resin adhesive shown in "Formulas" for this project. The epoxy resin adhesive adheres well to both the pewter and the polyester. Using epoxy resin adhesive, laminate the pewter pieces between the two bottom sections of each cone. Sand the pieces with wet 180-grit wet-or-dry sandpaper until the metal is flush with the surface of the polyester resin cone.

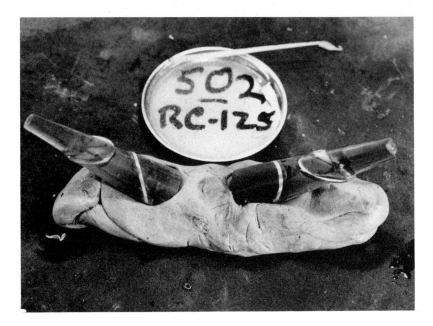

Step 10. Finally glue all the sections of the cones together with the epoxy resin adhesive system. You can prop them up in the silly putty/asbestos mixture to set. Curing takes about an hour. To make a stronger cure, place the pieces about 10″ from an infrared heat lamp for another hour. Sand the cones with wet 180-grit wet-or-day sandpaper. Then buff them with Learok 765, 884E, and 339E. Drill a 1/16″ hole a short way into the top of each cone.

Step 11. Make sterling silver loops and glue them into the holes with the polyester resin system (this "glue" won't show). Make little decorative "jewels" on each of the earring findings with epoxy resin adhesive shown in "Formulas" for this project. Use sterling silver jump rings to attach the cones to the findings.

Belt buckle by the author.
macramé belt by Marie Clark,
Bradenton, Florida.
Pewter and fiberglass-
reinforced polyester resin.

REINFORCING A PEWTER BELT BUCKLE WITH FIBERGLASS

Fiberglass is well known in the boatmaking industry for its strength. Fiberglass-reinforced polyester resin systems, weight for weight, are stronger than steel. Ordinarily, jewelry doesn't need to be metal strong. However, if you were to make a belt buckle out of pure polyester resin, it probably would break under pressure. You will learn in this project:

How to use fiberglass mat in combination with polyester resin.

How to enamel with polyester resin on polyester resin.

How to use pearlescence mixed with colors in polyester resin.

TOOLS AND MATERIALS

1. Jeweler's tools: saw and 1 or 2 blades, pliers, drill and 1/16″ bit, and rounded files.

2. Finishing tools: 180-grit to 300-grit wet-or-dry sandpaper, buffing compounds (Lea Compound C, Learok 765, 889E, and 339E), buffer with several 6″ muslin wheels; for hand buffing, use a slurry of powdered tin oxide and water on a buffing pad of cotton flannel wrapped around a wooden paint stick.

3. Cutting shears.

4. Coffee stirrers.

5. A roller-type vegetable slicer or wallpaper cutter.

6. Lacquer thinner.

7. 16-gauge or 18-gauge lead sheet used by plumbers, 6″ x 12″.

8. 18-gauge pewter sheet, 1′ x 1′.

9. Infrared heat lamp.

10. Wooden frame made from scrap pieces of wood.

11. A sheet of 10-mil Mylar.

12. 60/40 modeling wax (see Project 8 for how to make this) or a mixture of silly putty and Asbestos 244.

13. Korax 1711 mold-release spray or equivalent.

14. Fiberglas 181 cloth made by Owens Corning Fiberglas Corporation (see *Suppliers and Manufacturers*).

15. A 2″ common nail.

16. A belt.

17. Reichhold Chemicals Polylite 32-032 polyester resin.

18. Reichhold Chemicals MEK Peroxide (MEK-Px) catalyst.

19. Additives: Asbestos 244, transparent color pastes, and pearlescence.

FORMULAS

POLYESTER RESIN TO SATURATE FIBERGLASS

Polylite 32-032 polyester resin	100 grams
MEK-Px catalyst	1 gram
Color pastes (optional)	as needed

Mix well and use.

EPOXY RESIN ADHESIVE

Araldite epoxy resin 502	20 grams
RC-125 curing agent	5 grams

Mix the ingredients well for several minutes and use.

POLYESTER RESIN "ENAMEL"

Polylite 32-032 polyester resin	25 grams
MEK-Px catalyst	.25 grams (about 7 drops)
Pearlescence	as needed
Transparent color pastes	as needed

Weigh out and mix all the ingredients together. Be sure not to use opaque colors or thickeners when using pearlescence. The system must be very transparent and fluid to work properly.

---

20. CIBA-GEIGY Araldite epoxy resin 502.

21. RC-125 epoxy curing agent.

NOTES AND CAUTIONS

The resin system and fiberglass mat are available from the companies listed in *Suppliers and Manufacturers*. Other nonresinous items are available from your local art and craft supply store or hardware outlet. After trying some of the projects in this book, you've probably noticed that the first try at making a jewelry piece doesn't yield the nice results you see in these demonstrations. Remember that I made each piece described here many times before I was satisfied. Great care and patience are a necessity when you want craftsman-like results.

Be sure to wear gloves when you handle fiberglass mat. Also when you cut the fiberglass I suggest you wear a dust mask over your nose and mouth so that you don't breathe in the minute glass fibers which can become airborne during cutting.

Always have excellent ventilation when you work with polyester resins.

REINFORCING A PEWTER BELT BUCKLE WITH FIBERGLASS

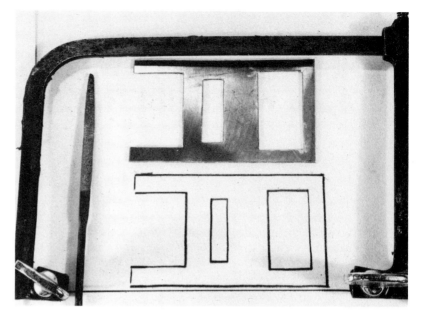

Step 1. My design for this belt buckle came out of a doodle and some design thoughts from Maitland Graves' book *The Art of Color and Design* (New York: McGraw Hill, 1951). Engrave your design on a sheet of matte-finish (polished with wet 400-grit, wet-or-dry sandpaper) 18-gauge pewter. Drill 1/16" holes in the internal areas through which to insert a saw blade, then saw the internal designs out of the pewter piece. Remove any major mars on the sawed edges with a needle file held at a slight inward angle.

Step 2. Deeply score, abrade, and clean one side of the pewter so that the hidden side of the decoration, which is to be glued to the body of the buckle, will adhere well.

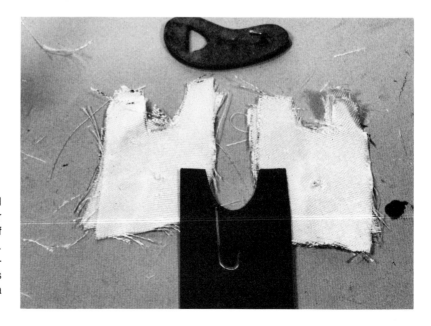

Step 3. Cut a piece of cardboard as a model for the fiberglass pieces making it ½" larger than the final buckle. Then cut 4 pieces of Fiberglas 181 cloth with sharp shears. Fiberglass 181 is quite expensive, but its advantages Fiberglas outweigh this factor. It's easily shaped, doesn't frazzle, and gives a trimmer appearance wherever it's visible.

Step 4. Belt buckles should curve gently so that they will fit the contours of the body. One way to obtain such curves is to make a curved pouring surface by stapling a 10-mil sheet of Mylar to an impromptu wooden frame glued together with epoxy. Even though the Mylar is self releasing from most of the resins mentioned in this book, I find it releases better by spraying it lightly with Korax 1711 mold releases or the equivalent.

Step 5. Mix up the polyester resin to saturate fiberglass shown in "Formulas" for this project, and with a coffee stirrer, sparingly apply it to the Mylar. Then place a piece of fiberglass over the resin coating. Apply more resin until the fiberglass appears saturated. Apply a second piece of fiberglass cloth and follow the same procedure.

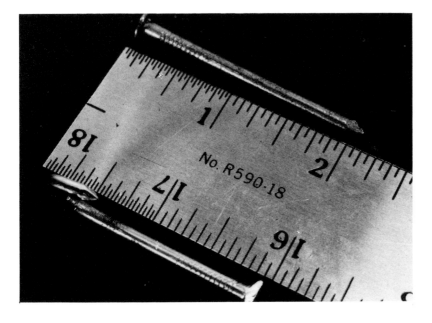

Step 6. Make a buckle hook from a common 2″ nail. Saw two parallel sides of the nail head flat. The remainder of the nail head acts as an anchor for the hook. Bend the end of the nail with vise-like gripping pliers.

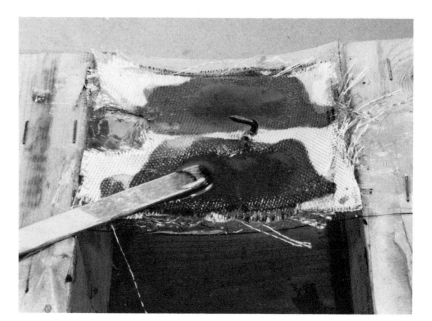

Step 7. Pass the bent end to the nail through two new layers of Fiberglas 181 cloth and place them on the other resin-saturated layers. Apply more colored polyester resin with a coffee stirrer.

Step 8. The body of the nail prevents the upper layer of fiberglass from making tight contact with the cloth below the nail. To solve this problem use a roller-type vegetable slicer to help force air bubbles out of the fiberglass cloth. Be sure to place the slicer in lacquer thinner as soon as you finish rolling or you'll have problems later when you try to remove the hardened resin. Then roll up several pieces of 16-gauge plumber's sheet lead, spray them with Korax 1711 mold release, and lay them on either side of the nail to act as a weight. You can also staple the Fiberglas 181 cloth together on either side of the nail body if a sticky stapler doesn't bother you.

Step 9. Around tight areas, a wallpaper cutter works as well as the vegetable slicer to eliminate air bubbles.

Step 10. Let the resin cure out. Then remove the lead weights and separate the piece from the Mylar form. Turn the buckle over, wipe it with tissues dipped in acetone to remove all traces of mold release, and lightly sand it with 180-grit wet-or-dry sandpaper.

Step 11. Glue the well-cleaned pewter to the fiberglass-reinforced polyester resin buckle, using the epoxy adhesive shown in "Formulas" for this project. Be very careful to apply the adhesive only to the pewter piece. Then place the glue-covered pewter surface on the resin-fiberglass buckle and clamp them tightly together. Be sure to remove any excess epoxy resin before it cures hard or the polyester resin decoration you apply later won't stick to it. I usually wait until the epoxy gets "leatherhard" and then cut it away at the metal/fiberglass/polyester joint.

Step 12. To prepare the two openings to be decorated with polyester resin, first scratch and abrade the fiberglass with a sharp tool so that there will be a good "tooth" for the fresh resin to hang onto. To prevent the polyester resin from running all over the pewter, make temporary containers around the openings using a moldable material such as the 60/40 wax described in Project 15, "Formulas," or silly putty mixed with Asbestos 244 shown in Project 14, "Formulas." I use the latter here since it self releases very well.

Step 13. Mix up the polyester resin enamel shown in "Formulas" for this project and pour it into the appropriate areas. Make a bar for the buckle from the excess pieces of the resin-fiberglass buckle body.

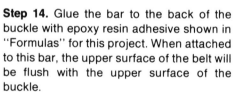

Step 14. Glue the bar to the back of the buckle with epoxy resin adhesive shown in "Formulas" for this project. When attached to this bar, the upper surface of the belt will be flush with the upper surface of the buckle.

Step 15. Attach the belt to the bar.

Torque neckpiece by Stanley Lechtzin,
Tyler School of Art.
Clear polyester resin and electroformed copper.
Photo courtesy of the artist.

DECORATING A SPRINGY FIBERGLASS BRACELET WITH EPOXY AND PEWTER

When working with these "new" materials, it's often necessary to develop novel methods to take advantage of their unique properties. This bracelet needs "spring" in order to be put on and taken off many times. Here is what you will learn from this project:

How to achieve metal-like "spring" using polyester resin reinforced with fiberglass.

How to use epoxy resins to adhere both cured polyester resin systems and pewter. In addition, these epoxy resin systems can be made flexible.

How to cast a rubber-like pearlescent cloisonné epoxy enamel and easily shape it to fit a curved cloison.

TOOLS AND MATERIALS

1. Jeweler's tools: saw and blades, drill and 1/16" bit, needle file, and a rawhide mallet.
2. Infrared heat lamp.
3. A hot plate or your stove.
4. Finishing tools: wet-or-dry sandpaper, buffing wheel and buffing compounds, and 000 steel wool.
5. Scrap pieces of wood to construct a box for rotating the mandril, old saw blades, and a paint mixer or similar rod.
6. 1" disposable paintbrush and coffee stirrers.
7. China marking pencil (a waxed, colored pencil).
8. Scotch tape, rubber cement, and rubber bands.
9. A small, sharp knife (X-Acto knife), and shears.
10. Any sharp tool such as a nail.
11. Straightedge and compass.
12. A piece of paper or lightweight cardboard.
13. A roller-type vegetable slicer or wallpaper cutter.
14. Three pieces of Fiberglas 181 cloth 7½" x 3".
15. 5-mil to 10-mil Mylar sheet 8" x 12".
16. A stretcher frame used by painters to stretch canvas.
17. A heavy-duty stapler.
18. 20-mil cellulose acetate, acetone, and a syringe.
19. 18-gauge strip of pewter, approximately 7" x 2½".
20. Non-flammable solvent for cleaning pewter (perchlorethylene) and lacquer thinner.
21. 16-gauge lead sheet, 8" x 3".
22. A mold-release agent such as Korax 1711 spray or MirrorGlaze wax.
23. Reichhold Chemicals Polylite 32-032 polyester resin.
24. Reichhold Chemicals MEK Peroxide (MEK-Px).
25. CIBA-GEIGY Araldite 502 epoxy resin.

26. Curing agents: RC-303, CIBA-GEIGY 840, DION EH-30, and Ajicure B-003.
27. CIBA-GEIGY Epoxide 7 or 8, reactive diluent.
28. Additives: transparent color pastes, pearlescence, Benzoflex 9-88 flexibilizer, and talc.

FORMULAS

POLYESTER RESIN BINDER FOR FIBERGLASS

Polylite 32-032 polyester resin	100 grams
MEK-Px catalyst	1 gram
Benzoflex 9-88	7.5 grams
Color pastes	as needed

Mix well and use.

EPOXY RESIN ENAMEL, 5-MINUTE CURE

Araldite epoxy resin 502	20 grams
Curing agent RC-303	15 grams
Pearlescence	.25 grams
Transparent color pastes	as needed

Stir the resin and curing agent together well for about 2 minutes, then add pearlescence and transparent color pastes. Don't use opaque color pastes with pearlescence. Remove surface bubbles by spraying the enamel with acetone in a Preval aerosol sprayer.

EPOXY ADHESIVE

Araldite epoxy resin 502	25 grams
Curing agent 840	25 grams
DION EH-30	0.5 grams
Color pastes	as needed
Talc	as needed

Mix the ingredients together well. To the epoxy adhesive formula above, add the desired color paste and adequate talc to make the epoxy resin system non-flowing.

SAWDUST-SATURATED EPOXY RESIN

Araldite epoxy resin 502	90 grams
Epoxide 7 or 8	10 grams
Curing agent B-003	40 grams

Mix the ingredients together and add as much heavy sawdust as you can until the resin is saturated.

BRACELET VARIATION, FLEXIBLE EPOXY SYSTEM

Araldite epoxy resin 502	50 grams
Curing agent 840	50 grams
DION EH-30	1.5 grams
Color paste or pearlescence	as needed

Mix the ingredients together well and use.

NOTES AND CAUTIONS

All the resin systems are available from the resin suppliers in *Suppliers and Manufacturers*. Pewter can be obtained from C. R. Hill Company. Other materials are obtainable from your local art and craft or hardware store.

This project required the fabrication of at least six bracelets to arrive at the demonstration which follows. Making a piece of jewelry for the first time will teach you how to improve it the next time. If you are a serious craftsman, I suggest you repeat the process of making a piece three times before you settle on the best procedure.

Although this project involves using polyester resin 32-032 reinforced with 181 Fiberglas cloth to make the bracelet body, you could easily substitute epoxy resin adhesive system 502/840/DION EH-30 (see the bracelet variation, flexible epoxy system in "Formulas" for this project) for the polyester resin. Epoxy resins are stronger and make better adhesives than polyester resins, and you'll probably

need only two layers of 181 Fiberglas instead of three if you use the epoxy resin system. The large quantity of flexibilizing 840 curing agent in the epoxy system, which incidentally is a "non-toxic" curing agent, will give good spring to the bracelet.

Naturally, you don't have to use pearlescence in the epoxy resin cloison. You can use transparent colors alone.

Remember that epoxy resins must be very carefully handled. Please don't get your hands in the "soup." If you become sensitized, you won't be able to work with epoxy resins again.

Have good ventilation; change the air in your studio at least six times per hour. Vapors from polyester resins in concentrations greater than 100 parts per million of air are hazardous to breathe. There's little worry about vapors from epoxy resins.

Wear a dust mask while cutting the fiberglass cloth.

DECORATING A SPRINGY FIBERGLASS BRACELET WITH EPOXY AND PEWTER

Step 1. Make a design for the bracelet with a straightedge and compass on a 7″ x 2½″ piece of paper or light cardboard. Use a sharp cutting knife (an X-Acto knife) to cut out the cloisons. With rubber cement glue the paper model temporarily to a strip of 18-gauge pewter.

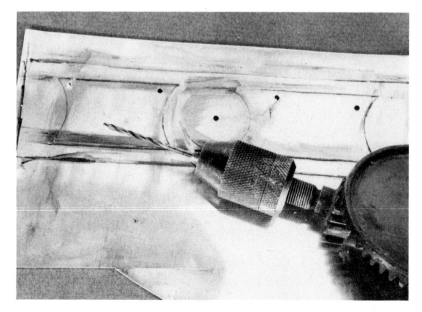

Step 2. Lightly engrave the outline of the paper model into the pewter sheet with a sharp tool and drill some holes in the cloisons so that you can insert the blade of a jeweler's saw to cut out the shapes.

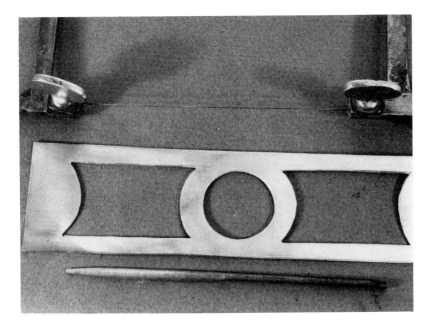

Step 3. Saw out the pewter design. Use a needle file to clean up the saw cuts and to file the interior edges. File the edges under at an angle to make a slanting "roof" to hold the resin more securely.

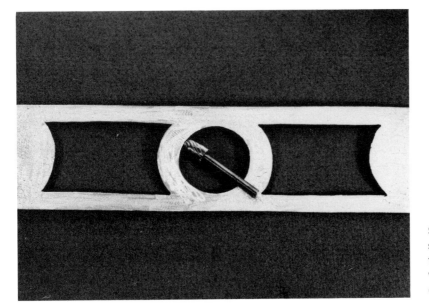

Step 4. For better adhesion, roughen the surfaces of the pewter with a burr attached to an electric hand drill, then clean them with a non-flammable solvent, such as per-chlorethylene.

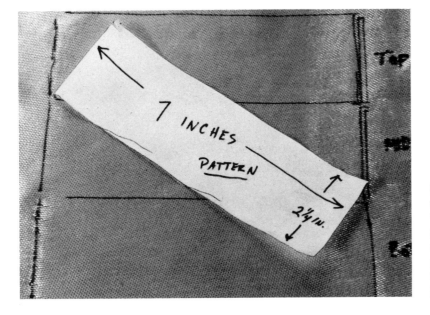

Step 5. Fiberglas 181 cloth, which is a woven material, is ideal for jewelry (see Project 19, Step 3). Use a China marker to outline three 7″ x 2½″ rectangles for the bracelet on the fiberglass, then cut them out with a pair of shears. *Be sure to wear a dust mask while you cut the fiberglass* or you may inhale invisible needles of air-borne glass.

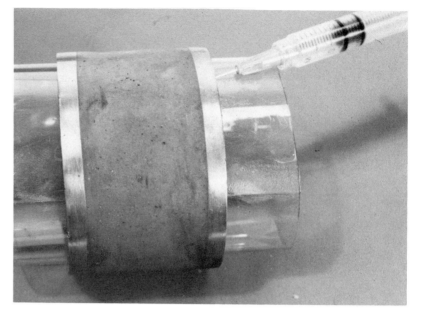

Step 6. Make an acetate mandril from 20-mil cellulose acetate, bonding it together with acetone squirted from a syringe (see Project 13, Step 1). You can use another bracelet as a model for size. Once the mandril is finished, it's wise to give the outside a light spray of mold-release wax (Korax 1711) so that the resins can later be removed more easily.

Step 7. Fill the inside of the mandril with sawdust-saturated resin shown in "Formulas" for this project. Pack the slurry in tightly while holding the mandril in shape with the forming bracelet.

Step 8. Remove the bracelet when the sawdust-saturated resin has set and drill a hole through the center of the sawdust so that the mandril can be rotated.

Step 9. From scrap wood construct a box to hold the mandril and its rotating bar. Glue the pieces of wood together with a mixture of two parts epoxy resin 502 and 1 part RC-303. You can staple broken pieces of saw blades to the top of the frame to act as friction bearings.

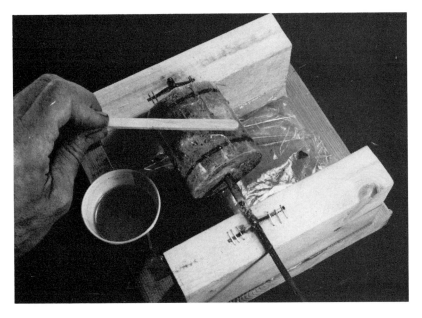

Step 10. Mix up the polyester resin binder for fiberglass described in "Formulas" for this project and apply it to the cellulose acetate mandril with a coffee stirrer. (If you prefer you can substitute the epoxy resin system mentioned in "Notes and Cautions" for this chapter.) Allow the resin coating to cure about 10" away from an infrared heat lamp. Turn the mandril frequently to insure an over-all cure of the resin. It's very important to precoat the mandril in this way to make sure that no fiberglass will come in contact with the skin of the wearer. When polyester coating cures, apply another fresh film of the polyester resin mixture to the mandril.

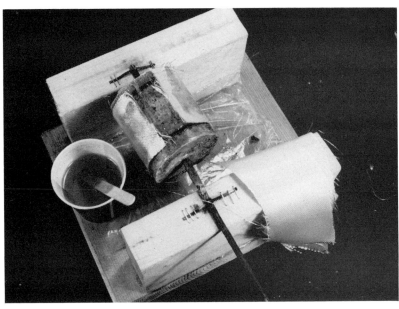

Step 11. Place a strip of fiberglass cloth around the mandril on top of the newly applied polyester resin. With the ever-present coffee stick, sparingly apply more resin to the fiberglass cloth, making certain that the cloth is well saturated (but don't waste the resin binder by using excessive amounts). As soon as one piece of fiberglass cloth is saturated, apply another piece and repeat the same procedure. Then add a third piece in the same manner.

Step 12. Use a roller-type vegetable slicer (see Project 19, Step 8) to remove any air bubbles, which can weaken the resin and fiberglass system. Wash the roller in lacquer thinner as soon as you're finished using it.

Step 13. Use steel wool to matte-finish one side of a 5-mil to 10-mil Mylar sheet. Stretch the sheet by stapling it tightly, matte side up, to a stretcher frame. Move the stretcher frame back and forth 1″ above a hot plate to warm the Mylar until it begins to crinkle. Remove the frame from the heat and blow on the Mylar to shrink and cool it. Continue this procedure until the Mylar becomes smooth and drum tight. Apply rubber cement to the Mylar sheet to make a releasing surface for the resin casting.

Step 14. Put Scotch tape along the four edges of the underside of the pewter plate, turn the metal over, and crimp the corners of the tape together to form a "boxtop." Apply rubber cement to the bottom of the pewter. When the surface is dry, press the pewter onto the stretched Mylar.

Step 15. Mix up the epoxy resin enamel shown in "Formulas" for this project and pour it into the cloisons in the pewter. Stir the resin a little while it's curing (it only takes about 5 minutes) to make a pattern in the pearlescence.

Step 16. After the resin has cured, spray it with Korax 1711 mold release. Then mix well a batch of the epoxy resin enamel without the color paste and pearlescence and pour it right over the freshly sprayed pewter and epoxy pearlescence. Let it cure.

Step 17. Apply another thin coating of this epoxy enamel to the hot resin surface and place a smooth, flat sheet of plumbers 16-gauge lead on top of it. (If you don't have lead, you can substitute pewter.) The lead holds the pearlescence in place and keeps the pewter and epoxy bracelet decoration from coming apart at this stage. The epoxy enamel coating should cure in about 5 minutes. Remove the Scotch tape and wrap the pewter bracelet around the mandril, using the lead as a collar and holding the bracelet in place on the mandril with rubber bands. This pressure insures good contact among the various elements being glued. Place the piece about 10" away from an infrared heat lamp. Heat curing makes the 502/ RC-303 system fingernail hard and speeds up the hardening of the epoxy enamel to make it stronger.

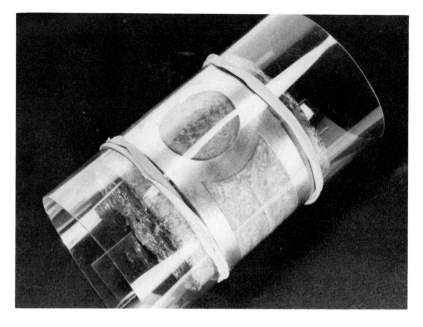

Step 18. Remove the lead but don't cut the bracelet loose from the acetate mandril. Sand the bracelet with wet, 180-grit wet-or-dry sandpaper until the resin surface is flush with the pewter. Mix up the epoxy adhesive shown in "Formulas" for this project as above, adding color paste and talc until you have a non-flowing paste. Cover the exterior edges of the pewter design carefully with this mixture. Wrap a cellulose acetate collar around the bracelet. Again place the bracelet 10″ away from an infrared heat lamp and let it cure for about an hour or until the new resin is fingernail hard.

Step 19. Remove the acetate collar and check the surfaces for blemishes. If there are any little holes, make up fresh resin to fill them. Heat cure the resin. Then sand the bracelet with wet, 180-grit wet-or-dry sandpaper.

Step 20. Saw through the bracelet and remove it from the cellulose acetate mandril. This should be easy to do because of the mold release you sprayed on the mandril initially.

Step 21. With a file shape the ends of the bracelet to a gentle curve. Then buff it with Lea Compound C to remove all scratches and any excess resin, and clean it with Learok 765. Finally use 000 steel wool to achieve a matte finish.

Pins by Walter Schluep, Montreal.
Sterling silver and epoxy resin enamel.
Photo courtesy of the artist.

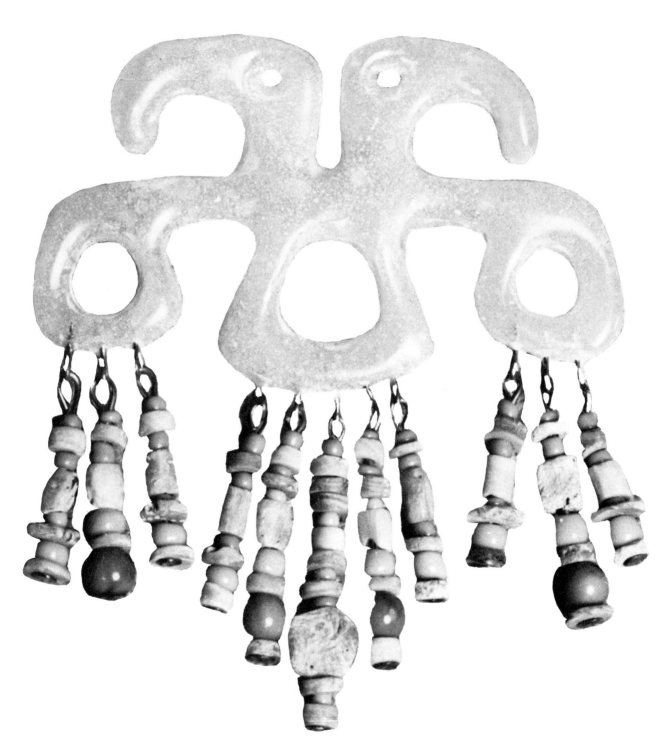

Brooch by Gretchen Anderson, Honolulu.
Cast epoxy resin and ceramic beads.
Photo courtesy of the artist.

GLOSSARY

"A" stage. A designation used to describe the beginning reaction in the curing of a thermosetting resin system. The evolving product is not thermosetting; it is soluble in certain solvents, and its three-dimensional molecular network is not yet formed.

Accelerator. A compound, or mixture, which makes a chemical reaction proceed more quickly. In polyester resin systems, cobalt naphthenate hastens the decomposition of the MEK-Px, initiating the polymerization of the polyester-styrene molecules.

Acetate. Shortened term for cellulose acetate, the principal ingredient in one of the tough thermoplastics generally used in the form of sheets or in ribbons of transparent tapes.

Acetate sheet. Shortened term for cellulose acetate sheet, a self-releasing plastic sheet for use with epoxy, polyester, and silicone resins.

Acetone. A very effective organic chemical, used as a solvent for all the uncured thermosetting resins mentioned in this book. It's highly flammable and should be used with adequate ventilation.

Acidic. One of the terms used to describe how a chemical behaves in the presence of water. For example, wine vinegar, which contains a chemical called acetic acid, is acidic.

Acrylic. A thermoplastic, synthetic resin such as Plexiglas (Perspex in U.K.), Lucite, and Acryloid. These are trade names for polymethyl methacrylate. The two most important starting chemicals in acrylics are called methyl acrylate and methyl methacrylate monomers.

Additives. A general term used in this book to denote any dry and non-oily substance which can be added to any of the liquid resins which have been discussed.

Adhesive. A material which, when placed between two substances, bonds, glues, or adheres one of these substances to the other. The making of a good adhesive involves much chemistry and physics.

Ajicure. The trade name of the epoxy curing agents: B-001, B-003, N-001 manufactured by the Ajinomoto Company.

Alkaline. One of the terms used to describe how a chemical behaves in the presence of water. Baking soda (bicarbonate of soda) is mildly alkaline. It's used to neutralize or react with acidic substances.

Alkyd. A name for the combination of alcohols with an acid. It's often used in the paint industry to describe polyester resins which are modified with oils such as fatty acids and vegetable oils to produce coatings.

Alloy. A mixture of metals which are melted together to form other metals such as sterling silver which is 925 parts of fine (pure) silver and 75 parts of copper.

Alphalap "PS". A cotton-base material with a precision cut rayon nap which is recommended for use when hand polishing plastics with slurries of tin oxide, aluminum oxide, or cerium oxide powder and water. This product has a contact adhesive backing. It's available from J.I. Morris, 394 Elm Street, Southbridge, Massachusetts 01550.

Amide curing agents. A series of epoxy resin curing agents or hardeners which are also flexibilizers or plasticizers. They're usually less toxic than the amine curing agents.

Amine curing agents. Curing agents for epoxy resins based on the presence of nitrogen and usually having an odor similar to that of ammonia. They're generally very caustic and should be washed off immediately with soap and water if they come in contact with the skin. For eye contamination, wash your eyes for 15 minutes in running water and then see a doctor.

Anti-oxidant. A product added to delay the oxidation or decomposition of another product, such as CIBA-GEIGY'S Irganox 1010 and Irganox 1076.

Araldite. CIBA-GEIGY's trade name for their epoxy resins such as Araldite epoxy resin 502.

Araldite curing agent 840 or General Mills curing agent 140. Polyamide curing agents for epoxy resins. They are considered to be nontoxic and also act as plasticizing or flexibilizing agents.

Asbestos 244. A modified asbestos fiber developed by Union Carbide, under the name Calidria resin grade 244 Asbestos. It is used for maximum thickening efficiency and thixotropy for certain resins, such as polyester and epoxy. *Use with care! Wear a dust mask when mixing dry powders into resin mixtures.*

Asbestos fibers. Plastibest 20, 30, and 7-FT-1 are asbestos fibers manufactured by Canadian Asbestos Company Limited for use as a reinforcement with polyester or epoxy resins. These fibers may be mixed in the resin instead of fiberglass. *Use with care! Wear a dust mask.*

Assemblage. The fitting together of a group of items.

"B" stage. The second stage in the curing of a thermosetting resin; at this stage, when the resin comes in contact with certain liquids, it won't completely dissolve, but it will swell. The spatial three-dimensional molecular network is partially formed at this "B" stage.

B-001, B-003, and N-001. Epoxy resin curing agents or hardeners developed by the Ajinomoto Company who claims they are nontoxic and non-yellowing when compared with the usual epoxy resin curing agents.

Benzoflex 9-88. The principal plasticizer or flexibilizing agent used in this book. It's manufactured by the Velsicol Corporation and is available from the special suppliers listed in *Suppliers and Manufacturers.*

Bezel. A collar usually made of metal, which holds the stone in the mounting of a jewelry piece.

Bleach. As used in this book, bleach is a product which decreases the yellowness of a product. An example is HH 772 Bleach which is added to the HH 772 acrylic syrup to make the acrylic less yellow.

Bonding. Another word for adhering or gluing.

Britannia Metal. *See* Pewter.

"C" stage. The final stage in curing a thermosetting resin. When the three-dimensional network of a molecular polymerization is complete, the polymer won't melt, and doesn't dissolve in the usual lacquer thinner solvents.

Cabosil. A trade name for a special grade of silica sand or silicon dioxide. The product is so finely divided that one gram is supposed to have about 200 square feet of area. Cabosil is used as a thixotropic, or thickening agent in epoxy, polyester, urethane, and silicone resins.

Canvas stretcher. A set of convenient wood framing pieces which fit together to make a frame for stretching canvas, silk, or polyvinyl alcohol (PVA), Mylar or cellulose acetate film which is used for casting polyester or epoxy resins.

Casting resins. Resins such as polyester or epoxy which are clear and colorless and are poured into molds which are either self-releasing or to which release agents are added. Polylite is a polyester casting resin made by the Reichhold Chemical Company; DER 332 is an epoxy casting resin made by Dow Chemical Company.

Catalyst. In resins such as polyesters, epoxies, and silicones, a catalyst is a material used in small quantities to initiate or speed up the polymerization process. In these reactions, the catalyst is either destroyed or in some way combined with the cured resin system.

Caustic. A term used to describe very alkaline substances such as lye and epoxy curing agents such as RC-125. Caustic substances are very dangerous to the eyes. Goggles should be worn when using them. If you do get these substances in your eyes, flush them with running water for 15 minutes and consult a physician.

Cellulose acetate. An acetic acid ester of cellulose which comes from cotton linters. When certain flexibilizers are added, a strong transparent thermoplastic film is produced. This film is available in various mil thicknesses from 1 mil to 50 mils and is easily bonded to itself wich acetone.

Centipoise. A convenient term which is used to describe viscosity. Water at room temperature is considered to have a viscosity of 1 centipoise; SAE 10 motor oil is 100 centipoises, and molasses is 100,000 centipoises.

Cero-bend. Trade name for a series of low-melting alloys related to pewter. Some of these alloys melt at temperatures as low as 158° F.

Chemical reaction (plastics). All of the liquid thermosetting resins discussed in this book are converted to solids through the addition of catalysts or curing agents (hardeners) which chemically react to form new polymeric compounds.

Chemical resistance. Chemical resistance should be considered by the artist-craftsman when he's selling to the public. A resin or plastic is considered to be chemically resistant to a material such as water, smog, fruit juice, and so on, if optical and physical properties (appearance, weight, strength) are unchanged after the plastic has been exposed to these "chemicals" for a reasonable length of time.

Chlorinated solvents. A series of non-flammable solvents which, although they don't burn, are relatively toxic when inhaled. Among the most toxic is carbon tetrachloride and among the least toxic are perchlorethylene, methylene chloride, and ethylene dichloride, which are solution adhesives for acrylic sheets such as Plexiglas, Lucite, and so on.

Cloissoné. According to Webster, this term means, "inlaid between partitions."

Collage. A term which describes the gluing or bonding together of the same or different materials.

Color pastes. Concentrated dispersions of pigments or dyes in a non-drying vehicle. This paste, which can be transparent or opaque, must also be soluble in the resin to be colored.

Compound. A distinct substance formed through the reaction of two or more elements with each other. A "mixture" is a thoroughly commingled complex of two or more compounds, each of which still retains its own identity.

Curing agent. A chemical compound or mixture which, when added to a thermosetting resin, converts the resin to an infusible plastic. In this book, curing agent and hardener are synonomous and are used in epoxy resin systems.

Curing agent 956. This epoxy resin curing agent was developed by the Union Carbide Corporation under the name of ZZL 0816 and was modified by CIBA-GEIGY as curing agent 956. I've used this safety hardener for over 10 years with no failures. It's still very important not to let this product get on your hands, since it's possible to become allergic to it.

DC 200 silicone oils. A series of exotic synthetic oils manufactured by the Dow Corning Corporation. These oils are based upon silicon, a non-metallic element which is similar to carbon, the basic element of the organic compounds studied in organic chemistry. These silicone oils of varying viscosities are excellent mold-releasing substances, barrier creams, and low-temperature lubricants.

DER 332. The numerical designation of Dow epoxy resin which is a pure, water-clear epoxy resin. It is so pure that it's easily crystallized at room temperature. These crystals are dissolved by gently warming the resin until the crystals dissolve:

Dermatitis. A term used in this book to designate skin allergies, usually similar to the reaction to poison ivy, which can be caused by contact with any of the synthetic resins or polymers discussed. A good rule to remember when handling these resins and curing agents is: no physical contact no dermatitis.

Dibutylphthalate. One of the main plasticizers or flexibilizers used in the resin and plastic industry. Although it's not chemically combined with the resin, it doesn't easily bleed out, or migrate. Araldite epoxy resin 502 contains 17% by weight dibutylphthalate, which makes the resin non-brittle.

DION EH-10 and DION EH-30. Curing agents which generally are mixed with other curing agents for hardening epoxy resins. DION EH-10 is about three times slower than EH-30. These products are equivalent to DMP-10 and DMP-30.

DION-3-800 LC (DPM-3-800 LC). An accelerator developed by Diamond Shamrock for the quick curing of epoxy resin systems. It's used in this book in the proportions of 9 grams of DION-3-800 LC and 1 gram of DION EH-30 to make up curing agent RC-303.

DMP-10, DMP-30 (DION EH-10, DION EH-30). Rohm and Haas developed these two epoxy resin curing agents many years ago. They're also used to cure other types of synthetic polymers called polymercaptains and thiokols. The Diamond Shamrock Corporation now manufactures the same chemicals under the trade-names DION EH-10 and DION EH-30. In both instances, the "10" is a much slower curing agent than the "30."

DPM-3-800 LC. See DION-3-800 LC.

Dylite. See Styrofoam.

Elastomer. A rubberlike natural or synthetic product which when physically stretched returns to its original shape and strength.

Electroforming. The electroplating of metals and nonmetals by immersing either or both of them, after proper preparation, into metallic salt solutions through which direct electrical current is passed.

Embossing. The process which produces a relief from a surface by pushing up the surface or by adding to the surface through the adhesion of other substances.

Emulsion. The suspension of fine particles or globules of one liquid in another. There are two general types of emulsions: in one type, water droplets are dispersed in oils (for example, mayonnaise); in the other type, which are non-water soluble, substances are dispersed in water (for example acrylic polymer latexes or mediums).

"Enamel." Used in this book, "enamel" means a clear, translucent coating or an opaque, vitreous-like coating (thin or heavy) on materials such as wood, stone, metals, or plastics. (Usually an epoxy resin system is used for enameling.)

Enameling. Traditionally in jewelry, the art of fusing vitreous substances at high temperatures to metals such as silver, copper, and gold.

Engraving. The cutting or incising of lines or shapes into materials such as metals, waxes, plastics and so on.

Epicure 87 (RC-125). An accelerated epoxy resin curing agent manufactured by the Celanese Corporation. When 100 parts of epoxy resin 502 are mixed with 20 to 25 parts of Epicure 87, the resin/hardener system cures in approximately 20 to 30 minutes. This system is not particularly moisture sensitive.

Epoxide 7 or 8. Reactive diluents for epoxy resins. (Epoxide 8 is almost odorless). Being low-viscosity, relatively nontoxic chemicals which contain epoxy groups and are not very volatile, they are ideal thinners for epoxy resins. The classic epoxy reactive diluent, butyl glycidyl ether, is relatively volatile and toxic. Check your epoxy resins to be sure that these latter compounds aren't present.

Epoxy-metal alloy. In this book, this term signifies the combination of metal powders with synthetic resins such as epoxies, polyester, or polyurethane. Often it's possible to add over 90% metals by weight to an epoxy resin. This mixture after curing, buffing and polishing, can be chemically treated as metal.

Epoxy resin 502. This product is manufactured by CIBA-GEIGY under the trade name Araldite 502. It's a mixture of pure epoxy resin (CIBA-GEIGY Araldite 6010) and 17% dibutyl phthalate, a plasticizer or flexibilizer. This was one of the first epoxy resins which I worked with in 1953. It's an excellent resin for use, both professionally and non-professionally, in the art and craft area.

Ethylene dichloride. A chlorinated solvent, available from plastics distributors such as Cadillac Plastic and Chemical Company, which is a good adhesive for bonding acrylic sheet to acrylic sheet. It works by dissolving the thermoplastic acrylic polymer, thereby bonding it to itself. However, the strongest joints are made with such adhesives as Tensol 7, made by ICI, and PS 30, distributed by Cadillac Plastic and Chemical Company, (New York office) 1761 Edgar Road, Linden, New Jersey 07036, and HH 772 distributed by Polysciences, Warrington, Pennsylvania.

Ethylene glycol. Used primarily as a permanent antifreeze; however, when mixed with gelatin and water, it helps to make an excellent mold-making material. This material self-releases from polyester resins and certain epoxy resin systems containing curing agents such as Ajicure N-001, B-001 and CIBA-GEIGY HY 837, which are not particularly moisture sensitive.

Exotherm. A chemical reaction during which heat is given off. Most of the thermosetting resins discussed in this book are cured by the addition of curing agents or catalysts which generate heat when reacting with the resin.

Expanded polystyrene. This term describes two trade names: Styrofoam and Dylite.

Fadeometer. An instrument used to evaluate the lightfastness of dyes and other materials when exposed to sunlight. It's based on the carbon arc, which is the closest man has come to the controlled reproduction of ultraviolet light, the ingredient in sunlight which deteriorates organic substances. Its primary function is to give some idea of how articles or colors will behave when exposed indoors to sunlight. This and other types of sunlight-like tests can't be directly related to actual weather tests because of the infinite number of variables in any particular outdoor location. You should always use such light tests in a comparative way, that is to check something known against your unknown.

Fiberglas 181 cloth. A close woven fiberglass cloth which "drapes" easily around almost any surface.

Findings. Mechanical fittings for jewelry such as cufflinks, earring wires, chains, rings, and catches.

Flexibilizer. See Plasticizer.

Flux. In this book, a chemical paste or solution which is applied to a metal surface so that the solder will adhere to the metal.

Gel-coat. The outside decorative finish of a form. In the plastics industry a thin, usually somewhat thixotropic thermosetting resin coating which is directly applied to the "released" mold.

General-purpose polyester resin. This type of polyester is used where translucency or transparency is not important such as with fiberglass or other reinforcement, opaque colors or additives.

Gram scale or balance. The various ingredients used in thermosetting, room-temperature curing resins must be accurately measured. The use of a scale which measures grams is most convenient. (453.4 grams is equivalent to 1 lb. or 16 oz.) I recommend the Ohaus Scale shown in *Your Studio and Basic Equipment.*

Hardener. Used interchangeably with curing agent in this book to designate a type of substance which, when added to thermosetting resins such as epoxy and urethane, converts them from a liquid to a solid. In order to distinguish the different types of solidifying which take place in the resin systems, I've used the term "catalyst" for the organic peroxides which cure or solidify polyester resins.

Heat distortion point. The temperature at which, under the specified conditions set by the American Society of Testing Materials (test D-648), a standard test bar will be deflected. You can set up your own tests to compare and evaluate materials.

HH 371. A mixture of 90 grams of styrene and 10 grams of DION-3-800 LC which is used in small quantities to speed the gelling of polyester resins.

HH 572. A soft modeling wax which melts at 212°. 40% HH 572 when melted with 60% by weight of Sun Oil Company 1290 Y microcyrstalline wax produces a wax which is excellent for models and mold making.

HH 772. A liquid room-temperature-curing acrylic casting and embedding syrup which enables you to make your own Plexiglas-like sheets.

HH 1065 B. A curing agent developed for a slow cure with very little evolution of heat. The ingredients are equal amounts of menthane diamine, made by the Rohm and Haas Company, and ZZ1-0822, made by Union Carbide Corporation. This curing agent is available through the resin suppliers listed in *Suppliers and Manufacturers.*

HY 837. An epoxy resin curing agent with outstanding resistance to weathering compared to other curing agents used here. This is a new product manufactured by CIBA-GEIGY.

Infrared heat lamp. Lamps or heaters are most effective as accelerators in the curing of the thermosetting resins. The most reasonably priced heat source is the industrial 250 watt infrared reflector heat lamp. Do not purchase the red glass bulb; it's more expensive and no more effective.

Inhibitor. A chemical which is added to another chemical or mixture of chemicals to prevent or retard a reaction.

Inorganic materials. Inorganic materials are substances which don't contain carbon and generally don't burn.

Inorganic pigments. Colorants which have been dried out at relatively high temperatures to remove all excess water and organic materials such as carbon compounds. Usually these pigments are oxides, sulfides, and so on and are extremely colorfast in sunlight, weather, and heat. Companies such as BASF have available iron-oxide pigments which are practically transparent, although they aren't ordinarily classified as transparent.

Intaglio. In graphics, this term signifies the cutting into a plate of metal, wood, or other material in such a way that the incised figure is depressed below the surface of the material.

Internal release agent. A chemical or mixture which is added to a resin or plastic so that the resin or plastic won't adhere to the mold into which it's cast.

Internal Release 54. A product manufactured by Axel Plastics Research Company which, when added in quantities of 0.25% to a polyester resin, will prevent the resin from adhering to glass, vitreous surfaces, or polished metal surfaces.

Isocyanate resins. Resins based on the union of chemicals or chemical mixtures, which contain nitrogen, carbon, oxygen, and so on, with other alcohol-related chemicals.

Klean Klay 20. Recommended by Dow Corning as a modeling clay which works well as material from which Silastic RTV rubber molds can be cast.

Korax 1711. A mold-release spray which prevents the adhesion of a resin to the surface upon which it has been sprayed.

Lacquer thinner. A mixture of solvents usually xylene, toluene, methyl ethyl ketone or MEK (*not related to MEK-Px*), methyl isobutyl ketone (MIBK), and Cellosolve, used to thin oil paints and clean brushes. These same thinners can be employed to thin resins, such as epoxy and urethane, when they are used as coatings.

Lancast A. This is a well tested low viscosity curing agent available from CIBA-GEIGY. When mixed with Araldite 502 and DION EH-30 (Acc 064) it's a strong adhesive.

Lap Joint. A joint which is made by overlapping one piece of material with another and adhering the materials at this overlap. Much adhesion testing is carried out with lap joint gluing or bonding.

Leather-hard. A term which has been borrowed from the potters to describe clay which is dried sufficiently to be stiff, but which is still damp enough to be worked with a knife or joined to other pieces with slip. When resins such as epoxy or polyester haven't quite reached their final stage or complete cure, they too may be cut with sharp knives, burins, linoleum-block tools, or woodcarving tools.

Lexan. General Electric's trade name for its polycarbonate plastic sheet. This plastic is transparent and practically unbreakable. In jewelry, it can be used for strength in items such as necklace links. A similar product, which is almost as strong, is Plexiglas 70 made by Rohm and Haas.

Light stabilized. A resin is light stabilized when a chemical, such as CIBA-GEIGY's Tinurin 328, has been added which absorbs the ultraviolet light from the sun. These stabilizers generally don't last indefinitely.

Liver of sulfur (K$_2$S). An inorganic chemical which, when mixed with approximately 97% water, will give a brown to black coloring to metals which contain copper, such as sterling silver and bronze. A patina (the chemical coloring of metals) can be given to aluminum with the method of adding about 5% to 10% 300-mesh carbon black powder to the 300-mesh aluminum powder. After the blackened resin binder has cured out naturally, the piece receiving the patina must be buffed to remove the surface resin and expose the shiny aluminum. Where it's not buffed, the piece will remain black.

Mandril. A metallic or non-metallic rod, often cone-shaped, around which a ring or bracelet can be formed. The forming may be done by hammering, casting, or shaping with a mixture of fiberglass cloth and resin.

Mearlin Pearlescence. The trade name of an additive which will give a pearl-like appearance to a resin system.

MEK. The letters which signify methyl ethyl ketone, an excellent organic solvent or thinner.

MEK-Px. These are the letters which designate methyl ethyl ketone peroxide, an organic oxidizing agent which is diluted approximately 40% with a plasticizer and is primarily used to cure, or harden, polyester resins at room temperature. MEK-Px is considered a hazardous product and should be carefully handled following the manufacturer's cautions.

Menthane diamine. A very slow epoxy resin curing agent, which may be mixed with other curing agents to obtain different properties.

Methylene chloride. Chlorinated solvents such as methylene chloride and ethylene dichloride dissolve Plexiglas and are therefore used as adhesives for acrylic sheets.

Methyl methacrylate. One of the ingredients used in the manufacture of the acrylic sheets which are sold under trade names such as Lucite, Plexiglas (Perspex in U.K.), and so on.

MIBK. The letters which stand for methyl isobutyl ketone, an organic solvent or thinner, which may be used with epoxy resins (for example, to produce thin coatings).

Microballoons. Small, micro-size, hollow spheres made either of phenolic plastics or glass. They're used to fill resin systems such as polyester, epoxy, or urethane, thereby producing a mechanical foam which is both light and strong. Such foams are called "synthactic" and they can be easily cut, sawed, or sanded. Resins highly filled with microballoons are available from the resin suppliers listed in *Suppliers and Manufacturers.*

Microcrystalline Wax, 1290 Y. The Sun Oil Company trade name for its yellow petroleum wax which melts at 178° F

Microliths. Special, easily dispensed, light-stable pigments manufactured by the CIBA-GEIGY Corporation.

Mil. This term is commonly used as a measure of one thousandth of an inch. Ordinary paper is about 4 mils thick.

Mille fiore glass chips. Decorative, candylike glass canes which are used in enameling on silver and copper. They also may be used when "enameling" with epoxy resins. They are available from Leo Popper and Company, 145 Franklin Street, New York, New York 10013.

MirrorGlaze wax. A paste wax producing an excellent release surface. It's easy to apply, and it yields a high polish. Hundreds of people in the author's workshops have had successful results with this product.

Mixture. The result of a thorough blending of two or more compounds, each of which retains its own chemical identity.

Mod-Epox. An epoxy resin reactive diluent, manufactured by Monsanto, who claims that it speeds up the curing time, thins down the resin, and is cheaper than the epoxy or its curing agent.

Mold. Any surface upon which a substance can be poured to eventually make the reverse shape. Negative molds are cavities into which the resin is poured. Positive molds are the opposite.

Molding plaster (casting plaster). *See* Plaster of Paris.

Mold release. Any product which, when applied to the surface of a mold, will cause that surface to become nonadhesive to whatever is poured and hardened upon it. Examples of mold-release agents are Korax 1711 spray and MirrorGlaze wax.

Monomer. *See* Polymer.

Mylar. A Du Pont trade name for one of its plastic films which is self-releasing for polyester resins.

Neozapon. The trade name for a class of metalized organic dyes which are relatively lightfast and soluble in polyester, epoxy, and polyurethane or urethane resins.

Nonreactive. When a product or chemical doesn't chemically combine in a system, it's considered to be nonreactive. Generally, organic solvents which are added to paints are nonreactive and evaporate from the paints.

Opacifier. Any material which when added to a transparent product makes the product opaque.

Organasol. The mixture of a vinyl-like liquid, synthetic polymer and an organic solvent. When the mixture is heated the solvent evaporates and the polymer is converted into a solid.

Organic materials. Any substance which contains carbon is called organic.

Organic peroxides. This distinction is made since the usual peroxide with which we're familiar is called hydrogen peroxide. Hydrogen peroxide doesn't contain carbon and is, therefore, inorganic. The peroxides used in curing polyester resins are not soluble, are organic, and are generally more hazardous. They should be handled with care.

Organo-metallic (metal organic) compound. The chemical combination of metal and organic (carbon-containing) materials in one substance.

Oxidizing agent. A substance which readily releases oxygen while chemically reacting with certain other materials.

P 444 A. The Rohm and Haas polyester resin, which is extremely resistant to sunlight and weather. It contains not only polyester resin and styrene, but also methyl methacrylate monomer, which gives the product its excellent properties.

Paillons. A French term meaning little snippings of solder, about 1/32" square.

Patina. The chemical coloring of a metal surface. A patina can be duplicated with paints and other products which will give a similar effect and is still called "patina."

Pearlescence. Having a pearl-like appearance.

Permoplast X 33. One of the non-sulfur modeling clays which Dow Corning recommends for use with silastic RTV mold-making rubbers such as "E." Other modeling clays which contain sulfur inhibit the curing of this silicone rubber.

Peroxide. *See* MEK-Px.

Pewter. An alloy of 91% tin, 7½% antimony, and 1½% copper which melts around 425° F. Britannia metal, which has essentially the same formula, was developed in England in the late 18th century.

PHR. Parts per hundred parts resin by weight.

Phthalocyanine or "phthalo" pigments. This class of metallo-organic dyestuffs whose full name contains the word "copper," is among the most resistant to sunlight and weather. There are a series of copper phthalocyanine blues and greens which have different tints of red, green, or blue. Those who are very interested in color should check with companies such as CIBA-GEIGY for their recommendations. Often it might pay to grind your own color in a vehicle which is compatible with the resin. The "phthalo" blues and greens, although they are pigments, can be extremely transparent when used in resins.

Pigments. Products which don't dissolve when added to a liquid. They may be very finely ground and evenly dispersed when the proper equipment is available. Pigments may be either organic or inorganic, or a combination of both.

Plaster of Paris. A relatively inexpensive mold-making material. Casting (or molding) plaster is used most often to make molds. Potter's plaster is slightly finer, with a higher degree of absorbency, and is used in ceramic work. Both kinds of plaster are readily available in any art supply store which carries sculpture materials.

Plastic. The term "plastic" describes a vast area of synthetic polymers, many of which are very familiar. The word has a bad connotation in connection with the art and craft area. The use of the word "resin" is preferable in this context. Most of the materials used in this decorative area are called "resins" by the manufacturers. "Plastic" also refers to a state of malleability or flexibility in a substance.

Plasticizer or flexibilizer. A chemical or mixture, such as Benzoflex 9-88, which when added to a resin gives it added plasticity or flexibility.

Plexiglas (Perspex), Acryloid, Lucite. Trade names for acrylic products primarily sold as sheets.

Plexiglas 70. An acrylic product, recently developed by Rohm and Haas, which approaches the strength of Lexan and is many times stronger than regular Plexiglas.

Plique-à-jour. A term used in jewelry to denote a transparent enamel section in a metal ornament.

Polycarbonate resin. A relatively new synthetic resin which is cast into transparent sheets and shapes. Lexan, which is General Electric's trade name for this product, is extremely strong and unbreakable. It's used more and more for unbreakable windows.

Polyester resin (unsaturated). One of a family of synthetic resins which are readily converted from liquid to solid by the use of organic oxidizing agents such as MEK-Px. Polyester resins contain many different additives but in their liquid state they are primarily organic polymeric materials dissolved in styrene or other monomers.

Polyethylene. One of the most commonly used thermoplastic products available, manufactured from ethylene gas, which is one of the by-products of the petroleum industry.

Polyform. A somewhat new modeling material which handles like modeling clay. When placed in an oven for 15 minutes at 300° F., it's converted to a relatively hard, rubbery solid which can be cut, sanded, added to with the same material, and painted. Superficially, it appears to be a mixture of a plastisol (a heat-curable, one-part, vinyl-like substance) and materials such as talc, kaolin, and so on. Polyform is available through art supply stores. For more information write to: Polyform Products Company, 9416 West Irving Park Road, Shiller Park, Illinois 60176. This product might generate some interest as a mold-making material.

Polylite. The trade name for the Reichhold Chemical Company series of polyester resins.

Polymer. "Poly" means many; "meros" means part. Monomer means one part, and when many monomers are joined toghether they make polymers. The joining together of many straight chains or interconnected straight chains produces thermoplastics. These plastics can be melted at any time and shaped or reshaped under heat with no resin deterioration. Thermosetting resins are cross-lined, three-dimensional structures. This means that the straight chains of the polymers are connected by crossing from one chain group to another and then an additional floor of chains and crossings are placed over the first floor and more links are added to join the two floors, creating a rigid structure which will be very strong but not very flexible. Thermosetting resins can be softened and somewhat reshaped, but not melted.

Polymercaptain. A series of odoriferous organic chemicals and mixtures which contain a chemical grouping called the -SH-, or sulfur-hydrogen, group, DION-3-800 LC (DPM-3-800 LC), a polymercaptain, which is used in epoxy resin systems to accelerate the curing of the resin.

Polymerization. The chemical combination of many molecules into one solid mass. Often this joining up produces what is called "one giant molecule."

Poly-paint medium. A name signifying the combination of a polyester resin and other additives to produce a vehicle designed expressly for painting on Plexiglas, polystyrene, or cast polyester resin sheet.

Polystyrene sheet. A sheet plastic which is made from styrene. It's easily heat-formed and can be used decoratively with polyester resins or Poly-paint medium.

Polyurethane resin. A family of resins based upon a system or organic chemistry involving the reaction of molecules called isocyanates with polyols.

Polyvinyl acetate (PVA). A product which appears on the market as a water emulsion. It's usually mixed with other synthetic polymers and used as an adhesive or glue.

Polyvinyl alcohol film. A self-releasing, strong, moisture-sensitive film used to cover catalyzed polyester and certain other resins while they're curing. Once the resins are hard, the film is easily removed. It generally comes in 4-mil to 6-mil thicknesses with a matte finish on one side.

Pot life. The length of time a catalyzed or activated resin is usable.

PPM. Parts per million.

Preval aerosol sprayer. An aerosol valve with a screw-on jar for spraying water, acetone, and so on, available from a hardware store.

Promoter. A chemical or mixture of chemicals which speeds up the curing of a resin. In polyester resins, the promoter or accelerator most commonly used is called cobalt naphthonate. It should never be directly mixed with MEK-Px since an explosion will result. It's present in polyester resins in such great dilution that there's absolutely no danger.

PS 30. A ready-made adhesive distributed by Cadillac Plastic and Chemical Company. It's used as an adhesive for Plexiglas.

PVC. An abbreviation for Polyvinyl chloride, one of the thermoplastic resins having huge consumer uses such as piping and clotheslines.

RC-125. An epoxy curing agent distributed by the Resins Coatings Corporation which is similar to Epicure 87 manufactured by the Celanese Corporation.

RC-303. An accelerated curing agent manufactured by the Resin Coatings Corporation. It is based on Diamond Shamrock's DION-3-800 LC and DION EH-30 in proportion of 9 to 1 by weight. When one part of RC-303 is mixed with one to two parts of CIBA-GEIGY's Araldite epoxy resin 502, the system cures in about five minutes. This very flexible adhesive won't dissolve Styrofoam.

RC-840 or CIBA-GEIGY 840. A polyamine epoxy resin curing agent which is a relatively non-toxic flexibilizer. The hardener/resin proportion is not critical when using this hardener. However, read the manufacturer's recommendations if you want to vary from the suggestions in this book.

Reactive diluent. A low-viscosity liquid which thins down epoxy or polyester resin by reacting in the system and becoming part of the molecular structure when the resin hardens. The safest and best reactive diluents, such as CIBA-GEIGY's Epoxide 7 and 8 which are epoxy resin diluents, have a low evaporation rate. Styrene is a polyester resin reactive diluent which is not hazardous when used with good ventilation.

Reducing agent. A chemical which, among other things, counteracts an oxidizing agent or prevents premature oxidation. It's used, for example, to stabilize polyester resin, so that the resin won't harden in the container before the MEK-Px catalyst is added.

Release agent. Any chemical or mixture of chemicals, such as Korax 1711 spray or Internal Release 54 which is applied to a hard surface, or mixed into an uncured resin or other liquid, so that cast objects won't adhere to their molds.

Resin. This term is actually interchangeable with the term "plastic." This book takes the view that plastics stand for ready-made objects whereas art and craft forms use resins. The basic manufacturers refer to their epoxies, polyesters, silicones, and urethanes as "resins." Resin can also signify a formulated system.

Rotational casting. A method of casting in which the mold is rotated or turned while the liquid resin is curing.

RTV. Room-temperature vulcanizing. This term usually refers to the silicone rubbers or elastomers which cure or turn to rubbers at ambient temperatures.

Saturated polyester resin. In chemistry, saturated means that all available sites for attachment of atoms to other atoms in a molecule are filled up, as when all the seats in a theatre are filled. Generally, we think of the saturated polyesters as fibers. The liquid polyester resins discussed in this book are unsaturated polyesters.

Sawdust. A filler manufactured for use in the plastics industry. Very fine sawdust is called wood flour. Powdered ebony sawdust, which you would have to make yourself, is now being used with epoxy resins for black enameling in jewelry.

Self-extinguishing resin. Certain resins in each of the families discussed in this book can be manufactured or formulated so that they will burn only when a flame is applied to them. When the flame is removed, the resins will extinguish themselves. This is accomplished by chemically building the resin molecules so that they contain atoms such as chlorine or bromine. Additives such as antimony oxide and some phosphorous compounds are also put into resin mixtures to assist in achieving fire resistance. All resins which you use should be tested after they have hardened. Light a match and try to burn a sample. Also check with the manufacturers.

Self-releasing. Certain resins are, or can be made, self-releasing. That is, when these resins are used for molds, the castings won't adhere to them. Silicone resins generally are self-releasing to materials other than silicones. Often there are additives that can be mixed with resins, which will make them more or less self-releasing.

Sensitizing resins. Uncured resins and the curing agents or catalysts mentioned in this book which are generally very chemically active, may, upon contact, have an effect upon the human skin. Resin manufacturers continually caution users: no physical contact with the resin system and you'll get no dermatitis. Continual physical contact with these resins may cause you to become sensitized (allergic) so that rashes like those caused by poison oak or poison ivy may result. Once you become sensitized, you can't work with that resin family. If resin spills on your hands or body, wash with soap, and water; if the resin contacts your eyes, wash them copiously with running water for 15 minutes and go to see a doctor.

Set. Cure, harden, "C" stage, all equivalent terms which can be applied to any of the thermosetting resin systems.

Shrinkage of resins. All the thermosetting resin systems have some decrease in volume when the unfilled resin system is converted from a liquid to a solid. Polyester resins shrink about 7.5%; epoxies shrink about 0.5% after the gel, or "B" stage; silicone rubbers shrink about 0.5% when cured at room temperature. Read the manufacturer's literature carefully if you want to be absolutely sure about shrinkage.

Silastic. Dow Corning's trade name for many of its silicone products.

Silastic A. One of the Dow Corning silicone rubber mold-making products. Used with catalyst F this material cures in 5 to 10 minutes at room temperature yielding a mold which will withstand 500° F., the temperature around which pewter is molten. Silastic A isn't moisture sensitve but does tear easily and therefore must be handled carefully.

Silastic E & G. Two of a series of Dow Corning silicone rubber materials which are liquids until cured with special catalysts. Both of these silicone products have very high tensile and tear strengths. Silastic G, according to the manufacturer, is less sensitive to moisture and other sulfur compounds than Silastic E. These particular elastomers (rubbers) are being used for self-releasing molds in industries such as furniture-making.

Silastic 140 and Silastic 732. These two silicone adhesive sealants are constituted so that when squeezed out of a sealed container, such as a tube, certain inhibiting chemicals evaporate. In the presence of the air's moisture, these silicones cure to a rubberlike solid.

Silicon. This metal is obtained mainly from beach or silica sand. Alcan Metal Powders of Elizabeth, New Jersey, produces 300-mesh silicon powder. This powder, mixed with an epoxy resin system, gives a beautiful brown-black metallic enamel which can be highly polished to a niello-like surface. Niello is an enamel usually used on sterling silver by the craftsmen of India.

Silicone oil. An organic-silicon product which looks like a clear colorless mineral oil, such as GE-910 silicone oil and DC-200 series 20 CTS viscosity silicone oil, used in this book both as a mold release and as a viscosity lowering agent when added to silicone mold-making room temperature curing rubbers. It also makes a good resin barrier ointment for your hands.

Silicone resins. A family of products, based on combinations of atoms of silicon, carbon, hydrogen, oxygen, and so on, which can be converted to solids and put to use in greases, heat-stable fluids, release agents, gaskets, insulating varnishes, electrical appliances, and so on.

Skin mold. A thin mold made by applying thin layers of mold-making material after the previous layer has hardened. After the first layer, reinforcements such as fiberglass are often added to the additional layers. This is done when the model to be copied is very large or when the mold-making material is very expensive, such as the silicone RTV rubbers. Quite frequently the skin molds are backed with a plaster mother mold. This mother mold is a holding container which prevents the skin mold from distorting when it's being filled.

Solder. A metal alloy which melts at a lower temperature than the metal or metals which it's used to join. The solder primarily used in this book is a tin/lead alloy for soldering pewter.

Solvent. A liquid which dissolves other liquids or solids. Water is a solvent for sugar and alcohol. Lacquer thinners are solvents for epoxy resins and urethane resins. Mineral spirits are solvents for oil paints. Alcohol is a solvent for shellac.

Sprue. An opening which is made in a mold to allow passage of the liquid substance to cast. When there's a sprue, there must also be a vent to allow the air to escape while the mold is being filled.

Styrene. The most common reactive diluent for polyester resins. It's not dangerous to work with styrene when adequate ventilation is provided; 100 parts per million is considered safe by the health authorities. According to manufacturers, styrene is not considered explosive. (Methyl methacrylate monomer can also be used as a reactive diluent for Polylite 32-032 polyester resin. It acts as an inhibitor against the ultraviolet rays of the sun.)

Styrofoam. A specially prepared mixture of polystyrene and other chemicals, which is extruded to produce a foamed product containing a very high percentage of air. Other brands such as Dylite and Styropor are products formed from beads of polystytene which are expanded in closed containers under heat and moisture.

Synthetic polymer. A man-made substance made of many of the same or similar molecular "building blocks" as natural polymers.

Talc. One of the popular, inexpensive fillers for all types of resins and plastics.

Tensile strength. The pull, usually expressed in pounds, required to break or pull apart one square inch of a material.

Thermoplastic. A term applied to plastics or resins which indicates that they are capable of being melted under heat. Once they're in the liquid state, they can be molded and cooled to return to their solid state. Plastics such as polyethylene, vinyl, and acrylics are classed as thermoplastics.

Thermoset. Materials such as epoxy resins, polyester resins, urethane resins, and silicone resin which, when chemically reacted with curing agents or catalysts at room temperature (sometimes at temperatures as low as near freezing or as high as 350° F.) are converted to solids. These solids are non-melting but in most cases they may be softened, reshaped, braced, and cooled to hold the new shape.

Thinner. This term usually refers to solvents such as water, mineral spirits, lacquer thinners, and so on, added to paints, resins, or other materials. These solvents evaporate over a period of time, depending upon the thickness of the coating or film.

Thixotropic. Materials which are non-runny while standing. When the material is pushed, it's easily moved and remains exactly in the position or shape in which it was left by contact with the moving object. Additives such as Asbestos 244 and Cabosil (pyrogenic silica sand) when mixed in small quantities (1% to 4% by weight) with liquid resins make these resins thixotropic.

Tinuvin P, 326, 327, 328. Ultraviolet light absorbers which protect certain resins against ultraviolet, light-induced deterioration. These absorbers also extend the colorfastness of the dyes used to color these resins. Contact CIBA-GEIGY for technical literature and information as to where trial quantities may be obtained.

Titanium dioxide. The most frequently used white metallic oxide pigment available. Blended and ground into certain vehicles, titanium dioxide is the white color paste generally available for coloring plastics and resins.

Translucent. This term refers to a material which will allow some light to be transmitted through it. However, it isn't possible to see through a translucent substance (for example, tissue paper is translucent).

Two-part systems. A term applied to the resins discussed in this book. Most of the liquid thermosetting resins which can be made to harden at room temperature or above are composed of part A, the resin, and part B, the curing agent, hardener, or catalyst. When the two parts are mixed in the proper proportions, the resin system will harden or cure according to the manufacturer's data.

Urethane. *See* Polyurethane resins.

Vacuum chamber. A container in which catalyzed, high-viscosity polymers such as Silastic, RTV rubber are placed to remove unwanted air trapped in the mixture. These vacuum chambers such as the ones manufactured by Ace Glass Company, 1430 N.W. Boulevard, Vineland, New Jersey 08360, are now made of Plexiglas and are, therefore, unbreakable.

Vacuum forming. A method of heating a clamped sheet of plastic, pulling it down into a mold or over a perforated form which is lying upon a porous plate, and externally applying a vacuum which sucks the thermoplastic into the mold or around the form. The vacuum-formed plastic is then cooled and removed from the clamping mechanism.

Vacuum pump. A pump which will suck gas or air from a given area. To be effective in removing air from resins, 29″ of vacuum must be obtained in the pump tube.

Vent. A passage made in a mold to allow the air to escape while the mold is being filled through the sprue.

Vulcanization. A chemical reaction which takes place primarily in rubbers where the liquid rubber polymer, such as silicone, is converted to a solid rubbery material of greater tensile strength and increased elasticity in the presence of a certain curing agent.

Water-clear polyester resins. A designation for clear, colorless polyester resins, such as the Reichhold Chemical Company Polylite 32-032 clear polyester casting resin.

Note to British Readers: Many of the trade names mentioned in Suppliers' List and the Glossary are not available in Britain. Equivalent products do exist, however, and when in doubt readers are advised to contact the British suppliers listed here and to refer to the British Plastics Yearbook (IPC Business Books), which list products, trade names, and manufacturing companies, before purchasing materials.

SUPPLIERS AND MANUFACTURERS

Use the general resin suppliers listed below for samples, small quantities, and technical information. The manufacturers used in this book, unless otherwise indicated, should not be approached directly for any of the materials I've mentioned; but if you have some knowledgeable questions and want information which the general supplier cannot answer, the manufacturers will provide technical brochures and data sheets.

RESIN SUPPLIERS IN THE U.S.

The few general resin suppliers stock a large amount of resins, hardeners, catalysts, additives, and related products. They may not have the exact product you require in stock, but they will have an equivalent or will get what you want.

Polyproducts Corporation
Order Department, Room 30
13810 Nelson Avenue
Detroit, Michigan 48227
(313) 931-1088

Resin Coatings Corporation
14940 N.W. 25 Court
Opa Locka, Florida 33054
(305) 685-5751

RESIN SUPPLIERS IN CANADA

Suppliers in Canada do not carry as wide a resin assortment as the U.S. suppliers do. Check to see what they have; you may have to order from the U.S. suppliers.

CIBA-GEIGY Ltd.
131 Hymus Boulevard
Montreal, 730, Quebec
(514) 695-7914

Mia Chemical Ltd.
5240 Bradco Boulevard
Mississauga, Ontario
(416) 625-6200

SUPPLIERS FOR JEWELRY TOOLS

Allcraft Tool and Supply Company, Inc.
215 Park Avenue
Hicksville, New York 11801
Jewelry supplies, tools, and findings

Victor Bergeon
110 West 47th Street
New York, New York 10036
Best Fit jeweler's tools, motors, files

The Craftool Company, Inc.
1421 West 240th Street
Harbor City, California 90710
Jewelry casting tools, basic jewelry-making kit, buffers

The Foredom Electric Company
Bethel, Connecticut 06801
Buffing wheels, motors, and abraders

T.B. Hagstoz & Son
709 Sansom Street
Philadelphia, Pennsylvania 19106
Findings, jeweler's tools

C. R. Hill Company
35 West Grand River Avenue
Detroit, Michigan 48226
Jewelry supplies and findings, exotic woods and metals

MANUFACTURERS

The following list of manufacturers includes only those whose products have been used in the project demonstrations. This list would have to be expanded many times to include all the companies that make equivalent materials. Since this book is dedicated to eliminating secrecy in the formulation of resin systems usable in jewelry as much as possible, I list whenever possible the original manufacturer's name or number for the product. However, you should use equivalent competitive products, if you can get them more easily or cheaply from another source.

Ajinomoto Company of New York
745 Fifth Avenue
New York, New York 10022
B-001, B-003, N-001, relatively non-toxic curing agents

Alcan Metal Powders
P.O. Box 290
Elizabeth, New Jersey 07207
300-mesh metal powders such as aluminum, copper, brass, silicon, antimony, and tin; lower meshes also available

American Cyanamid Company
Intermediate Department
Bound Brook, New Jersey 08805
Cyasorb UV 9 for acrylic and polyester systems; Cyasorb 207 for epoxy systems

41-14 29th Street
Long Island City, New York 11101
Internal Release 54 and other mold-release agents

Cabot Corporation
Cab-O-Sil Division
125 High Street
Boston, Massachusetts 02110
Cab-O-Sil (Cabosil), a thixotropic, thickening, gelling, and matting agent for plastics

Cadillac Plastics and Chemicals
P.O. Box 810
Detroit, Michigan 48232
PS 30 acrylic adhesive

CIBA-GEIGY Corporation
Plastics and Additives Division
Saw Mill River Road
Ardsley, New York 10502
Araldite epoxy resin 502; reactive diluents Epoxide 7 and 8; epoxy curing agents 956, RC-125, 840, and Lancast A, HY 837; ultraviolet absorbers Tinuvin P and 328; Microliths—permanent, dispersible, almost transparent pigments

Conap, Inc.
184 East Union Street
Allegheny, New York 14706
TU-50 and TU-80 mold-making two-part urethane rubber systems

Contour Chemical Company
4 Draper Street
Woburn, Massachusetts 08101
Korax 1711 mold-release agent

Diamond Shamrock Chemicals
P.O. Box 2386R
Morristown, New Jersey 07960
DION (DPM) 3-800 LC, DION EH-30 (DMP-30)

Dow Corning Corporation
South Saginaw Road
Midland, Michigan 48640
Silastic A silicone mold-making rubber and Catalyst F; Silastic E and G; DC 200 silicone oils; Silastic 140 and Silastic 732 adhesives

Fischer Scientific
52 Fadem Road
Springfield, New Jersey 07081
(outlets all over United States)
Thermometers

Foster Manufacturing Company, Inc.
Wilton, Maine 04294
#306 coffee sticks, 1000 per box; minimum order 6 boxes

General Electric Company
Silicone Products Department
Waterford-Mechanicville Road
Waterford, New York 12188
RTV 700 mold-making compound equivalent to Dow Corning Silastic G, Silicone 910 oil equivalent to DC 200, 50 CTS silicone oil

Imperial Chemical Industries, Ltd.
Plastics Division
Welwyn Garden City
Herts, England
ICI Tensol #7 acrylic adhesive

Koppers Plastic Company
2050 Koppers Building
Pittsburgh, Pennsylvania 15219
Acrylic sheet, polyester resins

Lea Manufacturing Company
237 East Aurora Street
Waterbury, Connecticut 06720
Lea greaseless abrasive Compound C, Learok 765, 884E, 339E, 312 buffing and polishing compounds; you may order small quantities direct

Mearl Corporation
41 East 42nd Street
New York, New York 10017
Merlin Silkwhite and other pearlescent products

MirrorBrite Polishing Company
P.O. Box C.T.
Irvin, California 92664
MirrorGlaze Wax

J.I. Morris
394 Elm Street
Southbridge, Massachusetts 01550
Alphalap "PS" with contact adhesive for polishing metals and plastics with water slurries of tin oxide, aluminum oxide, and cerium oxide powers

H.A. Ness and Company
698 Weston Road
Toronto 9, Ontario, Canada
Soapstone, uncut and cut blocks; you may order small quantities

Ohaus Scale Corporation
29 Hanover Road
Florham Park, New Jersey 07932
Triple Beam Balance 2610 (scale)

Owens Corning Fiberglass Corporation
Fiberglass Tower
Toledo, Ohio 43601
Fiberglass 181 cloth

Polysand Division
Frederic B. Anton Enterprises
P.O. Box 1759
Beverly Hills, California 90213
Polysand Kit TR-34, sandpapers down to 8000 grit

Polysciences, Inc.
Paul Valley Industrial Park
Warrington, Pennsylvania 18976
HH 772 acrylic syrup, catalyst, and bleach

Leo Popper and Sons
143-147 Franklin Street
New York, New York 10013
Mille Fiore glass chips; you may order small quantities

Procter and Gamble
Industrial Soap and
Chemical Products Division
P.O. Box 599
Cincinnati, Ohio 45201
Epoxide 7 and 8, Reactive diluents

Reichhold Chemical, Inc.
RCI Building
White Plains, New York 10602
Polylite 32-032 (polyester resin) MEK-Peroxide

Rohm and Haas Company
Independence Mall West
Philadelphia, Pennsylvania 19105
DMP-30, Plexiglas, Methyl methacrylate monomer

Sun Oil Company
Industrial Products Department
1608 Walnut Street
Philadelphia, Pennsylvania 19103
1290 Y microcrystalline wax

Union Carbide Corporation
Mining and Metals Division
Box 579
Niagara Falls, New York 14302
Asbestos 244 thixotropic agent

Velsicol Chemical Corporation
Resin Products Division
341 East Ohio Street
Chicago, Illinois 60611
Benzoflex 9-88 flexibilizer

BIBLIOGRAPHY

JEWELRY

D'Amico, Victor, and Martin, Charles J., *How to Make Modern Jewelry*. Scranton: International Textbook, 1948.

Davidson, Ian, *Ideas for Jewelry*. New York: Watson-Guptill, and London: Batsford, 1973.

Neumann, Robert von, *The Design and Creation of Jewelry*. rev. ed. Philadelphia: Chilton, 1972.

Pack, Greta, *Jewelry and Enameling*. 2nd ed. New York: D. Van Nostrand, 1953.

Untracht, Oppi, *Metal Techniques for Craftsmen*. New York: Doubleday, 1968.

ACRYLIC RESINS

Rohm and Haas Company, *Plexiglas Design and Fabrication Bulletin*, rev. ed., Philadelphia: 1971, and other pamphlets.

EPOXY RESINS

Lee, Henry, and Neville, Kris, *Handbook of Epoxy Resins*. New York: McGraw-Hill, 1967.

CIBA-GEIGY, *Skin Disorders from and Protective Measures against Epoxy Resins*, booklet A/89UX–1, Ardsley, New York.

POLYESTER RESINS

Cook Paint and Varnish Company, pamphlet, P.O. Box 389, Kansas City, Missouri 64041

PLASTICS

Hollander, Harry B., *Plastics for Artists and Craftsmen*. New York: Watson-Guptill, and London: Pitman, 1972.

Modern Plastics Encyclopedia, annual. New York: McGraw Hill, 1971.

Newman, Thelma, *Plastics as an Art Form*, Enl. Ed. Philadelphia: Chilton, 1969.

Roukes, Nicholas, *Crafts in Plastics*. New York: Watson-Guptill, 1970.

FINISHING

Lea Manufacturing Company, pamphlets on buffing and polishing metal, wood, and plastics, Waterbury, Connecticut.

INDEX

Edited by Sarah Bodine
Designed by Bob Fillie
Set in 9 point Vega by Publisher's Graphics, Inc.
Printed and bound by Halliday Lithograph Corp.
Color printed in Japan by Toppan Printing Company Ltd.